Passing Orders

Passing Orders

Demonology and Sovereignty
in American Spiritual Warfare

S. JONATHON O'DONNELL

Fordham University Press
NEW YORK   2021

Copyright © 2021 Fordham University Press

All rights reserved. No part of this publication may be reproduced, stored in a retrieval system, or transmitted in any form or by any means—electronic, mechanical, photocopy, recording, or any other—except for brief quotations in printed reviews, without the prior permission of the publisher.

Fordham University Press has no responsibility for the persistence or accuracy of URLs for external or third-party Internet websites referred to in this publication and does not guarantee that any content on such websites is, or will remain, accurate or appropriate.

Fordham University Press also publishes its books in a variety of electronic formats. Some content that appears in print may not be available in electronic books.

Visit us online at www.fordhampress.com.

Library of Congress Cataloging-in-Publication Data available online at https://catalog.loc.gov.

Printed in the United States of America

23 22 21   5 4 3 2 1

First edition

for Elizabeth Anne Bailey, *in memoriam*

Contents

	Introduction: Paradise Has Walls	1
1	Nations unto Light: Spiritual Warfare as Orthotaxic Religiosity	23
2	Jezebel Assemblages: Witchcraft, Queerness, Transnationality	52
3	The Islamic Antichrist: An Eschatology of Blowback	81
4	Leviathan's Wake: Demonology and the Passing of Order	109
	Conclusion: Paradise Refused	141
	Acknowledgments	159
	Notes	161
	Bibliography	193
	Index	211

Passing Orders

Introduction: Paradise Has Walls

"Around 8:30 AM the phone rang." So pastor Ray Pritchard opens his 2007 book *Stealth Attack*. It was his wife calling, it was September 11, 2001, and a plane had hit the World Trade Center. "I don't remember much else about that day," he continues. "Eventually I made my way to the church and met with the staff. That night hundreds of people gathered in the sanctuary to sing, to weep, to pray." Pritchard proceeds by outlining what was yet to come: the names of al-Qaeda and of Osama bin Laden, the anthrax scare, the color-coded alert system, the invasion of Iraq. "The world changed forever." President Bush "was right" when he declared that the United States was at war, the pastor decides, "and he was right again when he said that the war against terror would last for years, and it might not end in our lifetime. As I write these words, despite significant progress on many fronts, there is no end in sight."[1] Yet, while Pritchard may have begun mentally writing the book "sometime during that long day," *Stealth Attack* is not about 9/11 but "a small contribution to a conviction that arose from the ashes" of its wake. "It's a new look at an old war," he explains, "a struggle that has been going on between good and evil since the beginning of time. It's about spiritual warfare in an age of terror."[2]

For Pritchard, America's global war against terror becomes the modern reflection of a more ancient but equally global conflict. There "is a close link between the physical and the spiritual," he explains, and "what happens in the unseen realm directly affects the world around us." As such, "I have looked at the shattering events of the early years of the twenty-first century to help us understand our place in the great cosmic battle between

God and the devil, light and darkness, good and evil. In that battle we are all frontline soldiers," he concludes, "and no one gets a vacation."[3] The understanding this comparison provokes is not unidirectional. While the language of the demonic frequently lends itself to conceptualizations of America's foes,[4] for Pritchard those foes also permit a reconceptualization of the demonic. "Are you familiar with the term *asymmetric warfare*?" he opens the following chapter. "There is no better picture of Satan's strategy than the modern concept of asymmetric warfare. Though heavily outnumbered by the armies of the Lord, and having lost his personal battle with God, he now uses unconventional warfare to bring down the Lord's people."[5] Indeed, "Satan is the ultimate terrorist who led the first rebellion in the history of the universe. His attempt to unseat God was the first insurgency." The War on Terror becomes the frame through which to reimagine the War in Heaven: a Long War in which victory is both ultimately assured (the enemy is outnumbered, outgunned, and already defeated; *mission accomplished*) and yet constantly deferred, "there is no end in sight."[6]

This book, like *Stealth Attack*, is about "spiritual warfare in an age of terror." Through discourse analysis of "spiritual warfare manuals" like Pritchard's—a hybrid of self-help guide, military tactics manual, and demonological treatise—published chiefly following the Cold War (1989–2000) and in the Bush and Obama phases of the War on Terror (2001–2016), I use spiritual warfare and its demonologies as an extended case study for unpacking notions of temporality, territoriality, and sovereign power in the contemporary United States. The manuals examined in this book are varied. Many are primarily self-help texts, instructing the readers in how to discern demonic influence in their personal and familial lives, while others—more steeped in prophecy and conspiracist discourse—aim at diagnosing demonic influence in global politics or world history. Some are aimed at Christians who doubt the existence of the supernatural and seek to change this, while others are concerned with expanding the expertise of those already within the fold. While varied in scope, however, all manuals share an underlying worldview that galvanizes knowledge production, ritual action, and activism alike: humanity is living in the end times, Satan and his hordes have been unleashed, and God has given the faithful spiritual gifts with which to fight the enemy. For adherents, this conflict constitutes the foundation of reality, with all ideological systems and phenomenal events—from individual sickness, to systemic poverty, to the rise and fall of nations—being rendered superstructures built atop its base.[7]

This book does not make claims about the validity of spiritual warfare.

It is not a work of theology concerned with the limits of correct doctrine, nor does it aim to adjudicate whether demons are metaphysically "real" or not. It is sufficient that spiritual warriors believe them to be and, perhaps more importantly, engage with the world in accordance with this belief. At the same time, I am not concerned with the philosophical problem through which demonologies are usually framed: the problem of evil, of why there is "evil" (moral, natural, metaphysical) in the world—although as demons are evoked as one solution to this issue, it is necessarily part of my scope.[8] Rather, I follow a growing interdisciplinary body of research on late antique and early modern demonology that frames "the demon" as an object of discourse: that is, after Michel Foucault, an object systematically constructed through cultural, linguistic, and ideological practices.[9] As such, this project analyzes how the production of (knowledge about) "the demon" in the spiritual warfare discourses of late twentieth- and early twenty-first-century America, "connects with power, regulates conduct, makes up or constructs identities and subjectivities."[10]

At the heart of my analysis is the interrelation between *demonology* as a discursive tradition that posits the existence and activities of evil spirits and *demonization* as a sociopolitical reality in which traits associated with those spirits (willful deviance, ontological invalidity, inevitable failure) are mapped onto real-world populations.[11] And, conversely, how qualities associated with those real-world populations (asymmetric warfare, diversity, ad hoc coalition-building) are integrated into understandings of such spirits. In doing so, I interrogate how certain groups and persons become constructed as "with" demons—in the sense of both affliction and affiliation—and how this "with" acts to both consolidate and destabilize structures of sovereign power. Tracing intersections of spiritual warfare's imposition of this "with" with the political imaginary and material practices of American empire, I explore what it means to *name* a demon, to name some*one* or some*thing* as demonic, what structures this act of naming seeks to impose, what potentialities it attempts to strip and to induce. In the process, I address a series of questions about the sociocultural function of demonologies in America today, which for now I leave open: At a time in which dehumanization has increasingly become central to the global religious and political landscape, what work is "the demon" as a discursive object called on to perform?[12] How do the discursive traditions built around this object—demonologies—feed into and on the broader systems of power that saturate both the national landscape of the United States and its transnational impositions, including but not limited to misogyny, queer- and transphobia, settler colonialism, antiblackness, and Islamophobia? Finally, and perhaps most pressingly, how might the demonized—those of us positioned as "with" demons—respond productively to the structures of sovereign power that thus interpellate us?

Walled Heaven, Waning Sovereignty

Analyzing post-9/11 security discourses, the political theorist and sociologist of religion Michael Barkun argued that after 9/11 the United States developed a cultural fixation on invisible dangers, "dangers thought to be posed by invisible adversaries who might wield invisible weapons."[13] One was the terrorist, hidden in plain sight with concealed bombs and biochemical weapons. The undocumented migrant was another, an alleged harbinger of crime traversing borders that "should" be stable. A third was the pandemic, invisibly transmitted from foreign places and/or unleashed by terrorists. While these fixations all predate the War on Terror, reflecting common images of threat to American unipolarity,[14] 9/11 raised anxieties around them to new heights. Combined with technological advance and shifts in domestic politics, these anxieties facilitated new systems of securitization and sovereign power. Taken collectively, Barkun argued, these figures of invisible threat traced patterns of "pollution and defilement" that (re)organized the social imaginary of twenty-first-century America, representing "potential defilers who bring impurities into what was a previously unsullied community," removal of which would herald the restoration of order.[15] Like impurities, they required cleansing; like demons, they required exorcism.

The demon is among the oldest and most paradigmatic of invisible enemies, its genealogy intersecting with constructions of both the stranger and the pandemic. Indeed, as the stranger, it functions much like the alien in that it amalgamates the collective dangers of an "outside" into "the singularity of a given form," one that *"we imagine we have already faced."*[16] Framing the demon as exemplary of broader notions of the monstrous, Jason Bivins discusses it as threatening to the "sovereignty and boundedness of the flesh," signaling proximity to "bodily and epistemic limits."[17] Such an (un)bounded body does not need to be personal, but can be communal, national, even global. Perhaps unsurprisingly, therefore, both the rhetoric and logics of exorcism saturated post-9/11 discourses of cultural identity and military adventurism, offering what communication theorist Joshua Gunn called "a promise of recovery through the purging of something previously hidden or unnamed from a given body."[18] As a strategy of global exorcism, the War on Terror's foundational promise was that America would (unilaterally and infinitely) hunt down and defeat "evil." Whether such evil was secreted away in the earth (as in al-Qaeda's Tora

Bora cave complex) or "harbored" by nation-states (Afghanistan, Iraq), it aimed at the subjugation of the possessed (land, people) for the purposes of their purification.

As that against which America's "messianic imperialism"[19] mobilizes, the demon (and the demonized, those onto whom demonic activity is mapped) is central to declension narratives: jeremiadic narratives of moral, spiritual, national (and imperial) decline for which dark forces are blamed and in which the demonized are rendered (to borrow Stanley Cohen's concept of the folk devil) "visible reminders of what we should not be."[20] These dark forces are usually framed as coming from outside, or—when internal—as owing allegiance to that outside. This projection of threatening alterity enables the creation of a phantasmatic image of a walled enclosure—a *paradise* in its etymological sense, a garden possessed and maintained by sovereign power[21]—the sustaining of which becomes inextricable from articulations of security, sovereignty, and the stability and authenticity of states and selves. Demonologies in the United States arise when the borders of flesh and nation are (perceived to be) ruptured, disrupting concepts of cultural unity and exceptionality by "introducing pluralism and ambiguity into the national narrative."[22] As such, the conjuration and exorcism of demons becomes one way—to draw on Erin Runions's cogent summary of Wendy Brown's *Walled States, Waning Sovereignty*—that the United States "theatrically maintains a sense of bordered cohesion, through military walls and homeland security," policing movement "at least to look as if it is fortified against the deterritorializations and political breakdown in national sovereignty."[23]

For Brown, writing in 2010, the US-Mexico border was among the most visible of walls that marked the precarious (in)security of the nation-state following the Cold War. This is perhaps even more true today, as the border becomes coded in secular and theological conservative rhetoric as the paradisiacal solution to perceived threats of demonic dissolution. Robert Jeffress, the charismatic pastor of First Baptist Dallas Church and member of President Donald Trump's evangelical advisory board, for example, conjured this association in late 2018 in defense of Trump's plan to erect a southern border wall, remarking that "even Heaven itself is going to have a wall around it. Not everyone is going to be allowed in," and concluding unironically that "if walls are immoral, then God is immoral."[24] Jeffress' was neither the first nor last invocation of this theme. Two years before, Republican congressmen and members of conservative thinktanks convened a panel at the 2017 Conservative Political Action Conference on "If Heaven has a gate, a wall, and extreme vetting, why can't America?" Later, on February 11, 2019, congressman Steve King (R-IA) made headlines by tweeting an Arkansas grocery store ad that made the next leap in correlation: "Heaven has a wall, a gate and a strict immigration policy. Hell has open borders"—a right-wing evangelical meme that had circulated in several variations since at least mid-2018.[25] While these instances were criticized for their interpretation of scripture, they represent a set of affective and discursive associations growing in subsets of the conservative spiritual warfare milieu. These associations, starkly manifested in more fringe elements through equivalences between the expulsion of "illegals" and advance of God's Kingdom and demonizations of Latin American refugees as carriers of diabolic "witchcraft,"[26] join a violent desire for the closure of the homeland to an apocalyptic longing for the closure of history itself.

In their eschatological reconceptualization of national security, these figures and groups literalize a metaphorical relation that feminist author Rebecca Solnit constructed when, reading the narrative of the Fall through the prism of the US-Mexico border, she called Paradise "the first immigration-restricted country." In Solnit's reading, "Adam and Eve are the first refugees, the fig leaves the first cancelled passports," and "the Angel with the Flaming Sword" that stops their return is "of course . . . a Border Patrol agent." Paradise is here constituted by the violence of a territorial sovereignty claim that forcibly divides inside from out: "the wall, the guard, and the gate" maintain "the difference between the garden and the world. Whatever is inside the wall, past the gate, protected by the guard is imagined as some version of Paradise, but Paradise only so long as its separateness is protected."[27] Neither the sovereign ruler who cancels the passports or commands the border agents nor the serpent that provokes Paradise's securitization appear in Solnit's reading, however, and we are left to guess at their assignments. Yet if God's role as the transcendent force that makes and enforces the law can be read as somewhat stable, Satan's is more ambiguous. Positioned as (in) the serpent only retroactively, the Devil unsettles clear distinctions between insider and outsider.[28] Enthroned as the "prince of this world" (John 14:30), he orchestrates and personifies the domain against which the garden maintains its identity as such.

Satan's unsettling relation to Paradise is perhaps best dramatized in John Milton's *Paradise Lost* when, having finally escaped Hell, the Devil arrives at Eden's gates. Initially, he skulks about its walls. Then, tiring of this circumambulation, bounds over them like a "prowling wolf" (IV.183). This is not his only bestial mode. Satan's state in Paradise is protean; he shifts through animal forms: first a cormorant, then an unnamed quadruped grazer, a toad, the infamous serpent. In a place he does not belong,

Satan passes as those that do. For John Tanner, these transmutations "express more than a tactical need for disguises," instead figuring the internal force of the Devil's nonbelonging, attesting to "deep anxiety about continuity itself," thereby suggesting that his fitful mutability "manifests demonic rejection of the idea of permanence figured in heaven."[29] Yet it is Paradise's continuity that is threatened by the trespassing of this passing figure. Satan traverses its borders and adopts the semblance of its occupants, unfixing its fixity. Rather than merely figuring the Devil's internal anxiety over celestial permanence, his capacity to pass into it and as its residents exposes a deeper anxiety about the possibility of such permanence, revealing eternity to be itself unstable and transient, exposing Paradise's imbrication in what Brown called the "tremulousness, vulnerability, dubiousness and instability" of (nation-state) sovereignty that a need for walls represents—not sovereignty's "resurgent expression" but "icons of its erosion."[30]

I unpack the register of passing and its centrality to Paradise's (in)security later. For now, what must be said is that, from the perspective of Paradise, the demon is that which both must and cannot be guarded against. Its passage marks the limits of Paradise and of the possibility of Paradise. It threatens the stability of eternity with the passing of time, placing an order figured as timeless and unified in relation to its own impossible transgression. At the same time, the demon also gives to Paradise its self-consolidating other, providing it with a narrative of self-legitimation that justifies the arguments that frame Paradise's walls as necessary for existence itself, enabling rigid demarcations of order from chaos, life from death, self from other—even and perhaps especially when such borders blur or are breached. Constructing discourses about demons—demonologies—is one way Paradise tries to explain (away) this blurring and breaching, to render legible, manipulable, and eliminable threats (real and imagined, always incarnated) to its security and perpetuity. As a discourse, demonology thus testifies to acts of performative violence that, as Jacques Derrida outlines, *make the truth*, inscribe "a truth whose power sometimes imposes itself forever: the location of a boundary, the installation of a state... the dominant and juridically incontestable public truth."[31] However, as he notes elsewhere, as "soon as truth is a limit or has limits, its own... truth would be a certain relation to what terminates or determines it." Truth is constituted by the possibility of its contravention.[32] Paradise thus comes to rely on its demons, on the threat of their existence and the strategies for their exorcism. And this need for demons, for demonologies, reveals its security and continuity to be ceaselessly contested, corrupted, and on the verge of collapse. Demons here come to operate deconstructively, operating within and against sovereign power, destabilizing the very structures that require them for consolidation.

To capture this process of (de)stabilization, the construction and deconstruction of truth and its limits, this work draws upon disparate understandings of "demonology." The first, more traditional or at least more normative, is that of study of religions scholar Bruce Lincoln. Demonology, he claims, works akin to a scientific "unified field theory." It amalgamates rubrics that are normally differentiated in modern and secular classificatory systems—"bacteriology, epidemiology, toxicology, teratology, criminology, Marxism, psychoanalysis"—in order to build a unified model of reality in the service of a singular goal: an "unflinching attempt to name, comprehend, and defend against all that threatens, frightens, and harms us."[33] Critical here is both demonology's aspirations to totality and the contours of the "us" in whose name its unflinching attempt is brought to bear—an "us" that is inextricable from existing structures of power. Demonology is not just a discourse of threat but one whose acts of naming operate as processes of discursive and material interpellation, constitutive of the subjects they name—a mechanism of power that both acts on and (thereby) activates bodies.[34] Demonology, in sum, imposes names to classify and control (thus constituting) unruly or willful subjects within disciplinary and securitizing regimes of sovereign power.[35]

This process of classification and control is also part of the logics of Paradise. Elsewhere, in his study of Achaemenian Persia composed in the shadow of Abu Ghraib, Lincoln identifies "the pursuit of paradise" as the leitmotif of the "incipient moment" of empire, one that empowered the imperial project through its desire not just to isolate its inhabitants but to isolate them in a space that was itself a microcosm of the world.[36] The paradise aspired "to include all species," and the ideology this aspiration generated and justified trusted "that this ideal would be achieved at history's end," while (if begrudgingly) "accepting that, until the empire had encompassed the globe, one would have to settle for something less than totality and perfection."[37] For Lincoln, the image of the paradise thereby legitimizes two phases of empire: one in which "a nation or a people organizes and energizes itself for the conquest, domination, and exploitation of its neighbors," and another in which, as "its troops meet with success, its control extends outward, and it draws resources back to the center to fuel its further expansion."[38] Paradise's walls are never static. Rather, they partake in strategies of encompassing, enclosure, and encroachment. And as I explore later, while spiritual warriors have rarely used the image of Paradise consciously in this manner—although, as Jeffress and others show, this may be changing—the paradise's imperial undercurrents are central to their demonologies, which operate through processes of classification and control, expropriation and erasure, framing perceived threats to "us" in the language of demonology to facilitate logics of extraction, assimilation, and annihilation.

Yet the demon is also constructed as a transgressive and unsettling figure, one exceeding demonology's attempts to classify and thus guard against it, passing into the edifices of Paradise, revealing their porosity and provoking their collapse. Here, in addition to Lincoln, it is useful to draw on the definition of "demonology" employed by liberation and queer theologian Marcella Althaus-Reid. In keeping with Paradise's imbrication with the logics of empire, Althaus-Reid positions demonology in opposition to *retention*: an "imperial meme" that "reproduces itself by reproducing a past," one "based on imperial knowledge of expansion and strategies of acceptance, such as re-territorialisation and processes of identity unification which include the erasure of the past (redeeming the past by changing it)." Conceptualizing the demon as that which retention seeks to "redeem" and (thereby) erase, she advocates a framing of demonology as "a theology the starting point of which is the knowledge of rebellious spirits, a theology that exposes and accuses the legal sacred order of being constructed and not natural."[39] For Althaus-Reid, the "legal" dimension of legal sacred order is primarily sexual, tied to capital-T Theology's imbrication with normative regimes of sexuality that queerness rebels against, albeit one bound to broader regimes of racialization and coloniality. In this work, I pursue this more expansive framing, unpacking the imbrications of sex, gender, race, and coloniality and their conjoined logics of demonization.

This expansion, I detail in Chapter 1, enables the formulation of a heuristic rubric that I term "orthotaxy," a mode of religiosity in which "correct" (*orthos*) patterns, arrangements, and orders (*taxa*)—personal, societal, cosmic—become privileged over correct beliefs or behaviors. Befitting conjurations of "legal sacred order," within spiritual warfare discourses this orthotaxic religiosity is given shape by a mobilization of ideas of "illegality" to conceptualize both the demonic and the paradigms of bodily autonomy and territorial (co)habitation associated with it. Framing demons as figures who "rule illegally, acting as illegal squatters," spiritual warfare makes violation of their will and seizure of their lands an act of reclamation from "the illegal usurper, Satan."[40] As I will demonstrate, however, such accusations of illegality are themselves what constitutes and consolidates orthotaxy as "right order." As postcolonial queer theorist Sara Ahmed has explored, accusations of willful subjectivity—subjectivity figured as willing "wrongly or too much"—are inextricable from a simultaneous, interdependent articulation of "sovereign will." The legitimation of this latter will *as* sovereign requires both "the rendering of sovereign will *as* non-willful will and the rendering of those who do not obey the will of the sovereign as willful will." Claims to sovereignty or to speak on behalf of sovereignty require a marking of others' wills as a priori rebellious, as nonsovereign; one way "of thinking of sovereign will *is the right to determine whose wills are the willful wills*."[41] Asymmetries are what permit this accusation of willful deviance and what allows a will to figure itself as non-willful—to pass as normative, as sovereign. Consolidations of orthotaxy and its concomitant accusations of demonic illegality in spiritual warfare mimic this relation, being co-constitutive and dependent on asymmetries of power—drawn along existing hierarchical axes of oppression—that determine ahead of time which ideological structures, forms of subjectivity, and deployments of violence are legitimate or illegitimate, divine or demonic.

Starting with "the knowledge rebellious spirits," this book centers this asymmetry and co-constitution in order to resituate and refigure demonology as a tool of critique, one which reframes and subverts the declension narratives of modern America. Alongside Althaus-Reid's queering of demonology, I draw here specifically on the work of feminist geographer Katherine McKittrick. Building on the use of "demonic" in mathematics and physics as well as in theology, McKittrick reframes the demonic as naming "a non-deterministic schema; it is a process that is hinged on uncertainty and non-linearity because the organizing principle cannot predict the future." She draws here on Sylvia Wynter's uses of the demonic, exploring how centering such a demonic element underscores how "subaltern lives are not other/marginal to regulatory classificatory systems but instead integral to them." Or, framed more theologically, how demons and the demonized are integral to the divine order that conjures them. But this integration holds deconstructive potential, as the demon introduces uncertainty and nonlinearity into the systems that summon it for self-consolidation and edification. As such, for McKittrick, the demonic "makes possible a different unfolding, one that does not *replace* or override or remain subordinate to the vantage point of 'Man'"—that is, Western bourgeois conceptions of the Human as purveyor of "unquestionable reason, value, and authority"—"but instead parallels his constitution and his master narratives of humanness."[42]

Subversively reframing spiritual warfare's demonologies as capable of signifying precisely such a "different unfolding," I expose the targets of their declension narratives as symbolizing other(ed) narratives of cultural contestation and temporal transformation: projects of dissent buried within proclamations of decline. These are projects of descension, of fall and refusal to be sure, but also of derivation—of descent as ancestry and archive—both in that "demonology" exists as part of a genealogy of description, management, and containment (theological, secular, colonial) by which it (re)situates the objects it names, and in that demons and the demonized themselves embody their own ancestries and archives, imbricated in but exceeding demonology's unflinching attempt to classify and control them. As I will demonstrate, such descension narratives target the places where the seams of demonology's unified field theories are most visible, exposing how the demons they name undo the systems of sovereignty and security they are conjured to reinforce, accusing those systems of being constructed and not natural. In doing so, they unsettle the boundaries of order by revealing Paradise's walls to be porous, not stable; its structures transient, not eternal; its forms and mannerisms replicable, not unique. They offer, in brief, "a new look at an old war."

Passing Orders

It is on the threshold between order's consolidation and deconstruction, between the narrative of decline seeking to reassert normative order and the narrative of dissent striving to disrupt it, that "the demon" emerges as a passing figure. This passing is multiple, at once spatial, temporal, and specular. The demon *passes through space*, traversing borders that should remain stable, but it is also *passing in time*, destined for destruction, and constructed through images of deceit and dissimulation, as *passing for what it is not*. The last of these is especially critical. The ambiguities and anxieties of imitation have long been core to Christian demonologies: Satan's relation to God is one of "near-perfect imitation and essential difference,"[43] the world order created by the Antichrist near time's end is a "counterfeit world order,"[44] the state of sinful humanity is marked as "a distorted, misoriented, false imitation of what the human should be."[45] Yet by positioning the demon as a *passing* figure I do not mean simply to suggest—apropos 2 Corinthians 11:14—that Satan "masquerades as an angel of light." Nor, crucially, do I intend to claim that people who "pass" (whether in terms of race, sexuality, gender, religion, and so on) are demonic—although certain demonizing parties often frame them as such, mobilizing fears of invisible enemies to police the limits of being and belonging. By positioning the demon as a passing figure, I wish instead to tease out the imbrication and implications of the registers of its passing, and thereby excavate its structural relationship to notions of temporality, identity, and sovereign power—one core to the discursive and affective work it is conjured to perform today.

The ties between sovereignty and identity are deep-rooted and constitutive. As Derrida argues, before "any sovereignty of the state, of the nation-state, of the monarch, or, in democracy, of the people, ipseity names a principle of legitimate sovereignty, the accredited or recognized supremacy of a power or a force."[46] Ipseity, from the Latin *ipse* ("itself") inscribes identity at sovereignty's heart, marking a principle of the selfsame, the recognition of those like oneself and thereby the power, authority and proprietary possession that comes with the codification of that one-self. Yet if the structure of sovereignty rests on identity as selfsame, then passing—and in theopolitical modes, demonic passing most of all—unsettles it at its foundations. Passing is about identities, Elaine Ginsberg writes, "their creation or imposition, their adoption or rejection, their accompanying rewards and penalties." It is about the borders built between identity categories and "individual and cultural anxieties induced by boundary crossing." Perhaps ultimately, it is "about specularity: the visible and the invisible, the seen and the unseen."[47] Given this framework, how might the register and archive of passing inflect upon an American demonology organized around the relation between the seen and the unseen, between material superstructure and spiritual base, between (allegedly deceptive) appearance and (a projection of) inner "truth" that must be discerned and subsequently dispossessed?

Passing presumes a disconnect between essence and semblance, which galvanizes regimes of securitization that attempt to discern the "truth" of marked subjects—a truth often figured to be dangerous, perhaps demonic and disintegrative in nature—and thereby situate such subjects within paradigms of discernment and diagnosis, and ultimately projects of displacement, dispossession, and destruction. In the United States, passing is archetypally associated with race, with the crossing of the "color line," but also with other categories such as sexuality and gender. How passing marks these categories in relation to wider "legal sacred order" is distinct, however. The passing of sexual minorities, for example—whether by being closeted or simply by conforming to societal gender expectations—has been framed as assuaging the anxieties of normative order. The existence of the "closet," for example, permits that order to enact a fantasy of totality and homogeneity, as Eve Kosofsky Sedgwick has demonstrated.[48] Demonology can function analogously, becoming a receptacle of deviancy that permits fantasies of normative exception. Exploring the depiction of Satan in Dante's *Inferno*, for example, Laurel Schneider frames the demon through Sedgwick's epistemology of the closet, positioning Hell and Purgatory (albeit more ambiguously) as "indispensable containers of the repressed fluidity and ambiguity of Heaven, the very repression of which makes Heaven's monolithic claim to superiority possible."[49] Demonology here consolidates normative order by conjuring the abject vessels of its ambiguities, fluidities, and desires. Many of the spiritual warfare discourses discussed exemplify this demonology of the closet, positioning the source of "deviant" identities (gendered, sexual, religious) in unseen forces that can be removed, resolving the split between the seen and the unseen by normativizing the former through exorcizing the latter.

Yet while the closet is often framed as reassuring to (hetero)normativity, the ability both for racialized subjects to "pass" as white and for transgender subjects to "pass" as cisgender more often evoke anxiety rather than alleviating it. Gayle Wald demonstrates how the color line has long served a "territorializing" function "through its ability to impose and regulate social inequality" in accordance with the "changing needs and interests of white supremacy"—needs and interests that passing unsettles by revealing race to be "more liquid and dynamic, more variable and random" than it is figured in hegemonic discourses.[50] The gender divide operates in distinct but analogous fashion. As Toby Beauchamp explores, post-9/11 security cultures have increasingly figured gender nonconformity "as inherently deceptive in ways that justify continued surveillance to locate its truth," discursively fusing the "concealed sex or gender" of trans or gender nonconforming people with the "concealed weapons" of suspected terrorists as threats to the (normative, static, pure) body politic. The overproduction of legal documentation required of transition facilitates this securitization, as it renders the transgender subject's capacity to "pass" contingent on the existence of trails of medical, legal, and related documentation that—from the perspective of the state—ensures possession of a subject's archive and (thus) their "truth."[51] In the case of both race and gender, the possibility of unmarked and undetectable passing unsettles categories that are discursive figured and materially enforced as ontologically distinct. Yet while gender is often a privileged site of anxiety within spiritual warfare, as discussed in Chapter 2, the broader archive of racial passing carries specific weight and generates specific anxieties that are critical to the concept's mobilization in contemporary demonologies.

Discussing the racialized logics of slavery in America, Harryette Mullen notes that such logics define "the black as a facsimile or counterfeit of the white in order to deny the rights and privileges of whiteness."[52] This framing of blackness as counterfeit rests upon an underlying system that figures blackness as ontological absence, an absence that Black theorists have framed as foundational to the metaphysical structures of our anti-black world, in which blackness becomes (in Frank Wilderson III's words) "the very antithesis of the Human subject . . . a position against which Humanity establishes, maintains, and renews its coherence, its corporeal integrity."[53] This denial of legitimate being—ontological negation—is core to the theological structures of demonology and (therefore) to the theopolitical structures of demonization. Christian demonology frames demonic evil at the lowest point of a hierarchy in which being (*ontos*) is bound to God (*theos*) as apex and guarantor of morality and existence. This synthesis of ontology and theology—ontotheology—underlies Western metaphysics, placing God as/at the summit of a moral-ontological hierarchy as absolute good and (therefore) absolute being. Situated as/at the nadir of this same hierarchy of being(s), demons occupy a state in which moral deviance from order correlates necessarily to ontological absence. The "incarnation" of ontotheological evil thereby enables a construction of bodies as similarly void of being—and void due to a priori willful deviation from right order. That such bodies often are and have been racialized has not escaped notice. Building on Alexander G. Weheliye's framing of racialization as the process of organizing human beings into those permitted full, partial, and no access to the category of the Human—itself drawing on the work of Sylvia Wynter and Hortense Spillers—Adam Kotsko traces a path from Christianity's construction of rebellious angels as condemned to rebel against God in perpetuity through medieval Christian demonization of Jews to modern demonization of Black people. Reframing racialization through demonization, Kotsko argues that the racialized subject is framed as inheriting "moral failing on the model of original sin" and (therefore) as an intractably and intrinsically criminal opponent of creation.[54]

I attend closely to the racializing elements of demonology throughout this book. For now, it is worth noting that neither Schneider nor Kotsko examine or interrogate the place that notions of "passing" play with regards to their frameworks. This is important, as the racializing and receptaclizing logics of contemporary demonologies not only create and maintain unjust hierarchies between human beings (although they do this) but bring with them an abject terror at the possibility of passing, at the potential for human beings demonologically coded as "distorted, misoriented, false imitation[s] of what the human should be" to pass as Human (Wilderson), as Man (Wynter), or as *Humanitas* (Mignolo). Moreover, as these divisions between the coherent, integrated Human and its others are framed as intrinsic and essential, individual instances of passing cannot ever be just that. Ascendant xenophobic discourses over (racialized) "illegal migrants" or "bogus asylum seekers" are illustrative here. Discussing the latter figure's deployment in British politics, Ahmed observes that the term "bogus" names a counterfeit coin and originated in slang for the apparatus of counterfeiture itself: the machinery that impressed spurious currency, currency deemed illegitimate and (so) inferior. The "bogus" asylum seeker, one assumed "to be *passing* their way into the nation" to "*falsely* accrue benefits," thus becomes framed not as "a lonely spurious coin" but "a singular impress created by a machinery that is intended to defraud the whole system."[55] The counterfeit—money, asylum, whiteness, heterosexuality, and so on—is figured as passing for value it does not "truly" possess, absence appearing as plenitude. This absence is not self-contained, cannot be contained, instead figuring a "singular impress" of—to tease out the diabolic undercurrents of Ahmed's image—a distinctly *infernal* machinery (*inferno* and *inferior* being linked etymologically, signaling what is below, or perhaps must be kept below for the system to sustain itself).[56]

However, it is because of its perceived inferiority and capacity for passing that the counterfeit becomes—as Mary McAleer Balkun writes—"the standard by which authenticity is determined."[57] It is because of the counterfeit's existence (actual or conceptual) that distinctions between reality and falsity, between (legitimate) essence and (deceptive) appearance, become not only sustainable but required. It is the capacity for a counterfeit to be (mis)identified as authentic that necessitates articulations of the latter's legitimacy. Structurally dependent on its alleged counterfeits, authenticity comes to adopt a similar (if disavowed) fluidity. As Mullen notes, for example, racism "reifies whiteness" by imagining a "pure" whiteness unmixed with blackness; "'Pure' whiteness has actual value," she notes, "like legal tender, while the white-skinned African-American is like a counterfeit bill that is passed into circulation, but may be withdrawn at any point if discovered to be bogus."[58] Yet this economy is itself artificial, its valuations sustained by processes of (il)legitimation and control. As Hamilton Carroll has demonstrated, although white masculinity "holds the privilege of definition: to be white is to be *not* black; to be male is to be *not* female," hegemonic whiteness requires "a complex process of maintenance" by which it is ceaselessly redefined, rebuilt and reconfigured. Indeed, due to its structural relation to its others, white privilege (and conceptions of normative authenticity broadly) is "a slippery, illusory base" positioned as "always under assault." As a result, "whiteness is engaged in a constant process of boundary maintenance and reconstitution" that marks not only whiteness but "those categories that function in opposition to it."[59]

Passing disturbs the foundations on which the opposition between "counterfeit" and "authentic" is built. It reveals, in Linda Schlossberg's words, how "identity categories intersect, overlap, construct, and deconstruct" each other; the "passing subject's ability to transcend or abandon his or her 'authentic' identity calls into question the very notion of authenticity itself."[60] From the stance of normative order, passing's threat is in what it reveals in its unrevealing: to pass is to go unmarked by difference, and the ability to pass for "straight" or "cis" or "white" calls attention to how whiteness, cisness, and heterosexuality themselves are also in a perpetual state of passing, one that figures them as normative, as beyond the alleged volatility of racial "tensions" or gender and sexual "deviancies." Normative categories are constantly redefined, rebuilt and reconfigured in response to assaults (real or imagined) on their normativity; frameworks such as whiteness, maleness and heterosexuality pass as natural by disguising the factors, marks, and learned behaviors that occasioned their production.[61] They obscure their contingency by framing others as lacking independent, legitimate substance, as dependent—indeed, parasitic—on the normative category, as evil is framed as parasitic on the good. Passing figures—those seen to transgress the ontological bounds of sovereign order—are therefore rendered threats to Paradise's perpetuity.

In the anxieties over waning sovereignties and ethnonationalist identities that saturate contemporary America, notions of legions of (in)visible folk devils generated by infernal machinery both trouble and justify the systems that attempt to exclude them. They provoke the development of mechanisms designed to secure the edifices and the pursuit of Paradise. "The figure of the passer," Ahmed writes, corroborating Beauchamp, is "generated by a system as a *mechanism for legitimating itself*; it is how legitimacy is legitimated."[62] The counterfeit is the standard for authenticity, allowing it to differentiate itself from its inferior and infernal others and to police the limits of its Paradise. These mechanisms act to obscure the fact that social categories of supremacy are not only currencies untethered to any measure of value beyond that ascribed to them, but also that they are ceaselessly redefined, their characteristics re-pressed. The possibility of passing calls this assumed unmarked value into question and so, as Beauchamp explored, necessitates the passing of orders that might permit the counterfeit's detection—the development of surveillance systems that will make the passing figure always detectable. For spiritual warriors this logic of surveillance that renders the counterfeit always already knowable as such ultimately comes to possess an apocalyptic dimension closely tied to passing's temporal register. The counterfeit is marked for transience by an assumed gap between its inner essence and its outer manifestation that is seen to doom it a priori. It is passing in time as well as through space: when detected, it becomes a passing phenomenon, is "withdrawn" from circulation. There is an assumed inevitability to this discovery that grounds order's assurances of authenticity and legitimacy. An authentic is thought of as stable and constant, its record is clean, it *is* what it *seems to be*. But as Derrida contends, while the classical philosophical definition of truth is the "indefinite survival of the 'stable,'" there may be no reason— no absolute, ultimate, structural and structuring reason, beyond any and all possibility—why either a lie or its desired effects might not remain undetected unto infinity.[63] That is, there may be no reason to presume that a counterfeit will ever be detected, or must even be detectable.

Yet if the counterfeit—structurally speaking—might neither be detectable nor its effects rectifiable, then its constitutive lack of being or belonging may never be exposed, its impact never undone. Given time, it might even be mistaken for the truth that it claims to be. Given time, it might even become truth or at least accepted as such. As I will demonstrate, it is this possibility that the counterfeit might never be detected, that the passing figure might not inevitably pass on, which haunts demonologies in America today. Resultantly, such demonologies are oriented around notions of discernment and systems of knowledge production, on creating a "unified field theory" that would permit the detection and defeat of passing figures (racialized, sexualized, gendered, colonial), but also towards an eschatological horizon—on the end of time itself. For if there is no absolute reason a lie should not remain undetected until time's end, time's apocalyptic finale becomes positioned as that which reveals the truth *sub specie aeternitatis*, ending all possibility of being or seeming otherwise. The temporality of this revelation is shared by theological and secularized apocalypticisms alike, rooting both victory and defeat in claims of originary and essential (im)perfection. While the former can claim "that the ending of the story has somehow been hidden or revealed in the narrative since the beginning of creation," the latter can argue "that the state which eventually collapsed was somehow 'doomed' or 'flawed' from the beginning." Either way, the end is figured as "less of a surprise than a logical outgrowth of a trend . . . [that] can be traced back to the beginning or the founding of the state."[64] The revelation apocalypse brings is therefore not simply one of truth but of all that passes, of all deemed to be counterfeit by the arbiters of that truth—a judgment always already imbricated in the asymmetries of sovereign power.

Eschatology here operates as a tool of projected or post-hoc delegitimation, enacting an imperial inscription of a prelapsarian past actualized through the exposure and erasure—or rather, designation and destruction—of passing figures. This is not a move to eliminate the need for passing's "near-perfect imitation" as a tool of either subversion or survival—that is, an end to the pain to which material realities of passing are often linked—but rather of the "essential difference" it was constructed as masking. Anchoring the proper and expropriating ordinances of time, the apocalypse's anticipated revelation of which orders are true and which false, which eternal, which passing, sustains biopolitical and necropolitical systems of what Elizabeth Freeman terms chrononormativity: those techniques by which "manipulations of time convert historically specific regimes of asymmetrical power into seemingly ordinary bodily tempos and routines." Imbricated in a revanchist nativism seeking to reassert the rhythms of racial hierarchy and cisheteropatriarchal norms and the perpetuation of a racializing, colonial capitalism for which there is allegedly no alternative, chrononormativity enacts the violence of (re)temporalization by which bodies are forced into modes of maximal production, a production of value and futurity in which "teleologies of living" structure familial and collective logics of inheritance in service of "a *legacy*," a "properly political future" that may be ethnic, national, or otherwise.[65] In the regimes of spiritual warfare discussed here, demons—and those of us "with" demons—do not or cannot assimilate to these modes of (re)production. They resist teleology, inhabiting the queer rhythms of a world beyond the cultivation and curation of the garden. Paradise's securitization is thus always a securitization of its temporal sovereignty. Encroaching on and enclosing alternative temporalities, the pursuit of Paradise forecloses on their possibility of survival, casting them into zones of no future based on ascriptions of ontotheological absence tied to accusations of willful deviance. Exposed in the instant of eschatological disclosure, all other orders are—before the judgment throne of sovereign will—rendered merely passing orders.

The Broad Road

This work follows the trace of these passing orders, these counterfeit orders that pass for "true" ones, which provoke the passing of orders that might safeguard order from its own passing. It does so across four core chapters. Chapter 1 sets the stage contextually and theoretically. It outlines the central features of spiritual warfare demonologies, teasing out their structure to posit a framework for understanding spiritual warfare's mode of religiosity as "orthotaxic"—as fixated less on correct belief or practice than on correct arrangements and orderings of (social, spiritual, political) reality. I demonstrate that such "correct" orderings are justified as normative through a posited possession of three related attributes: *integrity* (it is whole and wholesome, unblemished, complete-in-itself), *incontestability* (systems of being and believing are invalidated simply by diverging from it), and *inevitability* (it is the unavoidable culmination of the historical process). These attributes are formulated in juxtaposition with the demonic figure of the "*arche*," or "territorial spirit," which is conjured to represent illegitimate territorial and temporal orders, both ideological and material, that simultaneously contest, consolidate, and threaten to counterfeit normative order. Drawing on deconstruction and postcolonial and decolonial theory, I contend that spiritual warfare's demonologies operate as attempts to exert mastery over both space (property, territory, bodies) and time (history, teleology, and the archive)—attempts inextricable from broader structures of American exceptionalism, empire management, and the enduring epistemic violence of modernity's inextricable imbrication with its colonial dark side.[66]

Having established the context of US spiritual warfare demonologies and the paradigms of order they are conjured to reinforce, the work then engages in case studies of three demonic figures commonly discussed in contemporary spiritual warfare texts in order to unpack the work that "the demon" is called on to perform. My reasons for structuring these chapters around specific demonic figures are several, but foremost is that scholarship addressing the sociocultural and political uses of demonology, whether historic or contemporary, generally treat all uses of demons as interchangeable.[67] While this approach has merits for examining the structural role of demons for identity construction, and is also deployed within this book, as Runions demonstrates in *The Babylon Complex* specific demonic figures (e.g., Babylon) can also be deployed to manage more specific anxieties (e.g., around empire, freedom, and control). *Passing Orders* follows in Runions's footsteps by demonstrating that in addition to the work performed by "the demon" broadly, specific demonic figures are strategically deployed to manage distinct anxieties and represent distinct relations of power and ideas of difference. While some of the work performed by these disparate figures overlaps, they are often differentiated in themselves and in regard to the populations they are mapped onto. That is, different(ly) demonized groups are predominantly figured as "with" different demons. The spirit of Jezebel, for example, is almost never associated with Muslims.[68] Conversely, the spirit framed as behind "Islam" is never associated with feminists or queer or trans folk.

Chapter 2 inaugurates the case studies by exploring demonologies of the Jezebel spirit. Adapted from the Queen Jezebel of 1 and 2 Kings and her symbolic recurrence as a false prophet in Revelation, Jezebel transcends her textual image as a mortal woman to become a transnational and transhistorical demonic spirit whose influence infiltrates all arenas of American life. Inheriting and disarticulating complex theological-textual archives and embodied histories of racial-sexual ordering, the Jezebel spirit reflects anxieties over the destabilization of borders, opening both self and state to the dangerous influence of foreign bodies. Drawing on queer theory, the chapter explores how conjurations of Jezebel construct her as revealing the boundaries of bodies to be always already porous and perforated, manifesting as a fear of nomadism and a loss of futurity figured as the reproduction of sameness. Ultimately, it argues that Jezebel represents a structural disinheritance of the reproductive futurism of an America built on concepts of stable, sovereign unity. Constructing and conducting an emergent vision of the body politic through a deviant body politics, Jezebel manifests as networks of process and flow, messy multiplicities that eschew any societal reproduction along unitary lines and contest their theologically prescribed role as abjected vessels to be colonized, coerced and ultimately annihilated by reinscriptions of "right order."

The Jezebel spirit comes as close to ubiquity within spiritual warfare texts as any demon. Even texts primarily concerned with other conjurations of demonic alterity will either invoked her name directly or else make gendered and sexualized references to the loss of national sovereignty, individual autonomy, and patriarchal values that she is figured as responsible for. These other demons are framed as usurping the ground of America through the cracks Jezebel opens, but in different ways. Chapter 3 focuses on one of these by exploring a rising subset of texts that place the Islamic Antichrist at the heart of their end times tales—an Antichrist that is singular and corporate, an individual Antichrist and an Islamophobic vision of "Islam" itself. Drawing on postcolonial and critical race theory, the chapter explores anti-Muslim spiritual warfare discourses as they work to conjure a phantasmatic "Islam" as inverted mirror of and reaction to Euroamerican imperialism, born from the self-defensive dissimulation strategies of asymmetric conflict and the force of anticolonial and antiracist rage. Merging Islamophobia and antiblackness, these demonologies position the relationship between colonizer and colonized, between whiteness and blackness, and between Christianity and Islam in analogous relation to that of the divine and demonic, with the latter assuming the position of a derivative and destabilizing imitation. Critically reading these demonologies, I argue that the Islamic Antichrist reflects (white) Christian America's disavowed systems of messianic imperialism. He subverts their claimed authenticity and authority through colonial mimicry and decolonial violence, ultimately exposing the terrifying and terrorizing foundations of an ontotheological order in which any attempt by those consigned to nothingness to exceed or escape the realm of pure function will only ever appear as an attempt at usurpation.

Chapter 4 follows from the question of foundations by interrogating spiritual warfare discourse around the Leviathan spirit. It traces Leviathan's genealogy in the chaos dragons of Near Eastern cosmology, from whose corpses the world was made, and their inscription as a figure of sovereign power, linked to biblical narratives of Egypt and cemented in Thomas Hobbes's political philosophy. Framed as inherently multiple, Leviathan is called on in spiritual warfare texts to figure disparate and often conflicting movements that threaten to usurp the "proper" temporal sovereignty of Christian America, foremost of which are resurgent revolutionary politics, secular state apparatuses, and revitalized Indigenous traditions. Working through deconstruction, decolonial criticism, and settler colonial studies, the chapter explores how Leviathan disrupts "settled" narratives of time, rupturing a present by embodying histories that refuse to be over and other sovereignties that contest spiritual warfare's claims to territorial and temporal rule. It argues that Leviathan destabilizes the colonial imposition of truth on which orthotaxy's claims to authenticity are built, exposing how the interplay between orthotaxy and its demonized others causes the division between counterfeit and authentic to blur and break down. In the absence of an apocalyptic ending, the once-and-for-all advent of truth that vanquishes all ambiguity and possibility of an otherwise, orthotaxy threatens to blend into the very legion it strives to defeat.

These figures—Jezebel, the Antichrist, Leviathan—who appear almost jarringly disparate, have been chosen to convey both the scope of spiritual warfare demonologies and their underlying similarities. Each figure demonstrates a part of the shifting contemporary American demonological landscape, inscribing and reinscribing different archives and genealogies that are (always imperfectly) subsumed into spiritual warfare's unified field theory. Moreover, while each of these demonic figures acts to contest the structures of orthotaxy through processes of passing and counterfeiture, each can also be framed as challenging one of orthotaxy's foundational attributes more than others. To preempt my conclusions, demonologies of Jezebel undermine *integrity*, articulating anxieties of process and flow that expose an integrated body politic as always already absent, the sovereign's throne as always already empty. Those of the Antichrist challenge *incontestability* by constructing a discourse of competing unity, an uncanny other so (un)like the self which threatens to replace sovereign order with its abject simulacrum. Finally, Leviathan unravels claims to *inevitability* by exposing the haunting of definitive futures by the possibilities it has deemed to be over, but which refuse to remain settled. Embodying and articulating joint projects of descension, each demon(ology) reflects a different crisis in attempts at consolidating sovereign power. They dissolve its thresholds, contest its right to rule, and impede its ends. In doing so, they reveal the structural dependency of sovereignty on its demons: its need for passing orders to safeguard it from its own passing.

Constructed as dissimulated and transient, each of these passing orders is framed as predestined for collapse by the radical difference spiritual warfare posits between (legitimate) appearance and (illegitimate) essence. Yet despite (or perhaps because of) this difference, these allegedly demonic orders display remarkable capacity for resilience and resurgence, survival and subversion. Challenged by the demonic capacity for mimicry, orthotaxy can itself only attempt to replicate a divine order that remains forever external and elsewhere. Evoked and reevoked time and again to combat multiple and recurrent conjurations of its Old Enemy, orthotaxy is revealed as passing for what it is not, working according to a ceaseless process of imitation and alter(itiz)ation that cannot but alienate it from the immutable truth it claims to represent. Stripped of claims to indivisible wholeness, incontestable right, and inevitable fulfillment, orthotaxy becomes just a possible order (perhaps not even a passable order) passing for a value that neither it nor any other order can truly possess. Ultimately, *Passing Orders* asserts, at the heart of demonologies—in their securitizing anxieties over counterfeiture and ardent eschatological anticipations—lies the terrifying realization that all things pass, and all things will pass.

1 / Nations unto Light: Spiritual Warfare
as Orthotaxic Religiosity

"*Quis es tu, mendax, pater mendacii? Quod est nomen tuum?*" the exorcist asks the demon possessing an Ursuline nun in Loudun, France, on May 10, 1634: "Who are you, liar, father of lies? What is your name?"[1] The deliverance of a proper name will create a point of reference and delimit terrain in an established demonological hierarchy, demonstrating the bond between the name and the *nomos*, the law. Mastery begins, Jacques Derrida reminds us, with "the power of naming, of imposing and legitimating appellations."[2] The exorcist demands answers in Latin, the language of learning, in order to master the language of an other, imposing order onto the radical alterity whose irruption here takes the form of the demonic. The imposition of order is of the utmost necessity for, as Michel de Certeau traces in his reading of the possessions at Loudun, what is symbolically at stake in this exchange is the very edifice of Christian truth. The liar must be made to testify to that truth, the lie made semblable and appropriable by it. The discourse of exorcism must therefore constrain the liar to speak this truth, the other to acknowledge the authority of the sovereign self. The demon, for its part, does not or cannot acquiesce—either to the demand itself or to the language of order in which that demand is given. "I forgot my name," it replies in the vernacular French, after a long silence: "I can't find it . . ."[3]

In the events at Loudun, Certeau traces a conflict over regimes of knowledge: between religion and science, in which traditional discourses of exorcism vied for validity against emerging systems of medicine; between Church and State, in which a centralizing French state tried to exert control over ecclesiastical and provincial authorities. Mapping these struggles, Certeau charts the contours of an epistemic rupture—of the confrontation in a society between the certainties it is losing and those it is attempting to acquire. At the heart of this rupture lies the figure of the demon. The demon—the truth of the demon—as the object of disparate regimes of knowledge becomes the site on which the legitimacy and authority of those regimes is determined. Yet this object is an ambiguous one, highlighting the tension at the heart of the discursive tradition that seeks to name and categorize it. On the one hand, the exchange Certeau relates and the broader systems of power-knowledge in which this exchange (if not only this exchange) occurs encapsulates the "unflinching attempt" to "name, comprehend, and defend against all that threatens, frightens, and harms us."[4] On the other hand, it illustrates the demon's propensity to resist or exceed that very "attempt to name" and thereby categorize, comprehend, command, and control it: its tendency to not be able (or willing) to locate its name within the rubrics imposed upon it, and in doing so "expose and accuse the legal sacred order of being constructed and not natural."[5] Critically, this ambiguity is woven into the very fabric of demonology's attempt to understand its object: as liar, the demon defies the stability of meaning and the sovereignty of truth to which it is forced to testify.

The tension Certeau charts in the possessions at Loudun opens a path toward mapping the contours of demonology more broadly, not only in early modern France but also in the contemporary United States. In both the demon testifies to a rupture in the order of things, demonology to those regimes of power and knowledge conjured to contort and conceal that rupture—to (re)establish epistemic certainty and explain (away) the fractures forming in the edifices of Paradise. As perhaps the premier locus of religious demonology in America today, evangelical spiritual warfare is the circle in which these regimes are summoned, its components giving shape to a mode of religious expression less grounded in claims to correct (*orthos*) belief or behavior (although these are constitutive parts) than on arrangements, patterns, or orders (*taxa*). These concepts of "correct order" or *orthotaxy* are constructed around three interlocking traits they are figured as possessing: integrity, incontestability, and inevitability. Such traits are discursively, materially, and affectively constituted in contrast to demonic others through the mobilization of onto-epistemological paradigms of demonology and sociopolitical practices of demonization—mobilizations that seek not simply to demarcate or even defend against difference but rather to subject it to processes of epistemic extraction and erasure through the mechanisms of a colonial worlding.

Living in a Demonized World

"Is there a cause and effect connection between an invisible invasion of demons and the disintegration of a society?" Thomas R. Horn poses at the start of his 1998 *Spiritual Warfare: The Invisible Invasion*. "If individual demon possession exists, could nations also come under siege to dominant demonic powers? If people who preside over legislative bodies abandon the moral laws of God, would they thereby espouse a social system that invites a regional increase in the influence of supernatural evil?"[6] If there was doubt as to the rhetorical nature of these questions, Horn proceeds to answer them. Demons, he claims, "play an active social role in every age of history," and by working in "close collaboration with certain unregenerate architects of society" they have even "at times" gained control of "the machine of municipal government." The 1990s was one such time. Refracting the broader antiurbanist sentiments of American conservatism, Horn localizes demonic activity in the cities. At a time when the United States "is considered the most advanced, civilized, high-tech nation in the world," he cautions, "spiritual regression and moral decay abound." Indeed, "something sinister seems to struggle against the moral character of American cities, eroding our social and cultural strength from within." Enumerating dangers familiar to culture warriors of the period, Horn lists "Idolatry, drug abuse, alcoholism, violence, Satanism, homosexuality," and the lingering specter of "socialism." Confronting such threats, "an objective evaluation of our moral dilemma must take into account not only the visible agents of city and state governments but also the unending interaction between spiritual and human personalities. This unseen realm of demonic powers energizes and motivates ever-present and sometimes vocal human counterparts." Ultimately, "What we see happening in America's cities illustrates a present darkness operating with evil intentions concerning our nation's future."[7]

Horn, a former pastor with the Pentecostal Assemblies of God, here captures concerns at the heart of many spiritual warfare discourses, highlighting their imbrication in paradigms of American exceptionalism. *Spiritual Warfare* is an archetypal jeremiad, representative of that quintessentially American genre that accuses the nation of having lapsed in its covenant with God, necessitating urgent course correction if it is to avoid divine judgment. In its juxtaposition of America's place as the pinnacle of civilization and its enumeration of its decadence, the text combines fears of national decline with assumptions of national supremacy. Horn assumes a correlation should—but does not—exist between America's geopolitical authority and its moral rectitude. With its exceptionalism under threat, however, he does not situate blame for the "disintegration" of American society only in the hands of the chosen people, but on the presence of unseen evil—on demonic spirits permitted residence through society's sins and which then (in concert with knowing and unknowing humans) reproduce and reinforce such sins to maintain that control. The doom of America is not (solely) the result of the sins of the elect, but on those structures—and the architects thereof, human and otherwise—that provoke and sustain their sins, the removal of which would allow the nation's privileged position to be restored. These structures are multiple and not always mutually compatible: advances in LGBT and reproductive rights; the growth of multicultural pluralism; the international drug trade; the threat of criminal and terrorist violence, and more. United only by opposition to "Christian America," this array of real and imagined threats caused Horn and others like him to posit an enemy grander and more unified than any single struggle, conjuring the image of "a world system out of step with God—a fallen planet under Satan's dominion, a place in need of redemption."[8]

Siting the source of national decline in the orchestrations of literal demons might seem at first idiosyncratic. However, growing numbers of evangelical Christians in America and across the globe are conceiving of themselves as actively engaged in a spiritual war with the forces of darkness for the souls and future of humanity. Such ideas about spiritual warfare are not a recent innovation. In the fourth century, Christian monks journeyed into the wilderness to battle demons and thus temper their selves into singular images of divine unity, while urban Christianization became increasingly coded as a struggle between a singular divine truth and the myriad demonic lies comprising the pluralistic and polytheistic urban landscape of late antiquity.[9] In early modern Europe, witchcraft demonologies crafted heuristics such as confession that allowed a measure of command and control over the unseen forces that were seen as threatening a fragile and porous self.[10] The advent of secular modernity and its "buffered self"[11] is often thought of as facilitating a decline in demonology as a school of theological inquiry, inaugurating an "afterlife" in which the demon endures more as an object of literary or artistic expression than of lived experience.[12] Narratives of disenchantment were never quite as successful as proclaimed, however.[13] Occulture and alternative spiritualities continue to occupy and carve out space in ostensibly secular nations,[14] while discourses of postsecularity and political theology have begun calling attention both to a "return" of religion to the public sphere and the spectral endurance of theological concepts in more secularized forms.[15] Emerging from and reacting to these contexts, contemporary spiritual warfare discourses reject disenchanted notions of reality as part of Satan's scheme—indeed, to paraphrase Baudelaire's generous gambler, the greatest trick he ever pulled—and advances a blend of ritual action (chiefly prayer) and political activism to retake lost ground from the "illegal usurper, Satan."[16]

Spiritual warfare discourses in America today often trace their origins to the early twentieth-century Pentecostal revivals—specifically the 1908 Azusa Street revival—and later postwar growth of charismatic Christianities in traditional denominations.[17] However, from the mid-1980s the paradigm began to spread through American evangelicalism broadly, signaling the rise of postdenominational neocharismatic ministries and what Christerson and Flory term "independent network charismatics," for which church growth and denomination-building were subordinated to the proliferation of specific modes of Christian expression, modes for which spiritual warfare is core.[18] Popularized in the writings of evangelists such as Cindy Jacobs, Eddie and Alice Smith, George Otis, Rebecca Greenwood, and C. Peter Wagner, among others, this emerging paradigm was framed as a "third wave" (in Wagner's term) of charismatic revival, succeeding those of Pentecostalism and postwar charismatic Christianity. This paradigm drew on the charismatic tradition of "signs and wonders" to propagate a narrative that humanity was living in the end times, Satan's legions had been unleashed upon the earth to demonize believers, and God had given the faithful spiritual gifts to aid them in this climactic, final battle. Such gifts included but were not limited to healing, prophecy, speaking in tongues, and—most importantly here—the ability to discern and expel demons from their lives and environs. This was accomplished with an ensemble of related practices, including deliverance (exorcism) rituals, intercessory prayer, and "spiritual mapping." The last—which Sean McCloud categorizes as an evangelical form "of geomancy that discerns where and why demons control spaces and places, ranging from houses and neighborhoods to entire countries"[19]—was perhaps the third wave's most defining and controversial teaching, and one that continues to shape spiritual warfare discourses in the decades since its formulation, even for those outside or opposed to the third wave proper.[20] Of the territories spiritual warfare maps, the "city"—as material, conceptual, and affective space—is especially critical. As Cindy Jacobs claims, the "city gates were symbols of authority. . . . Satan works hard to gain entrance to cities." He does so, moreover, through a city's collective sins: the city's gates "that open to him do so because of the sin of people in the cities."

The city gates become a "gate of hell." This does not mean the city is lost, however, for "When we found our cities on God's laws or reclaim them according to those laws, then the gate of hell cannot prevail."[21]

This figuration of "the city" as a prime battleground against demonic forces for the soul of the nation, which can only be taken through their (re)foundation on God's law, exemplifies a particularly religious strand of antiurbanism. By *antiurbanism* I do not mean a mere rejection of the urban but an ideologico-affective complex that situates itself in opposition to both "the density and heterogeneity" of urban life and "the sense of public that grows in urban soil"—the forms of collectivity and collective action that urbanity necessitates and inspires—and so constructs the city as "the loss of intimate social relations replaced by anonymity, and of nurturing communities replaced by alienation."[22] Figured as inherently atomistic and alienating, the antiurbanist city is positioned as the antithesis of true community, constructed as emotionally and spiritually nurturing, intimate and integrated, and the sole locus of legitimate social action. In spiritual warfare discourses, this antiurbanism is bound up with the well-documented tendency among evangelicals to perceive themselves as "not at home in and different from the world."[23] Larry Richards, writing in *The Full Armor of God*, outlines the reason why in relatively simple terms: "Satan spins lies that appeal to 'the cravings of sinful man, the lust of his eyes and the boasting of what he has and does' (1 John 2:16). Such attitudes and values are woven into what Scripture calls the *kosmos*, the 'world,' which we might render here as 'human culture.'"[24] This sense of the world as "under the control of the evil one" (1 John 5:19) provokes, in sociologist Anna Strhan's analysis, the cultivation of an individual and collective desire "to be 'other,' different from those around," while also "conscious that maintaining that distinctiveness is an ongoing struggle."[25] As Derek Prince writes, the duty of Christians is to continually live life so that "we challenge the world with a glimpse of the Kingdom."[26] Medina Isiah is more proscriptive: Christians must be firm in losing their attachments to "this world's ideas, principles, and moral standards. . . . The Word of God is clear, it commands us to not be shaped by, or mimic, the ways of the world."[27]

Within this antiurbanist demonology, few spaces become more archetypal of the *kosmos* to be rejected than the cosmopolis, which comes to be symptomatic of a specific conceptualization of space. Theorists of space have long demonstrated how space is both a product and productive of dynamic social relations, producing sites of becoming that give rise to new emergent relations of centrality and marginality, domination and resistance.[28] As Katherine McKittrick outlines, geography—as "space, place, and location in their physical materiality and imaginative configurations"—is bound up with racial-sexual patterns of domination that create and naturalize a normativity that is conditioning and seductive, but not absolute. "The production of space is caught up in, but does not guarantee, long-standing geographic frameworks that materially and philosophically arrange the planet according to a seemingly stable white, heterosexual, classed vantage point," she writes. This vantage point is figured as unitary and transparent, naturalizing racial, sexual, and economic hierarchies as given by "repetitively spatializing 'difference,'" unevenly situating the world within a given ideological order so the location of nondominant groups become where they "naturally" belong, fixed and stable.[29] Cities often exemplify and exacerbate this unevenness, "reiterat[ing] social class distinctions, race and gender distinctions, and (in)accessibility" through fostering flows of capital, spaces, infrastructure, and people in ways that privilege and mirror white, capitalist, and heteropatriarchial geopolitics.[30] Yet while urban inequalities are often parts of spiritual warfare demonologies, such inequalities are often framed as results of heterogeneity itself—or at least as an absence of a particular (divine, sovereign) unity. As such, spiritual warfare (whether in principle or practice) often comes to reinforce rather than challenge the unitary vantage point from which relations of domination are naturalized.

This naturalization is dependent upon the specific ways that spiritual warfare's vision of selfhood is constructed in relation to singular divine power in opposition to a demonic figured as diverse and (therefore) divisive. "God puts a high premium on unity and hates division," Steve Sampson writes.[31] However, the unity sought is not just any unity, but tied to God as singular truth. "As much as we want unity," Jennifer LeClaire cautions, "we can't compromise truth for the sake of unity. That's really not unity at all."[32] The fostering of integrated unity in relation to a truth guaranteed by sovereign will becomes the foundation of legitimate action and communal rejuvenation while drawing clear lines between territories of self and other, priming the latter for conquest and colonization. Drawing on the image of Hebron, where Abraham entered Canaan, Sandie Freed writes that "Possessing new land requires unity, holiness and accountability. In order to take our land of Hebron today, God requires an army that is in covenant with each other."[33] This idea of the covenantal army geared towards territorial ownership and societal transformation, galvanized by the cultivation of an ipseity in alignment with (and solely accountable to) sovereign will, highlights the first attribute of what I am terming orthotaxic religiosity: *integrity*—the concept of being both whole and wholesome, unblemished and complete-in-oneself.

This integrated unity is personal and societal, founded on ideas of God as singular and omnipresent in contrast to demons as multiple and contingent. "Unlike the Holy Spirit, who is everywhere at once and can speak to millions of people simultaneously," Alice Patterson writes, "the devil can only be in one place at a time. By himself Satan would be totally ineffective, but in cooperation with other powers of darkness he erects structures to deceive and manipulate entire nations."[34] As I discuss later, notions of demonic contingency and cooperation are critical to the demonization and delegitimization of projects of resistance. For the moment, I wish only to note how this framing mirrors antiurbanist ideas of the city's sense of public life. Lacking innate community mediated by the omnipresence and simultaneity of God, demons are framed as forming ad hoc alliances to build structures that, while having definite and widespread effects, lack truth and (thus) all authenticity, validity, and survivability. Demonic systems are linked not by a sovereignty that is "everywhere at once" but by contingent, even rhizomatic, networks of present darknesses cooperating in and across regional ecologies—even and especially when they command ostensibly vertebrate systems like municipal governments or nation-states, systems that themselves become cast as regional cells in willful resistance to a centralized yet omnipresent totality of divine will and rule.

Architectures of (Dis)Order

Understanding the discursive function of regional "powers of darkness" is key to understanding contemporary spiritual warfare, as these are the primary figures through which its demonologies are conceptualized and enacted. The scriptural basis for such powers is derived from Ephesians 6:12, a ubiquitous verse in spiritual warfare manuals: "For our struggle is not against flesh and blood, but against the rulers, against the authorities, against the powers of this dark world and against the spiritual forces of evil in the heavenly realms."[35] In his comprehensive *Believer's Guide to Spiritual Warfare*, Thomas White explains that this passage holds the Apostle Paul's codification of "Hell's Corporate Headquarters"; that is, the unseen demonic hierarchy. At the bottom reside "spiritual forces of evil." These represent the spirits "that commonly afflict people," including but not limited to spirits of "deception, divination, lust, rebellion, fear, and infirmity," against which the majority of everyday spiritual warfare is directed. Above these are the "powers of this dark world," which "operate within countries and cultures to influence certain aspects of life," and above these the "authorities," a word that "carries a connotation of both supernatural and human government" and figures "forces that '[stand] behind' human structures." Finally, at (or near) the summit are the "rulers," also known as "principalities," territorial spirits, or by the Greek *archai*: "high-level satanic princes set over nations and regions of the earth."[36] LeClaire frames these as "the CEOs or five-star generals of the demonic realm, reporting directly to Satan himself."[37]

The precise occupants of each rank in the hierarchy are fluid, with demons classified as merely spiritual forces of evil in one location or text becoming principalities in another as spiritual warriors seek to map distinctive territorial ecologies. Moreover, Satan—ostensibly the pinnacle of this infernal hierarchy as "prince [*archon*] of this world" (John 12:31)—is personally absent from most texts. As such, although he is undoubtedly understood to exist in spiritual warfare discourses, the Devil comes to reflect more of an organizational rubric for amalgamating, categorizing, and demonizing difference than a discrete entity who engages in the lives and environs of everyday people. This is the purpose of lesser demons, and ultimately of the *archai* themselves, for while most spiritual warfare manuals and practices are focused on the deliverance of individuals from demonic oppression the possibility of this oppression is figured as dependent upon the regional presence of an *arche*: a "principality is what assigns demonic spirits to operate in the disobedient," Charisma House's annotated *Spiritual Warfare Bible* states.[38] These territorial spirits "rule illegally and have a direct effect on the people living in their assigned areas," Jacobs explains, elaborating that they "work to 'brainwash' citizens from having the mind of Christ and thus neutralize the power of the Kingdom of God," such as by fostering "moral decay or addictions" in the populace.[39] Ultimately, Bob Larson writes, it is through the structures organized by the *archai* that Satan is able "to build a literal architecture of evil in human lives, an infrastructure that can serve his purposes."[40] The goal of personal spiritual warfare is then "to locate and go after the [demonic] strongman who has engineered the unwelcome superstructure inside you."[41]

Much like the etymology of the word itself, an *arche* in spiritual warfare "coordinates two principles in one," as Derrida once outlined. One is "the principle according to nature or history, *there* where things *commence*—physical, historical, or ontological principle." The other, is "the principle according to the law, *there* where men and gods *command*, *there* where authority, social order are exercised, *in this place* from which *order* is given—nomological principle."[42] The principalities conjured in spiritual warfare manuals encapsulate both principles, naming a point of commencement and of commandment, an origin as well as an order.

Understanding *archai* in this way clarifies the highly *structural* nature of spiritual warfare's demonological imaginary, where failures of personal and collective evangelization become rooted in the existence of elaborate and mutually sustaining ideological, affective, and institutional complexes. Larson's use of "superstructure" here is noteworthy, highlighting how in spiritual warfare the material world is understood as built atop a spiritual base—something McCloud has explored in depth. Drawing on Wagner's claim that third wave practices enable believers to see "the world around us as it really is, not as it appears to be," McCloud argues that spiritual warfare deploys a "'supernatural' hermeneutics of suspicion" analogous to materialist hermeneutics like Marxism or psychoanalysis. Yet, when it "lifts the obfuscating veil" of reality, spiritual warfare finds neither "the material conditions of existence" nor "the repressed memories of childhood traumas," but a clash of unseen, spiritual forces—good and evil, light and darkness, angels and demons—the conflict between which becomes reality's condition of possibility.[43]

This hermeneutics manifests in spiritual warfare missionary paradigms, as spiritual conflicts come to be represented and reflected in material political, military, and ideological ones. Jacobs's narrative of missioning in the USSR is illustrative. "July 1990 brought a crashing of walls between nations," she begins, "a time of unprecedented answers to prayers" in the wake of which she journeyed alongside six other women into the USSR "to meet with Soviet women, intercede on their behalf and touch the lives of those who have had little, if any, personal ministry." Handing out tracts in Moscow, Jacobs and her companions find nobody will take them within Red Square. Discerning demonic influence, they pray to God to break the demon's power, and "within moments all the tracts were gone from our hands." She concludes, surmising that "After our prayer Satan could no longer blind their eyes. We had taken possession of territory Satan wanted to control."[44] Similar examples are found in texts by other spiritual warriors. Wagner, for example, frames the 1945–52 US occupation of Japan as the "most serious setback for Japan's territorial spirits," because "Emperor Hirohito publicly denied [his divine] status" and the government formally separated itself from Shinto. This weakened ties between the Japanese and their traditional gods and so "Christianity grew well for what are now known as the 'seven wonderful years.'" In a related example that highlights the more fractious, competitive nature of demonic spirits, Wagner relates a conversation with Cho Yonggi, founder of Yoido Full Gospel Church in South Korea, in which Cho framed the success of Christianity in Korea (contra Japan) as tied to the damage to traditional Korean religion done first by the Japanese occupation and later by communism. Conflict between competing demonic spirits weakened Korea's own indigenous powers, permitting easier evangelization.[45]

Extending the base/superstructure image into more Gramscian territory, spiritual warfare might here be understood as a supernaturalized conflict over hegemonic perceptions of reality—a war over what ideas and concepts are given credence in a society, which sociocultural bodies are granted legitimacy by these concepts, and how these collectively impact occupants of specific territories, making certain actions and possibilities thinkable and others unthinkable. The clearest example of this understanding is in Francis Frangipane's 1989 *The Three Battlegrounds*. Frangipane defines spiritual warfare as, at heart, a battle over "*one essential question: Who will control reality on earth, heaven or hell?*" However, since Heaven and Hell lack physical weaponry, "When it comes to angelic and demonic warfare, the battle rests not in physical weaponry but in the *power of agreement* between mankind and the spirit realm."[46] As the engineers of "unwelcome superstructure[s]," *archai* are critical to how this "power of agreement" is materialized and territorialized, facilitating a theopolitical imaginary that envisions nations as "an ontological bond between a people and a territory" that takes both proper (divine) and improper (demonic) form.[47] Jacobs explains: "There cannot be two ruling entities over a nation. Depending upon our intercession, the righteousness or sin of a nation, and other spiritual factors, either the angel of the Lord or a fallen angel will be enthroned over that country."[48] The results of rule by an *archai* are figured as universally negative, meaning that—in Freed's words—"entire nations are cursed with poverty and infirmity; they have bowed down to false images, and a death structure of iniquity is established."[49] Engaging in a blend of intercessory prayer and political activism, spiritual warriors can overthrow these structures, establishing "God's rule into [sic] an area, taking it back from the illegal usurper, Satan."[50] Jacobs calls this process "dominion intercession," and it is spatial and temporal in nature.

Drawing parallels between contemporary charismatic deliverance and early modern exorcism, Renaissance scholar Armando Maggi notes that the removal of demons from objects, places, and people has always entailed a restoration of time as much as a reclamation of space. Dominion is central here, as the exorcist's power over demons was linked to the dominion over the earth Adam received from God in Genesis 1:28. Joining dominion over territory to the stability and staticity of a prelapsarian world creates a framework in which, Maggi contends, "demons signified the present time dominated by decadence and pain, whereas an exorcist evoked the order of the past"—and, importantly, the postapocalyptic restoration of that past.⁵¹ In spiritual warfare today, this intercession is not just personal but regional or national, allowing spiritual warriors to disrupt the improper bond between a people and the *archai* structuring their lifeworlds, restoring them to a state of lost purity. As Matthew Lee, Margaret Poloma, and Stephen Post write, spiritual warriors frame this as a mission for positive change "driven by a conception of 'the good' that proponents see as consistent with the will of God."⁵² And given the results that spiritual warriors assign to living under death structures, one can see why. Wagner, for example, claims the Japanese sun goddess Amaterasu (reframed as an *arche*) was responsible for the attack on Pearl Harbor, the collapse of the Japanese "bubble economy," and even the "3/11" Tohoku earthquake and nuclear disaster.⁵³ Jacobs, meanwhile, credits Saddam Hussein's 1990 invasion of Kuwait to attempts by the "prince of Persia"—adapted from Daniel 10:13 and 20—to recoup the empire of Nebuchadnezzar, adding in a later edition that "other *empire spirits*" in the region are trying to "regroup and take back ancient territory such as that conquered and ruled by the Ottomans." In case her intended target might be unclear—given which nation was accused of empire-building in the 2000s—she clarifies: "Islam sees its mission to be conquering the whole world in the name of Allah. Satan wants to fill the earth with terror and terrorists."⁵⁴ In two continent-wide examples, British-born Ghanaian minister Dag Heward-Mills claims "Africa is dominated by territorial spirits of poverty, superstition and war. That is why the continent, although blessed with human and natural resources, is plagued with backwardness and under-development." Similarly, he asserts "Europe is dominated by territorial spirits of atheism, homosexuality and immorality."⁵⁵

In these examples, the necropolitical dimension to spiritual warfare's "conception of 'the good'" starts to become clear, bringing into focus how the discernment and designation of death structures can work to create the subjects they name, framing certain lifeworlds as deviations from divine order and worthy only of dispossession and destruction. And here it is crucial to recognize that the principles of the principalities are deemed a priori illegitimate. "They rule illegally," as Jacobs wrote. If the *arche* is "*the place* from which *order* is given," then this cannot be a legitimate order; if it is "*there* where things *commence*" then all it commences (physically, historically, ontologically) must be erased. Here the second attribute of orthotaxic religiosity is made clear: *incontestability*. Orthotaxy is framed as being absolutely sovereign: it alone holds rightful rule over territory, and other systems of being and belonging are invalid simply by diverging from it. The kingdom of darkness is not a kingdom proper—that is, a legal territory ruled by a sovereign ruler—but a counterfeit that will eventually be unmasked and undone. And contextualized with regard to the regions listed earlier—Japan, the Middle East, Africa—this ascription of illegitimacy also adopts a distinctly (neo)colonial countenance, one reinforced by two interconnected ideas that emerge from spiritual warfare: its understanding of idolatry and conception of ancestral sin.

Unlike in other modes of Christianity, "idolatry" in spiritual warfare does not mean the worship of beings that are *not real* but rather of beings that are *real but not true*. Deities like Amaterasu or Allah—here seen as distinct from the Christian God—metaphysically exist but are demonized, the worlds they signify—Shinto and Islam, respectively—given spiritual power but denied epistemic and ontological validity. Spiritual warfare here epitomizes what decolonial theorist Walter Mignolo, writing on the colonization of the Americas, discerned as the "real project" behind the "extirpation of idolatry." This extirpation, he claims, was "not a religious issue, but an epistemic one. The eradication of other forms of knowledge was the real project at stake,"[56] rooted in what he calls the "hubris of the zero point"—the hubris of believing that one's knowledge is produced not from a situated location but the neutral center, *sub specie aeternitatis*. This epistemic hubris is reinforced by spiritual warfare notions of hereditary curses or generational iniquity, which claim that the sins of one's ancestors continue to impact the present, carried in the blood, opening one to demonic oppression through the sins of the father. While such ancestral sins can include bloodshed, murder, and sexual violence, one of the most frequently identified is idolatry—particularly with regard to racialized or colonized communities.

Anthropologists have discussed the racial dynamics of ancestral sin discourses. Writing of Guatemala and South Africa, respectively, both Andrea Althoff and Melissa Hackman observe that while issues plaguing Black and Indigenous populations like poverty or sickness are credited to ancestral idolatry, the crimes and atrocities of white settlers are rarely if ever framed as causing issues for their descendants.[57] Settler societies might sometimes have to atone for past violence, but systemic and structural issues faced by colonized populations are never a result of such acts of violence but of the lingering specter of traditional identities and ways of life. This is clear in Heward-Mills's framing of Africa, where problems stem not from histories of slavery, colonization, and ongoing exploitation under global capitalism, but from "superstition"—for which the only true cure is Christianization[58]—and also in more localized national or regional demonologies. Such framings corroborate not only Mignolo's claims about idolatry but also—by linking evangelization to economic success—situate spiritual warfare solidly within the matrix of what he terms modernity/coloniality: of colonialism's constitutive place in/as the "underlying logic of the foundation and unfolding of Western civilization" and of modernity's "rhetoric of salvation (by conversion yesterday, by development today)" that must necessarily "marginalize or destroy whatever gets in the way."[59] This alignment exposes spiritual warfare's imbrication in what Lincoln termed empire's incipient moment, the pursuit of Paradise. For this Paradise to be (re)created, competing architectures must be delegitimized, their architects dethroned, their archives appropriated into a singular, teleological narrative of history.

The Demonological Frontier

Practices of delegitimization, dethroning, and appropriation orient spiritual warfare theopolitics, fostering a framework that seeks not simply to (apropos Lincoln) "defend against" threatening unseen forces but to assault them. Discussing late antique urban Christianization, Dayna Kalleres argues that rather than being used simply "to mark alterity, to emphasize otherness or monstrosity . . . to measure and maintain a deliberate distance," as in Jonathan Z. Smith's category of the demonic, demonology often worked to proactively navigate political, socioeconomic, and cultural contexts. Analyzing the *In sanctum Julianum martyrem* of John Chrysostom (d. 407), she notes that rather than create distance from the demonic, John "depicts frightening images of the demons' power to corrupt and invade the human body in order to galvanize Christians to act; he offers a plan to move closer to the demons' location and engage with them directly in spiritual warfare." Moreover, "he provides a reliable antidemonic weapon"—the relics of the titular martyr Julian.[60] Kalleres calls this process, through which Christians were pushed towards active, antagonistic engagement with the demonic *diabolization*, and although deployed for analyzing late antique demonologies similar practices are at work in contemporary spiritual warfare. While they do not offer relics, spiritual warfare manuals perform an analogous function, teaching readers how to orient themselves towards and combat the demonic. Such manuals constitute the material hub of a new science of demons, one that is cartographical—concerned with mapping territories and spheres of influence, of discerning precisely where demonic spaces begin and end, and how they might be revealed—and colonial—aiming at the conquest and conversion of these spaces, assimilation of their traditions into spiritual warfare's knowledge regimes, and cultivation of new modes of subjectivity aligned with sovereign will. And, exposing the imbrication of this cartography within the matrix of modernity/coloniality, it relies on a twofold temporal narrative that joins perfection of demonological knowledge to irreversibility of territorial enlightenment.

As Hawaii-based pastor Richard Ing shows, spiritual warfare joins a surety of legitimacy to an uncertainty of specific knowledge that renders its demonologies exceedingly plastic. Satan divides the world into different areas of control, he claims: "countries, regions, cities, towns, neighborhoods, homes, churches, families, and individuals. I don't know the exact borders of these areas, but I know they exist."[61] Spiritual geography is here positioned as an imperfect but increasingly evolving science, a framing echoed by Frangipane when he writes that "our culture and the boundaries of worldly knowledge must not be allowed to rule over us, for old limitations are destined to go."[62] Despite this, discerning the identities and territories of *archai* draws heavily on "worldly knowledge." Jacobs contends that one "can find evidence of demonic influence by studying the music, culture, architecture, and art" of a region. Indeed, in "America it is not hard to discern the ruling spirits over some of our large cities through the architecture." For example, while once "the tallest structure in a town or village would have been the church" in modern cities "the tallest buildings will invariably be banks." Demonic influence might also be situated in cultural or historical prominence rather than only physical height: the blood shed at the Alamo in San Antonio "gave legal entrance to the spirit of murder and spirit of violence." Folk art is positioned as particularly revealing of demonic residency. "In Resistencia [in Argentina]," Jacobs relates, "we found three panels painted with the symbols for the spirit of death [which ruled over the city]. Sometimes [in other cities] the paintings are sensual and may indicate a spirit of lust or sensuality."[63]

Interrogation of regional folklore, art, architecture, music, and cultural practices functions here as enemy reconnaissance. This is crucial since, while demons "play an active social role in every age of history," as Horn stated, the boundaries of demonic territories and the archives of *archai* are in a state of adaptation, evolution, and flux. Data about their territories and traditions must therefore be acquired, classified and systematized, permitting the naming, comprehension, defense, and offense against those that frighten and threaten to harm "us." Even the ascribed identity of *archai* themselves are subject to alteration. As LeClaire writes self-deprecatingly in her 2016 *Waging Prophetic Warfare* (billed in a foreword by Jacobs as a "fresh revelation . . . revisiting and reexamining the teachings that have gone before"), "Early on in my spiritual warfare training, I had limited revelation and a limited arsenal. I was lacking in solid spiritual warfare fundamentals. I thought everything was Jezebel or witchcraft."[64] Earlier materials are therefore revisited and revised as new revelations arise. Whereas in Certeau's Loudun the restoration of right order rested on a placing of demons into preexisting demonological taxonomies, spiritual warfare's evolve and adapt, maintaining an underlying structure but adjusting to new knowledge and contexts, divine revelations, and demonic encounters.

This construction of an imperfect corpus of data that can be filled through empirical observation situates spiritual warfare discourses in the broader intellectual trajectories of Western modernity, even as they shun modernity's more secularizing trajectories.[65] Like other modernized systems of knowledge production, spiritual warfare figures knowledge as progressively realized and systematized through the formulation of taxonomies, systems of ordering and classification oriented around the discernment of causal regularities and universal standards that are applicable across social and societal modes.[66] Understood as active agents of history, the discernment of demons becomes an unveiling of the hidden mechanisms of history itself and their exposure and elimination becomes a narrative of progressive enlightenment waged through territorial conquest. As Frangipane explains, "Satan has a legal access, given to him by God, to dwell in the domain of darkness." This darkness is a domain of absence, but "its cause is not simply the absence of light; it is the absence of God, who is light."[67] Reclaiming territory thus becomes an erasure of darkness by light—and thus by God, truth, and presence. "When we possess the land over our cities," Jacobs explains, "we gain control of their political, physical, and spiritual arenas. . . . As we pierce the darkness over our cities, more and more of God's light and glory will pour into them."[68] While demons have "legal" rights to territories of darkness, these territories are merely passing spaces in which demons are positioned as transient and nomadic residents. They will eventually be filled (and so erased) by God's light: "When light is turned on in a dark room," Frangipane writes by way of analogy, "darkness becomes light."[69]

This narrative of progressive enlightenment indicates the third and final trait of spiritual warfare's orthotaxic religiosity: *inevitability*. That is, it positions itself as the ultimate and unavoidable result of the historical process, guided by the hand of providence itself. Eventually, they foresee, spiritual warriors will perfect the unified field theory of their demonology and God's light will overcome the present darkness, asserting rightful ownership over the world. With its dualism and logics of possession, spiritual warfare reflects what Derrida once named *heliopolitics*: the "ancient clandestine friendship between light and power . . . between theoretical objectivity and technico-political possession." As he observed, metaphors of light often served to obscure mechanisms of oppression through appeals to truth, masking acts of violence with claims to objectivity.[70] While Derrida is here addressing Western philosophy, the dynamic he names is highly relevant to spiritual warfare—especially as tied to its (neo)colonial cartographies of knowing. The heliopolitics of spiritual warfare manifest in its expropriating will to truth, its drive to synthesize diverse rubrics of knowledge, assimilating the archives of the *archai* it encounters to craft an ever-more-perfect body of data that will permit the discernment, delegitimation, and defeat of invisible invaders and their more and less visible agents.

Grounded in the assumed neutrality—the hubris—of the zero point, spiritual warriors figure their intercession as benevolent, a remaking "consistent with" God's will as the necessary ground for human flourishing, especially given the negative consequences they ascribe to rule by demonic *archai*—commencers and commanders of death structures that bring poverty, infirmity, and demise. Yet, as Mignolo and McKittrick both show, unitary and transparent geographies that depict how places "just are" further the uneven spatialization of difference, (re)producing space through sexual, racial, and colonial hierarchies. Orthotaxic frameworks of integrated unity, incontestable right, and inevitable victory partake in these uneven productions. Accordingly, any imposition of consistency with divine will carries consequences for all who cannot or will not conform to that will, for those whose territories of darkness (bodily and geographic) are not structurally permitted to contest the heliopolitical imposition of truth. Later chapters focus on these consequences, on the regimes they impose and resistances they inspire. Here, however, two examples suffice to represent the conjunctures of territoriality, time, and truth in spiritual warfare's heliopolitical imaginary, as these intersect with global and distinctly American regimes of racialization and coloniality: Haiti and Hawaii.

As Jeffrey Kahn details, Haiti has a specific relation to US regimes of sovereignty and securitization as the "Haitian"—later, "Haitian migrant"— has long been a figure of American political demonologies. Tracing the emergence of biopolitical regimes from the nineteenth century through the Cold War, Kahn demonstrates how Haiti became paradigmatic of a blend of "pathologized geography and sovereign power" core to the Caribbean borderlands of the United States and instrumental in developing the offshore borders and containment practices later mobilized in the War on Terror. Drawing on Mikhail Bakhtin and Michel-Rolph Trouillot, he excavates the "chronotopes of contagion that structure modernist regimes of historicity," binding space, time, and bodies by joining figurations of "decelerated or regressive temporality [to] stunted or degraded subjectivities that both produce and are produced by the decaying landscape in which they are embedded"—a landscape Haiti became archetypal of.[71] Spiritual warfare discourses theologically recode these paradigms, situating the root of the nation's penury not (just) in racial or cultural sources but in spiritual ones. This is effected with a rewriting of the nation's origin story, in which several hundred slaves gathered at Bois Caiman on August 14, 1791, under a leader named Boukman. Conducting a Vodou ritual, Boukman invoked spiritual forces to aid the slaves in their insurrection—one whose 1804 success made Haiti the Americas' first independent Black republic. Recalled and revised in times of national change and crisis, this story holds immense power for Haitian nationalists and spiritual warriors alike—but for opposite reasons. For the latter, Boukman's ritual was not (only) an instigator of national liberation but a diabolic pact, through which—apropos Larson—"In exchange for freedom from the French, participants pledged the ongoing allegiance of their nation to Satan."[72] Or as Clinton Lane relays in more detail: "Boukman, looking to heaven, denounced God because He could not deliver them from slavery and then gave the country of Haiti to the Voodoo spirits if they would deliver Haiti."[73] Reinscribed as territorial spirits, the Vodou powers become the foundation—the *arche*—of the Haitian nation, its penury paradigmatic of the death structures they erect.

In her comprehensive work on spiritual warfare in Haiti, Elizabeth McAlister observes that this narrative, which makes Haiti "the only nation to be dedicated to Satan" is a "backwards mirror image" of evangelical framings of the United States as a Christian nation with a providential destiny. As such, it not only justifies a neocolonial missiology that claims Haiti's penury will be alleviated via the excision and exorcism of its foundations, but augments a regional theopolitical imaginary in which Haitian impoverishment and American flourishing become naturalized results of divine order. Temporality is central here. Drawing on Trouillot as Kahn did, McAlister notes how the Revolution was so disruptive of European ontological and political assumptions about race and culture that it was "unthinkable." She goes further, however, by pointing to a theological element in this modernist historical imaginary: "the Revolution was unthinkable also because pagans could not vanquish Christians. A corollary to the politics of race, the reversal of Christian historical teleology," in which Christianity was to inexorably spread across the earth, was seen as similarly impossible.[74] The Haitian Revolution therefore becomes a (diabolically induced) rupture in developmental/soteriological temporality, one that is not just the antithesis and negation of (and so justification for)

American orthotaxy but one that threatens to pass into it, causing it to pass on, as Haitians and their traditions migrate north.

This concept of diabolic temporal rupture is not limited to Haiti, but is core to spiritual warfare broadly, as demonstrated elsewhere in framings of Hawaii, which similarly became key to US political imaginaries during the Cold War.[75] Whereas Haiti became symbolic of atavistic contagion to be policed, however, Hawaii became "an imagined racial and consumer paradise" and "gateway state" that mediated between Asia and the continental United States—the no less biopolitical proving ground for a new model of US multiculturalism that (as multiculturalism often does) disavowed its colonial and racializing history.[76] Perhaps accordingly, where Haiti was read as symptomatic of an existing diabolic rupture, discourses about Hawaii are chiefly concerned with this rupture's possibility. This is most clear in the aforementioned pastor Ing's *Spiritual Warfare*, which devotes a chapter to "The Hawaiian Religion." Acknowledging the injustices of Hawaii's annexation and the widespread expropriation of land by white Christians, Ing sees a threat of Kānaka Maoli (Native Hawaiians) returning to "ancient demon religions," and advocates for Christians to "ask forgiveness of the Hawaiian people for the sins of our Christian forefathers" to avert this. Echoing Althoff and Hackman's findings, this request not only does not entail returning stolen lands—marking forgiveness less as a mechanism for Indigenous restitution than for absolving white guilt—but Ing proceeds to declare that the "rallying cry of the Hawaiian sovereignty movement [itself] is a direct attack on Christianity." As with Haiti, this is because Hawaiian Kingdom nationalism is framed as drawing on traditions opposed to the providential teleology of (white) Christianity. By 1890, Ing claims, "almost 95% of the Hawaiian race was saved"; today, many are returning to gods who "of course, are all demonic in nature" and manifest in increasing promiscuity, homosexuality, and even human sacrifice—something that as Kānaka Maoli traditions grow in popularity, Ing assures us, "is just around the corner."[77]

Ing's framing, if perhaps fanciful, is both illustrative and ironic. As Kānaka Maoli scholar J. Kēhaulani Kauanui unpacks, not only are many Kingdom nationalists themselves Christian, but international legitimation of the Kingdom's original sovereignty was also linked to its Christianization and adoption of male-dominated leadership and Western gender and sexual norms.[78] Yet, while this complicates Ing's anxieties, it exposes the distinctly *settler* colonial dimensions at work within them. His narrative is one in which Indigenous traditions surrender to Christianity before being allowed to resurge due to the unrepented sins of the settler state.

The death structures these sins permit, however, are oriented not against settlers—who emerge curiously unscathed—but Native Hawaiians. The solution Ing proposes is therefore not to dismantle the settler state but to seek forgiveness for past atrocities in order to facilitate its continued existence: atonement becomes not simply a replacement for solidarity but a means of neutralizing resistance, perpetuating asymmetric relations of domination that have become transparent and naturalized, geographies of sovereignty, subjection, and subjugation that "just are." As Mohawk scholar Audra Simpson details, Western norms of knowledge production often entail claims that "the colonial project has been realized: land has been dispossessed; its owners have been eliminated or absorbed." In short, that it is "'settled' . . . 'done,' 'finished,' 'complete.'" Yet the "ongoing and structural project to acquire and maintain land, and to eliminate those on it, did not work completely. There are still Indians, some still know this, and some will defend what they have left. They will persist, robustly."[79] Spiritual warfare framings of Haitian and Hawaiian sovereignty mirror this structure, transforming both into diabolic insurgencies of things the settler project deems "over," ruptures in a narrative of orthotaxic inevitability that is ineluctably enmeshed in regimes of antiblackness and coloniality. Through its heliopolitical imaginary, spiritual warfare here reflects (on) the incompletion of the settler project, reinscribing and attempting to recuperate its subaltern realities of subversion and survival, sketching out ever more detailed maps of the shifting borderlands of a demonological frontier to facilitate their settlement and stabilization.

Under World

The demonologies of Haiti and Hawaii briefly outlined begin to demonstrate spiritual warfare's imbrication not merely within global structures of antiblackness and coloniality but in specifically American bio/necropolitical regimes of border security and settler colonialism. This is not only due to their geopolitical positions. While spiritual warfare is practiced and understood as "a global campaign operating in regional theatres of conflict," in anthropologist Dan Jorgensen's words,[80] these theaters are conjoined by asymmetries reflective of broader geopolitical forces, particularly ideologies of American exceptionalism and practices of US empire. America's unique position in the spiritual warfare imaginary—especially the third wave's—has been documented. In his history of spiritual mapping in the United States and Argentina from 1989 to 2005, René Holvast explicitly roots the paradigm in ideologies of Manifest Destiny and their framing of the "superiority of the US and its civilization."

Drawing on this inheritance, he argues, spiritual warfare constructs the United States as "a natural epicentre of divine initiative on earth," a position that becomes transparent and naturalized as the primacy of American evangelical mission theology and the prominent role of the United States in missionary work are rarely questioned either by practitioners or even their religious critics. Further, despite "being an 'international' movement, budgets, schools, initiatives, and personnel came predominantly from the US" and many key figureheads are "either citizens of the US or non-US citizens under the influence of the US through education or funding."[81] Pithily summarizing the Americanism he saw underlying spiritual mapping, Holvast writes that in the paradigm "the destiny of the Christian version of the US was manifest."[82]

If this Americanism is visible globally, it is attenuated in the manuals of US-based spiritual warriors. US historical and cultural images and idioms abound in such texts, while the (continental) United States is framed both implicitly and explicitly as "center" to a nonevangelical (or less evangelical) "periphery." Among the clearest examples of this are in framings of the ongoing War on Terror, which I have touched on in relation to Pritchard's post-9/11 framing of Heaven's Long War, of Satan as "ultimate terrorist" waging an asymmetric (and doomed) conflict against God. Pritchard is not alone, however. In *101 Answers to Questions about Satan, Demons, and Spiritual Warfare*, prominent evangelical author Mark Hitchcock devotes entry 56—"What are the main activities of demons?"—entirely to asymmetric warfare,[83] while third wave warrior Eddie Smith compares Christians' failure to see "the unseen warfare that rages around us" to Americans' failure to process the War on Terror as "*an ideological war, a spiritual battle that can never be won with guns and missiles.*"[84] Perhaps the most telling correlation, however, is found in Linda Rios Brook's *Lucifer's War*. Using the ongoing war in Afghanistan as an extended metaphor, Brook compares humanity's imbrication in the ongoing cosmic war to Afghani citizens who, while "the legal occupants of the land," are "powerless to summarily dismiss the armies" that fight there and whose "lives are [therefore] consumed by conflict they did not invite and for the most part do not understand." This is, however, not only a metaphor. Echoing Pritchard and Smith, the War on Terror becomes both a material reflection and a chance for chastisement, as it is—at "its roots"—an "ideological and spiritual war over views about God," an alleged truth at which "Western nations nervously balk."[85]

All these texts assume or express a set of binary oppositions that condition one another: God/Devil; Strength/Weakness; Righteousness/Evil; and, most obviously but most important, America/Terrorists. America's alignment with the position of righteousness and divine sovereign will is naturalized, its military and technological superiority bleeding into the omnipotence and omnipresence of God himself. Brook's reading is especially revealing here. By casting Afghani citizens as a neutral center, a metonym for a humanity torn between divine and demonic forces, she subtly delegitimizes domestic resistance to US occupation—not simply by aligning resistance with coded-foreign terrorists/demons, but that by positioning them as only human she renders attempts at liberation unaligned with US/divine interests a priori illegitimate, no less lacking in truth and thus destined for dethroning and dispossession than the demonized terrorists. Brook's text here subtly invokes the classic colonial inversion that casts native peoples not as indigenous but as "invaders" that land must be reclaimed from.[86] And in this context it is telling that *Lucifer's War* contains one of few explicit acknowledgments of spiritual warfare's coloniality. In an attempt to exculpate America from colonial ambitions, Brook proclaims that: "Unlike the war in Afghanistan, the opposing forces [of God and Satan] do indeed have a plan for colonization that will determine which kingdom will be established and ultimately rule the planet."[87]

Linking together the demon, the terrorist, and (if disavowed) the colonized, Brook points towards spiritual warfare's structural dependency on the figure C. Heike Schotten refers to as the "death-native." Reading settler sovereignty through Lee Edelman's queer dissident polemic *No Future*, Schotten demonstrates that settler sovereignty relies on a logic of futurism that seeks to secure the perpetual survival of the (settler) body politic and continually produces scapegoats as the "displaced, villainized obstacles" to this survival. These obstacles represent "death"—the end of the social order and its capacity for endless reproduction—and are archetypally figured as the "Indian," who represents the limits and destruction of the settler colony and whose domination (therefore) ensures its perpetuation. This creates a structural dependency, since the settler order is unstable it requires this obstacle as the receptacle for its instability, the "reason" behind its lack of fulfilment: "Settler sovereignty cannot . . . do without the death-native it brings into being; the native as death *must* exist in order to purchase life and survival for the settler."[88] Schotten views this structure not simply in settler colonialism "proper" but in the War on Terror that is its heir. Linked by accusations of "savagery" and fears over a collapse of normative order, "terrorists" are paradigmatic of this death-native, "obstacles to empire [that] become projected versions of Indians, [just as] Indians become retroactively legible as the first or foundational examples of 'terrorism.'"[89] Examining a theological substrate Schotten acknowledges but does not explore, however, allows us to view the "demon" as perhaps archetypal of such "displaced, villainized obstacles" conjured and condemned to ensure the survival and sanctity of sovereign order, among the first of objects "thrown across" (*dia-bolos*) the path of providential futurism to (vainly) contest its inevitability.[90]

Read in relation to one another, the settler state's dependency on the "death-native" and spiritual warfare's drive for new demonological frontiers—the discernment and dispossession of "death structures"—permits a reassessment of how US spiritual warfare is, as McCloud writes, "deeply involved in and largely dependent" on mission fields outside the United States itself.[91] This dependence is due to the importance of these mission fields for developing spiritual warfare's demonology, which by constructing nonevangelical traditions and figures as "actual demons or the abodes of demonic presence"[92] become fonts of data for its unified field theories. Reframed through Schotten's analysis of settler sovereignty, this dependency appears more structural, revealing how spiritual warfare discourses must ceaselessly seek out (thereby producing) demons as embodiments of the death of orthotaxy, demons who it must then continually dominate—spiritually, but not only spiritually—to secure its futurity. To mask its structural instabilities, orthotaxy's failure to secure its own integrity, incontestability, inevitability is displaced in the inscription of new demonological frontiers whose inhabitants are demonized as obstacles to eternity. In the process, the lifeworlds of demonized subjects are flattened, their diversity and complexity effaced and their resistances recuperated to make them comprehensible to and assimilable by a demonology whose operation here adopts a character of colonial worlding.

Worlding, or the "worlding of the world," refers to those forms of performativity that "map universes of knowledge, practice, and power,"[93] and within studies of religion is often used to conceptualize the cultural and material work (stories, rituals, transactions) believers engage in to shape their realities.[94] In Martin Heidegger's work on art from which the term derives, worlding refers to "a saying of world and earth, the saying of the arena of their strife and thus of the place of all nearness and remoteness of the gods" that is how "a people's world historically arises" as the "unconcealedness of beings" and, simultaneously, "the earth is preserved as that which remains closed." Ranjana Khanna explains, describing worlding as "an act of strife between being and nonbeing . . . an event through which the participants are brought into temporality and history, or, conversely, excluded from these and concealed timelessly into the earth."[95] Working with the violence inherent to Heidegger's formulation of "strife," Gayatri Chakravorty Spivak has refigured worlding in the context of colonialism as an act of "epistemic violence" by which imperialism inscribes itself onto colonized "space" through the "colonial presupposition of an uninscribed earth" upon which they could write the cartographies of their own world.[96] Drawing on Spivak's reframing, Khanna sees worlding as a "profoundly ideological" event that projects certain elements into existence (world) while simultaneously "remainder[ing] others as earth."[97] It is a process of naming as epistemic violence that both exhumes and entombs, renders some objects visible and utterable while consigning others to the realm of the unsayable. Khanna uses worlding to analyze the constitution of psychoanalysis within coloniality, to unearth "what was made possible and impossible to think in the projective saying"[98] of psychoanalysis, and I wish to engage in a similar project regarding spiritual warfare.

Spiritual warfare, in its discursive construction and materialization of a conflict over *"who will control reality, heaven or hell,"* operates by worlding, deploying discourse and ritual to reshape reality, rendering specific epistemic formations possible, desirable, permissible, speakable; others impossible, undesirable, impermissible, unspeakable. Its worlding is a colonial worlding. Through a heliopolitics animated by a settler imaginary, spiritual warfare figures nonevangelical worlds as "uninscribed earth" before violently rendering them legible and unconcealed as "world." Indeed, quite literally so, as *kosmos*. Demonology here reveals itself as a strategy of legibility in the sense described by James Scott: "a condition of manipulation."[99] Masking its epistemic violence with appeals to a revelation of objective truth—the illumination of the hidden truth of demons, of demons as active in history and of the mechanisms of history itself—the worlding of the world of spiritual warfare consigns nonevangelical traditions to the earth, to Hell (the etymology of *Hell* names, after all, the hidden, the concealed under the earth). Although nonevangelical worlds are, much like those of the colonized, "far from mere uninscribed earth,"[100] spiritual warfare's imaginary constructs a sovereign subject (the spiritual warrior) as having the authority to overwrite those worlds with his or her own. The discourses this subject articulates, however, do not simply seek to replace nonevangelical worlds, but rather transform them into the base matter, the earth, from which to shape their own.

In accepting the partial validity of nonevangelical worlds, by making them *real but not true*, these transformations are visibly palimpsestic, perhaps necessarily so—as the disconnect between worlds facilitates the conjuration of demons as willfully deviant, legitimizing the plundering of one reality for the epistemic perfection of another. It is in relation to these colonial dynamics that spiritual warfare's positioning of the illegality of *archai* as the commencers and commanders of nonevangelical traditions and territories must be situated. To dethrone an *arche* requires and results in the rewriting of its archive, its worlding and its earthing. As the organizing principles, the principalities, of passing orders, *archai* are figured as masquerading as what they are not: evil passing for good, illegitimacy for legitimacy, darkness for light, chaos for order. From the apex of regional hierarchies, *archai* pass orders down chains of commencement and commandment, ostensibly bringing ruin to inhabitants of their territories. For spiritual warriors they must thus be systematically deposed, the traditions they inaugurated effaced, overwritten with "a conception of 'the good' that [is] consistent with the will of God." This heliopolitical worlding both feeds and feeds on a narrative of enlightenment embedded in—to draw on Talal Asad's summary of its more secularized repetitions—"the idea that 'freedom' and 'America' are virtually interchangeable—that American political culture is (as the Bible says of the Chosen People) 'a light unto the nations.'"[101] But there is violence in this light, a violence embedded in the structures of Paradise and the soteriologies of modernity/coloniality that lead back there.

"The transparency of light," Althaus-Reid once wrote, "which carries with it the clarity of imperial logics and the white axis of its racial supremacy, gives a global identity to demons."[102] The discourses of spiritual warfare introduced in this chapter epitomize this transparency, since its heliopolitics encode and enforce paradigms of racial hierarchization and (settler) colonial power in order to (re)produce a vision of reality that appears unitary, transparent, and naturalized as what "just is," or perhaps—given the centrality of declension narratives—"should be." However, the demons explored herein are not merely global but distinctly American. Or rather, they are global precisely because they are American, because they emerge from the anxieties of a settler-state-turned-global-imperium as it seeks to world itself over territories and traditions that will always be more than uninscribed earth. Summoned in the conjuncture between racial capitalist settler state and global empire—between what Nikhil Pal Singh succinctly calls America's "inner" and "outer" wars[103]—the figure of the demon both ensures and unsettles regimes of racial ordering, sexual normativization, and colonial expropriation. It is what the settler state requires and fears, what Paradise must and cannot guard against. As such, the demon troubles and justifies regimes of securitization and stabilization—the quest for new frontiers, physical and philosophical—that permit the discernment and dethroning of that "present darkness operating with evil intentions concerning our nation's future." It is this present darkness, which unsettles the heliopolitical worlding of the city on the hill by secreting finitude and contingency into the ostensibly eternal edifices of Paradise, that later chapters explore.

Raising Hell

Frameworks of spiritual warfare juxtapose a paradigm of correct order—orthotaxy as God's will and rule—with a legion of heterogeneous orders, each commenced and commanded by demonic powers working through ad hoc networks of cooperation and competition. While Satan ostensibly exists at the pinnacle of these structures, the Prince of Darkness is decentered in spiritual warfare texts. Rather, with practices of deliverance, spiritual mapping, intercessory prayer, and political activism, spiritual warriors attempt to discern and defeat his "CEOs" or "five-star generals"—the "other powers of darkness," the *archai*. *Archai* operate as spiritualized personifications of hegemonic ideologies. Perceived as ruling over geographical territories, from homes to nations or continents, they condition the worldviews of a region and activities of lesser demons, shaping systems of authority, sociocultural dynamics, and the lifeworlds of those under their dominion. Expropriated from nonevangelical worlds, each *arche* manifests an archive that gives form and function to the architectures it is seen to rule. These archives are multiform, encapsulating histories, folklore, art, architectural patterns, music, culture, religious rituals, and ideas. The task of the spiritual warrior is to map these archives, interrogating them to discern the identities of the entities they enthrone. Such discernments may at times prove inaccurate, requiring fresh revelation and revisions of old knowledges. Ultimately, however, they will feed a growing demonological corpus, creating ever more detailed taxonomies by which the other may be named, comprehended, and exorcised in defense of the self.

In their attempt to create ever more accurate databases about the identities, tactics, and weaknesses of the Old Enemy, spiritual warfare's demonologies operate through a simultaneous expansion and solidification of borders enmeshed in the discursive structures of US settler sovereignty. The aim of spiritual warfare is to expand the kingdom of God on Earth. To this end, spiritual warriors attempt to discern the territories of darkness, reveal the truth of their diabolic natures, and ultimately "settle" them in light's name. This expansion is predicated on a radical differentiation between territories of light and of darkness, between an "us" that is frightened or threatened and all that which it must expel, exclude, and eliminate to defend itself. This process is not unique to spiritual warfare today.

Rather, it is part of the strategies of spatiotemporal dominion exercised in historical Christian demonologies, the messianic imperialist projects of late twentieth- and early twenty-first-century America, and the overarching structures of modernity/coloniality. Yet spiritual warfare unites and exemplifies these trajectories. It operates through the conquest of physical and conceptual territory, requiring the systematic dismantling of alternative orders and the lifeworlds they sustain. These orders are not—cannot be—fully erased, however, and so they are overwritten, consumed by spiritual warfare's orthotaxy, where their ascribed errors become the nutrients of its assumed truth, the earth of its heliopolitical world.

This pursuit of more perfect demonologies and the victory such perfection will ensure is driven both by a set of distinct orthodoxies (e.g., the existence and spatiality of demons) and orthopraxies (e.g., intercessory prayer, spiritual mapping). However, what animates and drives spiritual warfare is a concern with order. This concern is manifested in multiple different but overlapping ways, in a fixation on proper pattern recognition, on taxonomical formulation, and the working-out of spiritual warfare's "unified field theory" that would explain the organization and operations of the material and spiritual worlds. The clearest example of this concern, however, is in the attempt to create a system of "right order" through the territorial and temporal instantiation of God's rule—a (re)making of place and history as consistent with divine will—and the construction of myriad "architectures of evil" that spiritual warriors oppose to it and constitute it in opposition to. Although both contain ensembles of beliefs and practices, neither God's rule nor the demonic hierarchies and hegemonies contrasted to it are identical with them. Instead, in the spiritual warfare imaginary each represents an order, a pattern or arrangement: a *taxon*. Each *taxon* encompasses structuring and hegemonic concepts, the systems of authority they legitimate and the sociocultural dynamics these in turn foster. Ultimately, they constitute the horizon of a lifeworld, arranging bodies through affective and discursive linkages into particular modes of being, believing, belonging.

Energized by the discursive and material structures of American exceptionalism (more and less disavowed), the *telos* of spiritual warfare is to enable the "proper" ordering of reality. It is this mission to properly and perfectly order reality that leads me to classify spiritual warfare as an "orthotaxic" religiosity. Rather than "only" being concerned with the policing of proper beliefs and behaviors, spiritual warfare is chiefly concerned with the correct arrangement of reality. Proper beliefs and behaviors both emerge from and enable this arrangement; similarly, improper beliefs and behaviors emerge from and enable other arrangements.[104] Dethroning demonic *archai* is among the chief concerns of spiritual warfare because it is only by transforming its organizing principles that proper ordering of a territory can be realized. Delivering people from minor demons, while necessary, will bring but temporary respite if the structures that enable them remain in place. To this end, spiritual warriors must chart the territories and traditions of other orders and work to reveal the hidden truth of their Hell, to world what is concealed in the earth—to expose their "lies," their ontological status *as* "lie"—and thus unmake and replace them with "truth," to make their errant realities conform to the architecture of sovereign will.

As I have begun to explore, spiritual warfare's orthotaxy is constituted by three core characteristics practitioners see it as possessing: *integrity*, *incontestability*, and *inevitability*. Orthotaxy is constructed as the end of the historical process, one the rightfulness of which cannot be questioned and which thus constitutes the closed space within which (and only within which) unity, moral goodness, and human flourishing are not merely attainable but possible at all. It is important to state that these may not be the only qualities orthotaxic modes of religiosity operate with, merely those most visible in spiritual warfare. Nor, crucially, is it that spiritual warfare's orthotaxy "truly" possesses these qualities: rather it is constructed as doing so, and its normative supremacy over other orders is justified based on this possession. Spiritual warfare's orthotaxy is not only opposed to such alternatives, however, but is (therefore) dependent on them. The demons it conjures are the raw materials from which it shapes its world. But demons are by nature willful subjects. They contest the consolidation of sovereign will and the systems of order it maintains. Named, comprehended, and conjured to enable the defense of order, the demons of spiritual warfare are "rebellious spirits," who "expose and accuse" the architectures of sovereign power "of being constructed and not natural."[105]

Orthotaxy is simultaneously dependent on and destabilized by its demons, who trouble its assumed integrity, contest its right to rule, and reconfigure its ends. These demons reject its "unflinching attempt to name," comprehend, and thus command and control them, and it is by excavating this willful refusal to simply stay buried, under world, that it becomes possible to critically (re)world them, to unearth the narratives of dissent entombed within proclamations of decline. Worlding "involves a creation of strife," Khanna writes, "understanding worlding involves an analysis of that strife—critically worlding the processes of the previously earthed, thereby seeing the historical, political, and economic dynamics of strife through its unconcealment."[106] Critically unearthing the infernal currents that circulate under and inside, support and subvert, the foundations of spiritual warfare's world, the following chapters commit themselves not to bringing to light, which would only reproduce the epistemic violence of a colonial heliopolitics, but to raising Hell.

2 / Jezebel Assemblages: Witchcraft, Queerness, Transnationality

"*Where is the Prince?*" It is a question that is both a ritual and a name: Jezebel, *'izebel*. Its elements have been traced to *'y*, "where?" and *zebul*, "prince," linking it to the Phoenician ritual practice that expressed human concern over the death of the god Baal, as attested in the Ugaritic *Baal Cycle*, while others have claimed that the name is a layered parody: *'îzĕbūl* first becoming *'î-zĕbūl* ("No nobility"), before *zĕbūl* is then twisted into *zebel* ("dung").[1] Other etymologies have been proposed for her name, which has always remained ambiguous: "unexalted, unhusbanded, or the brother is prince," even "chaste."[2] When etymology is relevant to their designs, the spiritual warriors whose texts I analyze here deploy several definitions, sometimes at once, but prefer "unhusbanded"—gesturing toward the defiance of patriarchal authority and "proper" sexual cohabitation that they associate her with.[3] Yet in its form as a question lies the kernel of an anxiety that infiltrates spiritual warfare conjurations of Jezebel, encapsulating and exceeding them. "Where is the Prince?" she laments, she mocks, she probes. Does this name question the presence of her own "false" gods, whose absence finally condemns her, permitting the reassertion of a "legitimate" (masculine, monotheistic) authority? Does it refer to her Israelite husband, whose alleged domination—his symbolic castration—by his foreign queen paves the way for Jezebel's reign, and thus act as both the sign of her self-asserted power and the lament of her adversaries for the restoration of an absent phallus? Or perhaps like the archangel Michael, whose name encodes a rhetorical and negative question uttered in rebuke of Satan's rebellion—*mī kāěl*, "Who is like God?"—Jezebel's name might represent a performative act of similar (albeit oppositional) negation, one which might destabilize the singularity of sovereignty itself. "Where is the Prince?" Jezebel queries, unsettling the notions of patriarchal sovereign presence on which orthotaxy relies and which its partisan warriors continually attempt to reinstate.

Jezebel is a familiar figure in conservative Christian writings,[4] and since her deployment in America's late twentieth-century culture wars she has been the subject of numerous studies and attempted reclaimings.[5] In the narrative of 1 and 2 Kings, she is a Phoenician princess who marries the Israelite king Ahab and leads him and Israel into polytheism, and violently persecutes Israel's priesthood and the prophet Elijah. She is finally defeated by Jehu, who restores the normative, masculine order of Israelite monarchy and monotheism. Her name later recurs in Revelation, projected onto a prophet in Thyatira accused of leading Christians astray through "sexual immorality" and idolatrous worship (Revelation 2:20). As Lee Quinby notes, these twin figurations—sinful queen and false prophet—work together to form a composite image of Jezebel in contemporary America as "a calculating and murderous woman whose defeat carries apocalyptic urgency."[6] This image forms the template for her conjuration in spiritual warfare as the "Jezebel spirit," who assumes, expands, and recontextualizes the figure's portfolio and associations.[7] Identified as among the most powerful of demons, an *arche* for which human "jezebels" are mere vassals and vessels, Jezebel is framed as behind sociocultural phenomena and political projects as varied as queer and trans rights, feminism, drug addiction, abortion, toxic interpersonal relationships, pornography, Hollywood, foreign and/or syncretic religions, and the Democratic Party as a whole, among others. In the process, she becomes as ubiquitous in spiritual warfare as the figure is in conservative evangelicalism widely: "Anyone involved in deliverance ministry is aware of Jezebel's ubiquity."[8]

In this ubiquity, Jezebel's evocation is revealed to be central to the "anxious labor"[9] of securing the sexual-sovereign foundations of sociopolitical order. Her signification testifies to the foundational role that the circumscription of "proper" gender and sexuality have in maintaining hierarchies of domination—but also, read otherwise, the struggle to overturn them. This signification (dis)articulates her theological-textual archives and embodied histories of racial-sexual ordering, including both the Jezebel spirit's often disavowed relation to discourses on Black womanhood, her imbrication (as "the jezebel") in a history of the violent denial of "any semblance of bodily integrity"[10] actualized through slavery and its afterlives, and her more overt (and overtly deracialized) mapping onto contemporary reproductive, queer, and trans politics. Critically reworlding discourse on the Jezebel spirit excavates potentialities buried in these archives and embodiments, ones formed of transcorporeal and transnational bonds that might allow for the reimagining and reconstitution of bodily integrity on the other side of its fragmentation. Conjured to secure the foundations of normative order, Jezebel deracinates that same foundation, destabilizing any attempt to ground a body politic in claims of indivisible, integrated sovereignty and the (white, settler, cisheteropatriarchal) future this sovereignty is seen to guarantee.

Mother of Monsters

The prominence of Jezebel within spiritual warfare leads her to adopt a somewhat singular role. For John Paul Jackson, for example, Jezebel supersedes other territorial spirits, becoming "a celestial power that has worldwide influence," who "transcends specific geographical boundaries and can affect nations. Whatever region this power enters, it co-joins and collaborates with the ruling principality of that territory."[11] As such, rather than just being one variant of demon, Jezebel can be seen as the mother—or at least midwife—of what Jason Bivins calls that "thoroughly American . . . bestiary of monsters," which unsettles American exceptionalism by "introducing pluralism and ambiguity into the national narrative."[12] Reflecting this maternal function, even spiritual warriors who focus on other demons will devote space to declension narratives in which elements of Jezebel's portfolio (feminism, abortion, queer rights, religious and ethnic pluralism) serve as the impetus of alleged civilizational collapse, enabling further demonic encroachment. As with many qualities assigned to the spirit, this function is tied loosely to readings of the biblical Queen—specifically her worship of other (foreign, multiple, ergo false) gods, who become linked to the proliferation of unsanctified sexual practices. As Landon Schott intones: "Through the worship of Baal, came the god *Dagon*, for Baal was the son of Dagon. Baal, Dagon, Ashtoreth, and Molech combined for the erotic acts of perverted heterosexual relations, homosexual activity, violent sexual acts, body piercing (including genitals), body cutting, and an infatuation with blood . . . prostitution, and ceremonial orgies."[13] Jezebel's introduction of other(ed) gods and other(ed) sex are rooted in her ascribed resistance to patriarchal, monotheistic authority, which in spiritual warfare becomes perhaps her most defining attribute. "Jezebel will *not submit*," Schott instructs his readers: not to God, nor to any "natural authority," nor to "any man or leadership."[14]

Jezebel's refusal of submission renders her an archetypal willful subject, a figure who—in Sara Ahmed's words—"pulse[s] with desire, a desire that is not directed in the right way."[15] This charge of willfulness is intimately tied to the archive of Jezebel's racialization, where her conjuration as a spirit of illegitimate control, source of a "defect" in believers' "submissive fidelity to God,"[16] intersects with both the afterlives of Black slavery and American Christianity's enduring alignments with whiteness. In spiritual warfare discourses, however, the racialized dimensions of Jezebel's conjuration and archive are rendered opaque, sublimated into a generalized figuration of queerness framed through her biblical archetype's associations with the corruptive influence of sexuality on individual, nation, and cosmos at large. Queen Jezebel's marriage to Ahab is read as paradigmatic here, as her refusal to submit to normative cultural, gender, and sexual roles is seen to destabilize both the Israelite monarchy and the nation it represents. Jezebel is an idolater and (thus also) an adulterer, rejecting legitimacy and fidelity to venerate the ontotheological absences of her many gods and sanctify the polymorphous perversities they allegedly promote. Worse still, she turns her husband to idolatry, supplanting God's "legitimate" (nativist, male, monotheistic) authority with her own "illegitimate" (foreign, female, polytheistic) one.

Inscribed onto modern America, this biblical narrative is integrated into wider evangelical purity cultures and their imbrication in projects of nation-building, national belonging and (in)security, framing "sexual immorality" as "a legitimate threat to the individual and to the collective well-being of the American citizenry."[17] The figure of Jezebel and the spirit that bears her name energize and haunt such discourses, facilitating a paradigm in which "proper" gender and sexual norms are tied to notions of sovereignty and territory, of who rules or has a right to rule in both the household and the nation, catalyzing anxieties over the entwined stability of these positions. Jezebel's willful refusal to submit to (male) authority is central here, not merely for how it frames Jezebel but also her husband. In his book on the "Ahab spirit," Steve Sampson casts Ahab as at least partially culpable for Jezebel's sins: by surrendering to her will Ahab abdicated his divinely ordained role—as ruler, man, and man-as-ruler. His passivity, his inability to perform the active, masculine gender role that God intended, condemned him. This dynamic was evoked by Alice Patterson in 2010 to explain US politics, when she claimed that a Jezebel spirit ruled the Democrats, an Ahab spirit the Republicans, leading the latter to refuse to defend "biblical, moral values" against progressive policies like same-sex marriage due to not wishing "to be called intolerant, a bigot, uncompassionate, racist, or other names."[18] Ahab appears here as the illegitimate passivity permitting Jezebel's illegitimate activity—the "arms dealer that enables her wars."[19] As the force actively seeking to disrupt the ceaseless reproduction of cisheteropatriarchal monotheism, it is Jezebel who faces the warriors' true ire. "Jezebel is the guilty party," Patterson clarifies; and if only "men of God would take their rightful authority in their churches, workplaces, and families," Schott laments, "her tyranny would come to an end."[20]

Jezebel's primacy over Ahab is reflected in the degree to which her spirit often subsumes the functions of his, a subsuming closely related to how the sexist language that saturates Jezebel demonologies feeds a disavowal manifested in assertions that she is not a woman but a genderless spirit. While this is technically true (all spirits in spiritual warfare are genderless) it is a statement that only ever arises in relation to Jezebel,[21] and a reaction to the gendered history of her conjuration. Writing in 1989, for example, Francis Frangipane framed Jezebel as "the source in our society of obsessive sensuality, unbridled witchcraft, and hatred for male authority."[22] Two decades later, Michael Kleu and Madelene Eayrs repeated this formula with a subtle alteration: "When we speak of the spirit of Jezebel, we are identifying the source in our society of obsessive sensuality, unbridled witchcraft and hatred for authority."[23] This omission of "male" reflects less a shift in Jezebel's construction away from rejection of male authority, however, than toward a destabilization of masculine order more broadly. Frangipane continues that Jezebel was "more attracted to the uniqueness of the female psyche" due to "its sophisticated ability to manipulate without physical force,"[24] while Sampson—writing in 2006—also highlights her desire to create men "stripped of their manhood and authority . . . [who] have become eunuchs—slaves—to this demonic force."[25] Jackson follows suit, claiming Jezebel afflicts women and men alike but leaves the latter "weakened and emasculated," while Schott similarly cites the spirit as behind a rise in "dominant" women and the "emasculation of men in our society."[26] In a telling reflection of her alleged dominance, Jezebel here subsumes the Ahab spirit's own emasculating operations. This elevation of Jezebel to sole instigator of gender trouble also allows her vaunted genderlessness to be read more expansively, as marking her not just as a genderless spirit but a spirit *of* genderlessness: a spirit whose goal is the undoing of cisheteropatriarchal gender and sexual order and the uniform reproduction of the body politic this order was conjured to ensure. The Jezebel spirit is a queer(ing) spirit.

Jezebel's unsettling of normative marriage and the normative family are at the core of her queerness—a queerness manifested not only in her projected associations with queer communities but in her unsettling of stable and secure notions of identity and territoriality. By "queer" here, I do not mean only LGBT+ identities, which can be subject to recuperation, but rather the figure Lee Edelman and, building on him, Heike Schotten identify as signifying the abjected other of (hetero)normative order and the rejection of a future imagined as perpetuation of a sovereign self-same. This order and its futurity are dependent on what Edelman terms "reproductive futurism," which "generates generational succession, temporality, and narrative sequence, not toward the end of enabling change, but, instead, of perpetuating sameness, of turning back time to assure repetition—or to assure a logic of resemblance."[27] For Edelman, reproductive futurism is incarnated in the figure of the Child and opposed by the "queer." These figures should not be confused with really existing children or queers. For Edelman, the Child is not a child but rather a fantasy of the perpetuity of "the absolutism of identity" and "the fixity of what is" for which children are the premier cultural symbol.[28] Similarly, the "queer," Schotten explains, names those discursively and materially placed "before, beyond, or outside" the "oppressive, heteronormative ordering of time" and "its civilized progress narrative as specters of death, 'savage' and immoral others who become valid targets of necropolitical elimination" in the name of preserving "life itself."[29] This often includes queer and trans subjects, but also other figures like the "terrorist" or "Indian" who are similarly named, categorized, and comprehended as signifying the demise of normative visions of society.

While this queer(ed) figure adopts other forms in adjacent demonologies (explored in later chapters), in demonologies of Jezebel it is most often mapped directly onto queer and trans subjects, who—alongside those who have or conduct abortions, framed as "radical feminists"—become emblematic of Jezebel's war on the nation, as seeking to "distort" or even "destroy the meaning of male and female."[30] For spiritual warriors, abortion and queer rights—of which trans rights are framed as extension and exacerbation—are linked together by ideas of reproductive failure and (dis)inheritance. For Schott, "Homosexuals cannot produce, they cannot reproduce, and they cannot bear fruit." Indeed, homosexuality is "part of [Jezebel's] religion" *because* it undermines God's commandment that men and women reproduce.[31] Abortion is, likewise, positioned as integral to Jezebel's faith, for similar reasons. For LeClaire, "unwanted pregnancy that ends with the child's death is, arguably, a sacrifice" to Molech, while Schott assures readers that Baal worship included not only "child sacrifice" but "murder of the unborn (abortion) and newborn babies."[32] Abortion's central role here is not simply due to sacrificial associations with demonized Near Eastern traditions. Rather, according to Sampson, it is because as "a strategic position of power for Jezebel" it attacks "the very nature of God, which is *life*."[33] God is not just life, however, but a certain kind of life—life that can reproduce and be reproduced on normative lines. "There is no inheritance for an aborted child," Schott explains, linking this inheritance specifically to the perpetuity of the Church: Jezebel "brings a spirit of death to natural families and spiritual families," he continues. "It destroys the fruit of churches. It aborts the relationship between pastors and their spiritual children and destroys the future of churches and the legacy that God intends for His people."[34] LeClaire echoes Schott with her views on homosexuality, turning to well-worn tropes of bodily health: not only is the "spiritual cancer called sexual immorality . . . metastasizing across the many parts of the Body today," she writes, but "When one part of the Body suffers, every part suffers," beckoning not just societal sickness but divine cataclysm, like that suffered by "Sodom and Gomorrah, whose inhabitants gave themselves over to sexual immorality and will suffer the vengeance of eternal fire."[35]

The Church and the normative family here become the conjoined conveyors of cultural legitimacy and survival, merging the individual body with that of the Church as Body of Christ and the bodies social and politic of America, their collective fate sealed with jeremiadic tones. Jezebel is here cast as the antithesis of reproductive futurism, who aborts both actual children and the symbolic-social ties between generations through a promotion of non(re)productive lifeways. However, it is here that what Edelman framed as the nonidentity of the Child with really existing children is important, because while Jezebel is read as inherently abortive her biblical template in fact has children: Ahaziah, Jehoram, and Athaliah.[36] Nor are these children unknown to spiritual warriors. Jehoram features often as the recipient of Jehu's rebuke on the impossibility of peace so long as "the idolatry and witchcraft of your mother Jezebel abound" (2 Kings 9:22)—a claim I will return to. Athaliah, meanwhile, is often elevated to a demonic power in her own right, becoming Jezebel's "destructive seed" who sought to "destroy every legitimate authority to the throne," symbolized in her own marriage to the king of Judah and later purge of claimants to the throne (2 Kings 11:1).[37] Jasbir Puar helps us address this seeming paradox. Drawing Edelman into dialogue with Achille Mbembe's theorization on necropolitics, Puar argues for understanding "how a biopolitics of regenerative capacity already demarcate racialized and sexualized statistical population aggregates as those in decay, destined for no future," an ascription of predestination "based not upon whether they can or cannot reproduce children but on what capacities they can and cannot regenerate and what kinds of assemblages they compel, repel, spur, deflate."[38] Read through Puar's framing, demonologies of the Jezebel spirit act as a discursive nexus where this demarcation of populations meets the (settler) colonial heliopolitics of spiritual warfare, conjuring racialized-sexualized others whose soteriological (dis)possession is what secures eternity itself. Jezebel must be cast down not because she cannot have children, but because her children are not and cannot be the Child, their regenerative (in)capacities and the assemblages they compel and repel signify only death to sovereign will and the orthotaxy it ensures and is ensured by.

Schotten's rereading of Edelman via settler sovereignty, discussed in Chapter 1, is relevant here. Edelman's project called for a radical reclamation of the interpellation of queer bodies as having "no future"—an embrace that, Schotten rightly observes, is "an embrace of death." Responding to critics like José Esteban Muñoz, who critiqued Edelman for reproducing a vision of atemporal white gay male identity that threatened queer Black and Indigenous strategies of survival in the face of systemic violence,[39] Schotten contends that the futurism Edelman targets is precisely the racialized order of settler sovereignty and thus the "death" that must be embraced and enacted is, accordingly, the death of that specific order.[40] This order is not only cisheteronormative or settler colonial, however, but profoundly theological, as reproductive futurism and/as settler sovereignty incarnates an older and overtly providential teleology. Demonologies of the Jezebel spirit unearth this confluence, as spiritual warfare's narrative of futurity is bound not just to the Child as symbol of the eternal perpetuity of normative order but to this order's heliopolitical drive for conquest. "We must conquer Jezebel with repentance and with the spirit of Jehu," writes Sandie Freed.[41] This repentance-cum-conquest is, much like settler colonialism itself, not simply an event but the (re)instatement of an ongoing structure.[42] Freed's analysis of "Jezebel's seed," Athaliah, clarifies this, figuring her desire to destroy Judah not simply as part of a general desire to "destroy a people and a nation" by targeting "the legitimate heirs" but a desire to thwart Judah's capacity for "conquest," as represented in David as one who "possessed the spiritual DNA to conquer his enemies . . . all for the glory of God."[43] Jezebel and her children's queer(ed) refusal of reproductive futurism here meets Althaus-Reid's reframing of demons as opposing "retention," that "imperial meme" which "reproduces itself by reproducing a past."[44] Embodying this opposition, embracing (themselves as) the death of sovereignty and its "legitimate heirs," Jezebel, Ahab, and Athaliah come to personify queer(ed) futures that threaten to exceed the providential teleology of a nativist and cis-heteropatriarchal monotheism.

The Disintegrated Body

In the effort to foreclose on futures that exceed divine order, Jezebel must be dethroned. More than this, she must be destroyed. As if signifying her singular threat, Jezebel's death narrative—told in four acts across thirty verses, from God's sentence on her and Ahab in 1 Kings 21:14–24 to her actual demise in 2 Kings 9:30–37—is, as Wilda Gafney notes, "without peer in the scriptures."[45] When her time comes, Jezebel puts on makeup, a formal wig and fine clothes, and gazes through her window, awaiting death. Jehu, the newly chosen king, orders her servants to cast her down. They oblige. While Jezebel's adornment is often read as representing an attempt to alter her fate through seduction, for Gafney it reveals less an attempt to save herself—the servants who defenestrate her are eunuchs—than her "own sense of self." Jezebel is a woman, she explains, "a foreign one, doubly marginalized and doubly despised." As such, it "is as a woman, culturally constructed through the artifice of beauty, that she will go to her death." A "queen until the end," Jezebel faces death "on her own terms."[46] Her fate is gruesome and absolute: her blood covers the walls, her body is trampled by horses, dogs devour her flesh; all that remains are her skull, her feet, and the palms of her hands. It is also paradigmatic. As Tamura Lomax writes, "the details of Jezebel's death note the defeat of the woman who dares to claim autonomy over her own body, beliefs, desires, presentation, politics, and legacy. Natural hierarchy and female deviance are restored, with Jezebel's distorted body parts and absent torso and lower body serving as proof of both freakish abnormality and nonexistent reproductive capabilities."[47]

Jezebel's disintegrated body—a body constructed as incapable of the integrity orthotaxy demands, which must thus be fractured and fragmented, reduced to the nothing it already "is"—orients spiritual warfare's fixations on the threat of human—especially women's—autonomy, and opens a path to an interrogation of the spirit's disavowed racial archive. In the United States, the figure of Jezebel exists both as a biblical figure and a racial trope, with the latter ("the jezebel") representing "the epitome of race, gender, and sex pathology," a sign of "innate black female immorality and promiscuity" that rationalizes sexual violence and denies subjectivity, and has been "indispensable to white Western and global dominion and," at times, "North American black patriarchy."[48] The trope emerges from the slave plantations as a frame for the commodification of Black women's bodies, and specifically their wombs, as "simultaneously lucrative, imperfect, advantageous, grotesque, enticing, and wild/life," rendering them "quintessentially deviant enclaves upon which the abnormal could be staged, unrestricted curiosities would unfold, and unbridled access was enabled—sans any semblance of bodily integrity, and, to some, sans the mental capacity or the moral judgment to choose and/or refuse."[49] Lomax's work is concerned with the deployment of this trope and the metanarrative it enables in Black American life and the Black Church in particular—the translation of "white perversions" into "black possessions." It is thus notable that she mentions the Jezebel spirit only once, as only one example of the trope's endurance.[50] More notable, however, is the overt absence of the trope from many spiritual warfare texts themselves. As Jennifer Leath notes, even in Black churches Jezebel's spiritualization has often worked alongside her "racial history [being] made opaque."[51] This is doubly so for white spiritual warriors, even those that directly address race, for whom the trope is visible only in its invisibility.

However, even if Jezebel's racial history is obscured and people are marked as "with" her due to a "defect" in "submissive fidelity" tied more closely to her queerness, this archive lingers. The scant places race is explicitly addressed are a useful entry point here. While the racial history of Jezebel as tied to slavery is absent in Patterson's text, she does claim that the spirit was behind slavery itself, figured universally as "an ideology that devalues human life as a whole." Yet this claim serves not as a meditation on universal devaluation, let alone the unique violences of racial chattel slavery, but facilitates a transference of the violence of slavery onto constructions of abortion as a means of demonizing the Democratic Party. For Patterson, abortion succeeds slavery as both equivalence and escalation—a common trope among white (if not only white) conservative evangelicals—with Planned Parenthood clinics in "black inner-city neighborhoods" positioned as "not a sign of compassion but of *intentional, systematic racism* and *genocide*."[52] Ultimately, these claims scaffold a maternalistic lament that "the black community is unknowingly embracing the genocide of their own race" by voting Democrat, positioning them as requiring (white) Republican saviors.[53] Patterson is not unique here. Michael Brown's *Jezebel's War with America* deploys a similar framing, with the causes of an alleged "tremendous deterioration of the black American family"—"sexual immorality, baby killing, fatherlessness, homosexuality, and the breakdown of gender distinctions and roles"—being woven into a tapestry of pathologization that positions Black Americans as in thrall to demons (and possibly welfare) from which they must be delivered.⁵⁴ Queerness is a particular target for Brown, who blames the apparent crisis of the Black family on Black men on "the down low." Aware of how these claims might read, Brown then directly exhorts an imagined Black reader to "hear me loudly and clearly: I'm standing *with* you against our common enemy, Satan, believing that there is a great, nation-changing calling on your community, which is why the enemy so hates you."⁵⁵

Both Brown and Patterson here exemplify spiritual warfare's biopolitics of regenerative capacity, celebrating the possibility (and mourning the loss) of a normativized Black subject—against an assumed present of Black deviance—that can be integrated into orthotaxy's structures.⁵⁶ To return to Lomax, they demand "that black people make themselves over," requiring "black survival and black progress" to be grounded "in false sex and gender hierarchies," positioning "the black 'nuclear' family and hegemonic black sex and gender politics as the only option for black humanity."⁵⁷ At the same time, they reveal a broader demonization of (willful) subjectivity predicated on a denial of bodily autonomy—one enmeshed in spiritual warfare's (settler) colonial heliopolitics and foregrounding the influence of the jezebel's archive. Like places, bodies too are subject to spiritual warfare's constructions of ownership, legal or otherwise. Frangipane makes this clear by claiming that the reason demons cannot possess people—or at least Christians—only oppress or demonize them is because "*possession* implies ownership. If one has given his life to Christ, he has become the property of the Son of God."⁵⁸ Framed through this logic of possession, bodily autonomy becomes idolatrous, a deviation from sovereign will sinful not "merely" because it is a deviation from divine will but because (as such) it signifies an erroneous claim to autonomous subjectivity. In *Jezebel*, Schott links this claim directly to abortion, writing that the threat of the pro-choice movement lies not just in abortion itself but because it trades "righteousness for a woman's right to choose self-worship."⁵⁹ In his later *Gay Awareness*, he positions queer subjects as similarly demonized, in need of a normativizing deliverance that would free them from "the spirit behind homosexual practices [that] is designed by Satan" and thus permitting their entry into "a life of holiness" possible "Only within the boundaries of heterosexuality."⁶⁰

This specific focus on normative racial-sexual ordering finds a generalized manifestation in how Jezebel is framed—apropos Sampson—as dividing "a church body" because she drives people to "seek a place God has not granted them."⁶¹ Freed presents one of the clearest examples of this, narrating an incident at the church where she and her husband co-pastor in which a congregant believes herself to have prophetic words from God.

The Freeds "had tried on numerous occasions to give her loving correction, but she never received our counsel," and this time refuse to let her speak. She does so anyway: the woman "prayed aloud in the spirit—but it was not the Spirit of God speaking. The false tongue bore no witness, and there was no godly interpretation." Unwilling to let her give "false direction through illegal authority," Freed's husband snatches the mic "and took godly authority." The woman and her family then depart, wandering "from church to church, with Jezebel seeking a position of authority . . . because [she] will not receive correction and discipline."[62] The contents of the woman's revelation is not recounted, only that it was illegitimate due to its alleged deviation from sovereign will, here incarnated in the "godly authority" of the Freeds. The narrative illustrates, as Ahmed has shown, how the charge of willfulness "is useful as a technique for making those who are assumed as inassimilable . . . responsible for not being assimilated." Situating this observation in the context of citizenship and immigration discourses, she contends that "It is as if they [the migrant] do not enter a door (imagined as open, an open door functions as a sign of national good will) because of what they have failed to give up."[63] In Freed's tale, the woman's failure to respond to "loving correction" is placed on her as she refuses to surrender her claim to truth. This failure/refusal marks her as a willful part, dangerous because she refuses to properly take part, to become a proper part of the whole. As such, here—as elsewhere—"one form of will assumes the right to eliminate the others."[64]

It is this "right" to elimination, justified through a denial of any possibility of (bodily, moral) integrity, that inscribes Jezebel's racial history as and at the disavowed heart of her spiritualization. Reinscribing a theopolitical archive that long equated Africa and blackness with the Satanic[65] through spiritual warfare's heliopolitical imaginary, Jezebelian bodies become bodies of darkness—of absences for which the occultation of Jezebel's raced body is perhaps the most structuring and foundational. Like Athaliah, Jezebelian bodies inherit the non/being of their (spiritual) mother. Inserted into systems of violence that operate along the lines of race, gender, and sexuality—violence that might not always directly cause death, but nonetheless leads to it—these bodies are stripped of the capacity for self-determination and ontological resistance. They cannot possess themselves. They must be possessed. And it is only with this violent seizure of the other's self that the integrity—the wholeness and wholesomeness, the unblemished completion—of orthotaxy can be ensured. Spiritual warriors might object here—citing Ephesians 6:12—that their struggle is "not against flesh and blood," that their violence is directed not against people but against the demons that entrap them, that they stand "*with* you against our common enemy," as Brown insists. However, this division between flesh and spirit is unstable. This instability is manifested by both a history in which it was Christianity that constructed and imposed the idea of "flesh and blood" as definitional of (religious, racial) community, with lethal and lasting consequences in expulsion, slavery, and colonization,[66] and a present wherein spiritual warfare troubles the lines between seen and unseen worlds, energizing the coercive purification-by-normativization of flesh through the exorcism of sinful spirit(s). Narratives of defects in submissive fidelity—of failures to respond to the "loving correction" of power or excise sexual or gender identity in pursuit of a "holiness" promised and withheld by cisheteropatriarchal order—here demonstrate how, as Jakobsen and Pellegrini observe in regards to the evangelical injunction to "love the sinner, hate the sin," the "line between whom we are supposed to love (the sinner) and what we are supposed to hate (the sin) is impossibly movable and contradictory."[67]

Like the Queen, Jezebelian bodies are condemned for "what they fail to give up"—their cultures, their bonds, their dignity, their selves. As Lomax writes, "Jezebel lives on her terms and dies a martyr to her people, representing her gods, her husband, and her place as queen mother."[68] Both woman and foreigner, doubly marginalized and despised, racialized and queered by history, Jezebel's disintegrated body is intended as a cautionary tale, signaling what awaits those who dare refuse the heliopolitics of possession and those institutions and individuals that claim their mantle. "Jezebel *will not submit*," as Schott wrote: a refusal that seals her fate. But as Jezebel's children are condemned only because they are not the Child, her failure to submit—however disintegrative to the order she rejects—is not a failure of her integrity so much as the performance of an other(ed) integrity: her own, on her terms, for her people, her gods, her husband, her place. We might here revisit and revise Jezebel's willfulness—as Leath proposes, drawing on Cathy Cohen—as representing a "deviance that is not *for* its own sake, but *happens* by virtue of the integrity and dignity of inherent identity, and deviance that is *embodied* as resistance to oppression for the sake of the sociopolitical integrity of people and communities."[69] Jezebel's integrity is not the integrated wholeness of divine singularity but of social bonds and self-governance, and perhaps—at least in the context of spiritual warfare—the diffuse integrations of the Jezebel spirit itself, uniting transcorporeally, transhistorically, and transnationally all those who would dare "seek a place God has not granted them." Jezebel's body (politic) might here start to be rethought as a (dis)integrated body, an assemblage—"a series of dispersed but mutually imbricated and messy networks, draw[ing] together enunciation and dissolution, causality and effect, organic and nonorganic forces"[70]—of queered and racialized bodies, bound together by a history of fracture and fragmentation conducted and constructed through the imposition of her name. This rethinking would not seek to banish Jezebel—let alone exorcize her—but reconstitute her impossible agency in the wake of disintegration: a Jezebel, in Leath's words, "restored her original name, realizing a peaceable pluralism, and deploying her sexuality . . . in acts of defiance and political resistance."[71] And at the heart of this reconstitution, forming the warp and weft of these Jezebel assemblages, are her witchcrafts.

The Forging of Will

Witchcraft is a recurrent motif in Jezebel demonologies. Both singular and multiple, witchcraft refers not only to magic or sorcery but to wider relations of rebellion, seduction, and corruptive influence, and to the affective-linguistic force that enables and sustains such relations. It is linked to Jezebel through 2 Kings 9:22, wherein Jehu rebukes Jehoram, and formulated more broadly in relation to 1 Samuel 15:23, in which the prophet rebukes King Saul for his disobedience to God: "Rebellion is as the sin of witchcraft, and stubbornness is as iniquity and idolatry. Because you have rejected the word of the Lord, He also has rejected you from being king."[72] Drawing on this verse, LeClaire summarizes the "hallmarks" of witchcraft as "rebellion and stubbornness. If you are exhibiting these behaviors, you are effectively serving the idol of self and opening yourself to spiritual witchcraft."[73] In spiritual warfare, to serve oneself is to enter into rebellion, to oppose sovereign will and thus forfeit one's own (rightful) sovereignty over one's dominion, including one's body and one's will. Yet this framing of witchcraft as something one is *open to* as opposed to something one *does* is important. Despite or rather because of its associations with the self, witchcraft is not an individual act. Rather, it is something one channels, a force that compels and emanates from webs of willful hearts: "Where there are rebellious hearts there is witchcraft," Freed writes.[74] As I will demonstrate, witchcraft exceeds and extends between bodies—human and demon alike—binding them into transcorporeal relations of copresence, enfolding them into and as queer networks of power that resist and disrupt the expropriations of orthotaxy and the heliopolitics of its worlding.

For Sampson, "Witchcraft is nothing more than illegitimately controlling the will of another." In case readers suspect he is only writing against abuse of power, however, he clarifies that "from a biblical perspective, witchcraft is anything that usurps the authority and influence of the Holy

Spirit in a person's life."[75] Freed corroborates this, declaring "When we resist His direction and instructions, we are in rebellion—witchcraft!"[76] As with demonic illegality, witchcraft's ascribed *illegitimacy* is here key, as divine direction and instruction is frequently embodied in the "godly authority" of a rightful leader—like Freed herself. Extrapolating on the woman expelled from her church, Freed sites a key manifestation of witchcraft in "soulish prayers targeted against leaders in their church" and which can evolve into "charismatic witchcraft . . . prayer based upon an individual's isolated and personal insight, desire and will. This form of witchcraft hinders godly authority and a move of the Holy Spirit."[77] Freed also indicates witchcraft's affective dimensions: after the woman leaves "the atmosphere was disturbed—actually defiled" due to her lingering "false" prophecy. This idea of witchcraft-as-atmosphere is reiterated by LeClaire, who holds it to be "behind a metallic-seeming atmosphere"— one "as hard as bronze" that arises from "any number of principalities and powers exerting their force on the territory."[78] It is not solely felt, however. She continues that witchcraft is "a spiritual force that I believe operates with or without the power of death and life that is in our tongues," and "words of death are one of the fastest ways Jezebel's messengers get the job done because it takes the battle out of the realm of the imagination and makes it real." As examples of such death words, she specifies people saying she "will rot in hell for my biblical stand against homosexuality" and criticism of "false prophets" as acts of witchcraft.[79]

Marking critique of doctrinal positions as "witchcraft" might seem strange, but critical scholarship on early modern witchcraft is useful for contextualization here. As Alain Boureau discusses, one of the key doctrinal shifts that laid the groundwork for the early modern witch hunts was a reinterpretation of witchcraft as heresy. This fusion refigured witchcraft as a contagion, by which heretical beliefs—previously private—could be transferred magically by those in league with devils (figured as Jews, witches, magicians, and "sodomites"). This meant that "the victims and accomplices of the evil work were no longer" only those deemed morally or physically frail, "but all human beings in their fragile and porous constitution and in their openness to the supernatural."[80] Ideas of diabolic language were central to this new porosity. As Maggi unpacks, unlike angels whose words conveyed unmediated insight into sovereign will, demons' exile from divine presence also exiled them from language as conveyor of truth. As such, demonic speech was understood to be "a fire that devours both its listeners and speakers" and "to speak the devil's language *is* as well as *means* to devour the creation."[81] Contemporary spiritual warfare's notion of witchcraft is distinct from those of early modernity, but the hermeneutical frameworks and fears Boureau and Maggi here unearth help in refiguring its anxieties over (personal, national) boundaries and the devouring impact of exposure to alternative lifeworlds, especially when these are vocalized. LeClaire's exposure to the "witchcraft" of critique threatens her place in divine order, potentially devouring both her integrated selfhood and orthotaxy itself.

Even more than the "fragile and porous constitution" of individuals, the threat posed by vocalization exposes another fragility: the fragility of insulated normativity, of a racial, imperial, cisheteropatriarchal order that—finding its claims to sovereign supremacy contested—becomes stained, strained, and starts to shatter. This challenge to normative supremacy is manifested in a contemporary reinscription of how—as Maggi notes—Satan's rhetoric was "first and foremost a social occurrence," which could impact divine order only through support from human interlocutors: "his disciples, witches, magicians, sodomites, heretics, and Jews."[82] In short, the demonic threat to divine order was made possible through the existence and shared articulations of the demonized. While the dynamics of modern spiritual warfare's witchcraft are distinct, it is also construed as fundamentally social. This is illustrated not just in its ascribed communicability—transferring between bodies through language and affects—but also in the sense implied by Freed's notion of "charismatic witchcraft," of a witchcraft that passes as and so subverts charismatic Christian practice. Witchcraft mimics "proper" social-spiritual order, a mimicry that both produces anxieties over potential slippage into counterfeit practice and lays the groundwork for the delegitimization (and the deconstructive potential) of other traditions.

Witchcraft's potential to counterfeit divine order troubles spiritual warriors' attempts to enact that order. Jacobs, for example, frames the act of praying for things God has not willed for you as a form of witchcraft, a form of "psychic prayers out of our own human minds and not ones prayed from the mind of Christ." This is, she claims, "the basis of what witches do in their unholy intercession: They produce curses and false bindings on those for whom they pray."[83] Freed corroborates this analysis: "Witchcraft is a counterfeit of true spiritual authority,"[84] she writes, relating demons broadly to "bonds (bondage), shackles (prison) and chains" via the Greek term *desmon*, which "looks so much like the word *demon*."[85] However, chains are not solely the province of the demonic. Elsewhere, Freed also compares the harmonious unity and operation of the Church to a chain, one comprising people "to whom I must cling in order to walk into God's future plans for me." She elaborates: "Think of a chain and its links. . . . If one link of chain gets disconnected, then the whole chain is broken. No longer is there oneness—a unity or flow of connected links."[86] While seemingly confronted here by two types of chain—one carceral, another communal—these are perhaps not as distinct as spiritual warriors might wish. Binding people together across space and time, the latter constitutes a chain of generations linked to a providential future. It is the chain of reproductive futurism and of the Child Jezebel refuses to (re)produce, which necessarily enchains Jezebelian subjects—queered and racialized subjects—by denying them all capacity for the very "unity or flow" of kinship, history, and selfhood that it claims as proper only to itself.

As a rubric mobilized to deny queered and racialized subjects community and continuity as part of a soteriological fantasy of deliverance from a carcerality produced by that same rubric, the naming of "witchcraft" here reinscribes an archive of colonial and white supremacist subjugation. In the history of European nation-building, accusations of "witchcraft" were one means by which colonial administrators managed encounters with Indigenous practices, inscribing them as both superstitious and fictious while simultaneously subjecting them to legislative sanction and punitive surveillance.[87] The concept also came to be specifically tied to blackness, with notions "blackness as witchcraft"—and thus as material and spiritual threat—being deployed to justify white projects of domination and devouring.[88] These associations recur in spiritual warfare, as certain religious and spiritual traditions become especially tied to "witchcraft." Writing of South Florida, LeClaire targets "Santeria from Cuba, voodoo from Haiti and Rastafari from Jamaica—and God knows what other devils from various other parts of the world" as hallmarks of witchcraft's mark on the region, linked—leveraging Victorian associations of colonial subjects with homosexuality—to its volume of queer residents.[89] Freed is similar, writing that New Orleans is so deeply tied to Vodou merely being in the city is dangerous: "Visiting areas of New Orleans . . . where there is a great deal of voodoo practiced, can bring strong witchcraft assignments against people."[90] In a confusing but revealing example, Argentine minister Victor Lorenzo, who went on missions alongside Wagner and Jacobs, identifies the "spirit of witchcraft" ruling La Plata, Argentina, as manifested "in the magic and intrigue of Freemasonry" but proceeds to direct prayers against it "toward Brazil from which came the Afro-Brazilian spiritism."[91]

As Lorenzo's initial framing of Freemasonry suggests, it is not only Black Atlantic religions that are constructed as conveyors of witchcraft. LeClaire also targets Catholicism and Wicca, claiming witchcraft intensifies "during Lent when witchcraft deifies Mary . . . and during the Halloween season when Wiccans kick their witchcraft into overdrive."[92] Discussing one Friday during her stay with an underground church in "a closed Muslim nation," Jennifer Eivaz associates witchcraft with Islam. Relating her experience with strong mental disorientation she had "learned is a symptom of religious witchcraft," she explains that "I was informed later that the local Muslims meet on Fridays at the mosque to pray. I believe I was bumping into their prayers—that I was in the atmosphere of those prayers."[93] Nonetheless, Black diasporic traditions maintain a critical role, gesturing perhaps to that unique paradigm of transcorporeality Roberto Strongman identifies as at the heart of Black Atlantic religions; how the body is figured as "a concavity upholding a self that is removable, external, and multiple," creating queer confluences of human and deific identities in which the enfleshment of divinity becomes (contra orthodox Christianity) at once universal and quotidian. For Strongman, this multiplicity of selfhood challenges the unitary concept predominant in the West, permitting "the articulation of noncompliant identities that are usually constrained by normative heteropatriarchy."[94] In spiritual warfare, however, this unsettling multiplicity can only be demonized, its transcorporeality marking not simply challenge but counterfeiture—"witchcraft!" The concavity and multiplicity of self, blurring and blending human and deity, flesh and spirit, here marks merely an absence of (white) presence, a lack of heliopolitical possession that denies the rights and privileges that such presence ensures. The rubric of "witchcraft" enables a denial of the legitimacy of alternative lifeworlds, of identities and destinies that (not coincidentally) overlap with pathologizing politics that equate its diabolic growth with the transnational movement of racialized peoples, both permitted by and permitting of an alleged collapse of normative society due to Black matrifocal families—demonized in the specter of the "welfare queen"—and the diverse kinship relations of queer and trans communities.[95]

Spiritual warfare's juxtaposition between a priori (dis)integrated lifeworlds here reflect wider conservative demonization of nomadism, albeit literalized. As William Connolly outlines, in conservative discourse the "centered calmness" of "sites of tranquility" such as family, church, nation, and heterosexuality are contrasted with and constituted in contrast to "nomadism"—the "restless, mobile, unreliable, parasitic, narcissistic, and egoistic," the "feminine in the classic sense of the term"—and people figured as embodying this nomadism: "atheists, prostitutes, non-Christian minorities, inner-city blacks, the media, illegal aliens, gays, lesbians, left-leaning Jews, and unmarried women."[96] That such figures overlap almost perfectly with those demonized as with the Jezebel spirit is telling, if unsurprising. Yet more critical is that—while framed as such—the conflict conservatives posit between stability and nomadism is not as clear as they claim. Exploring what he calls the "evangelical-capitalist resonance machine"—the assemblage of religious, political, and media forms that form the ecologies and economies of contemporary American conservatism—Connolly contrasts their demonization of nomadism to their robust support for global capitalism, which is in many ways archetypally nomadic: transnational, mobile, and phantasmatic. Yet capitalism is framed as either a "civilizational necessity" offset by the heteropatriarchal stability of family-church-nation or "the most beautiful site of uncertainty and creativity the world has seen since its creation by God" (or both). Either way it "is exempted from critical engagement," with the role it plays in producing those same "nomadic" minority populations elsewhere demonized similarly obfuscated.[97] In short, the true conflict is not between the nomadic and the stable but rather between "legitimate" and "illegitimate" nomadic assemblages.

Spiritual warfare's concepts of "witchcraft" are among the clearest—if not only—places this conflict becomes clear. A web of willful hearts, "witchcraft" figures spiritual warriors' terror not just at the porosity of borders but the solidity and solidarity of alternative communities. The use of the rubric to demonize collective devotional actions demonstrates this, complicating their delegitimizations by portraying "witchcraft" as not only a cause and result of discord but also—to play with Freed's imagery—"a unity or flow of connected links" that binds peoples together. "Witchcraft" here comes to name the diverse kinship ties orthotaxy must dismantle to materialize itself as such. LeClaire related the saturation of witchcraft to the "number of principalities and powers exerting their force on the territory." Freed reinforces this by marking it as "a manifestation of all seducing spirits."[98] Fitting into the antiurbanist imaginary of spiritual warfare broadly and the long relation of race as a metaphor for discussions of the urban, it is the city that most embodies spiritual warriors' anxieties of "witchcraft."[99] For LeClaire, it is Miami: "home to a cornucopia of cultural rebellion," filled with "homosexuality, an active drug scene, naughty nightclubs and the like, as well as"—and here she repeats the diagnosis of her earlier work—"a diverse population that has brought Santeria from Cuba, voodoo from Haiti and Rastafarianism from Jamaica to our shores." In a telling attempt at humor, she adds: "You might say the principalities and powers here are as eclectic as the population."[100] Paralleling her framing of Queen Jezebel's pantheon, witchcraft is tied to a multiplication of sexualities and spiritualities, caused by an immigration of devils from pathologized geographies and dark continents knowable only by divine omniscience.[101]

As discussed in Chapter 1, the antiurbanist imaginary rejects "the density and heterogeneity" of urban life and "the sense of public that grows in urban soil," figuring the city as a "loss of intimate social relations replaced by anonymity, and of nurturing communities replaced by alienation."[102] Conjured into this imaginary, witchcraft might be reimagined as a supernaturalization, or rather demonization, of this "sense of public," the idealized (if not actual) vision of urbanity as a site of encounter and contact. A manifestation of spirits "as eclectic as the population," witchcraft is not the product of a singular will—even Jezebel's—but of a collective willful effervescence, an affective and atmospheric disruption of the (moral, structural) integrity of orthotaxy as it tries to replicate the homogeneity, simultaneity, and omnipresence of the divine. Witchcraft's threat lies not only in its disruption of this order, but in that—like orthotaxy itself—it interpellates, ties together, and mobilizes bodies in social and spiritual networks. Witchcraft transmits. It is "first and foremost a social occurrence." Against spiritual warriors' contestations, both witchcraft and its other here appear not as forces that uniquely break or bind but that break certain chains and bind others, foster certain connections and contest others. Pulsing "with desire, a desire that is not directed in the right way," witchcraft reflects not simply (urban) alienation from divine order, but formations of solidarity within and between communities of difference, joining the allegedly impossible and yet impossibly real bonds of all who transgress the boundaries of "our shores" and their assigned place in the hierarchy of being. Through and as these resonances, witchcraft constitutes the condition of possibility for another order, birthed through assemblages of transcorporeal copresence and collaboration whose willful parts fuse, enmesh, and enfold into one another—the unstable organs of a (dis)integrated body, which comes to bear a name distinct from but entwined with Jezebel's own: Babylon.

Anxious Labors

Babylon is a figure with remarkable polyvalence in America today: "Great city, successful empire, queenly Whore, ambitious building project, united charismatic power, and failed achievement." Her complex and often contradictory archive and mutable mobilizations have been unpacked to delightful effect by Erin Runions. Runions charts how Babylon has become "a site of identification and an object of intense counteridentification," one whose conjurations "Invariably . . . touch on the dangers of sex, the necessity of war, or the problems of governance," coming to signify "central fears of U.S. liberal democracy: that sexual, moral, ethnic, or political diversity will disrupt national unity or, conversely, that some totalitarian system will curtail freedom and force homogeneous unity."[103] Her similarity to the conjurations of Jezebel are immediately apparent; Jezebel and Babylon are often related in Christian eschatological scenarios based on their implicit and explicit parallels in the book of Revelation, where the former's name is mapped onto the prophetess at Thyatira and the latter appears as "the alluring, genderqueer, bloodfiend Whore of Babylon as an allegory for Rome."[104] However, while their interrelation is a common feature of spiritual warfare texts, its specifics often remain ambiguous. LeClaire declares them "religious running mate[s];" Schott that Jezebel "runs parallel with the great 'whore of Babylon.'"[105] For Frangipane, Babylon is "*the spirit of compromise with the world*" and Jezebel "*the unique principality whose purpose is to hinder and defeat the work of repentance*" (that is, the renunciation of worldly ways).[106] In a seeming conflation, Ing writes that "Babylon the great (Jezebel) has wiped out the prophets of God for centuries" but also that Babylon "is Jezebel, and yet she is much more. Her rulership extends throughout the world."[107] This parallels Jackson's framing of Jezebel alone as "a celestial power that has worldwide influence."[108] Subordinating both, James Gardner casts Jezebel as epitomizing "the spirit and power of Ishtar," the Babylonian goddess he also sees as behind Babylon herself.[109] LeClaire, referencing the legendary (and nonbiblical) Assyrian queen Semiramis as exhibiting "the first recorded manifestation of what we call Jezebel," also positions Jezebel as Ishtar, later claiming that the "spirit of Jezebel" is "founder of the Babylonian religious system" and thus of all (non-Christian) religions, since "Babylon is called the Mother of Harlots, which means she births other religions."[110]

Ultimately, little consensus emerges from spiritual warfare texts on *what* the relationship between Jezebel and Babylon is—whether they are distinct spirits, whether one is a form of the other (and if so, which), or whether they are both forms of another *arche* (such as Ishtar) entirely. What remains consistent, however, is that they *are* related. Whether conflated, subsumed, paired, or paralleled, Jezebel and Babylon are intimately entwined in the spiritual warfare imaginary, queerly conspiring and colluding in the realization of a cooperative network of territorial *archai*. Indeed, the queer ambiguity of their relationship in spiritual warfare can itself be read as part of their broader figuration. Exhibiting the blurry copresence of selves that spiritual warriors accuse the Jezebel spirit of fostering, Jezebel and Babylon fuse, and in this apparent loss of discrete identities come to embody in exemplary fashion the anxieties of Jezebel-related demonologies: material dependencies, religious syncretisms, a multiplicity of sex and spirits, and the loss of absolute sovereign singularity. Orchestrating bodies into queer bonds of kinship that eschew the normative reproduction of a future, the figure(s) of Jezebel-Babylon challenge—to borrow Kath Weston's analysis of psychological merging in queer partnerships—"culturally specific constructions of an essentialized self that can be lost and alienated as well as discovered and loved."[111]

The queerness of Jezebel-Babylon's relation is perhaps most comprehensively illustrated by LeClaire. Drawing on Isaiah 47:5—"Sit in silence, and go into darkness, O daughter of the Chaldeans; For you shall no longer be called, The Lady of Kingdoms"—she argues that "part of Jezebel's end time purpose is to seduce people to worship the Lady of the Kingdoms instead of the King of kings," clarifying that the Lady "is Babylon." This "end time purpose" is not incidental, not a result of demonic seduction generally, but the product of a specific relational dynamic. "Babylon is the worldwide religious, political and economic system personified in the book of Revelation as *Mystery Babylon*," LeClaire explains, and "I believe Jezebel is a principality and *Mystery Babylon* is the world's system through which it works . . . Babylon is full of idolatry and immorality because its systems were birthed through Jezebel."[112] Placing Babylon within the same matriliny as Jehoram and Athaliah, LeClaire strips her of the capacity for legitimacy, and thereby of both the chance for individual survival and the possibility of a legacy. However, it is not Babylon herself that is "birthed through Jezebel" but the systems comprising her, systems that collectively render her "a counterfeit of the Bride of Christ"[113]—a counterfeit Bride and counterfeit Body, an inferior, infernal Body built of necropolized and infernalized bodies. Moreover, although some spiritual warriors position Babylon as the "Bride of Satan,"[114] this is absent from most discussions of the Jezebel-Babylon partnership. Indeed, LeClaire's figuration of Babylon as the system through which *Jezebel* works, much as God operates through his own earthly Bride, makes a reading of Babylon as the Bride of Jezebel naturally follow.

In Jezebel-Babylon's queer conjugation, their challenge to orthotaxy's claims to integrity is rendered most clearly in (trans)national form, as transecting, transcending, and transing the boundaries of bodies, of genders, of nations. This comes to be reflected in what is perhaps LeClaire's most structuring binary opposition: that between the "Lady of Kingdoms" and the "King of kings." Encoding a conflict between profoundly gendered modalities of power, this juxtaposition opposes a masculinized absolute sovereign over lesser but still-sovereign rulers to a feminized image of transnational territorial assemblage. Babylon is not the Lady of *a* (singular) kingdom, nor is she a Lady of kings, an authority above and beyond mortal monarchs, but one of kingdoms. In their commentary on Isaiah, John Goldingay and David Payne comment on this word's specificity. It is "suggestive," they remark, that the states under Babylon's control are "kingdoms" (*mamlākôt*), not *'ammîm* ("peoples") or *gôyim* ("foreign nations"), implying that these might be "sovereign states that controlled their own destinies . . . ruled by a king or queen of their own."[115] They frame this word choice as indicating a relation of subordination—a reduction of sovereigns to servants. This reading coheres with Babylon's general figurations in America today, where she is evoked to symbolize a (perceived) loss of sovereignty and the coherence and control of borders, discursively "put to work in a time when subjectivity and politics are shaped by access to global markets no longer controlled by sovereign centers within nation-states."[116] As Runions explains, within this framework of (in)stability the narrative of the Tower of Babel—built, extra-biblical tradition asserts, by Nimrod, husband of Jezebel's "first recorded manifestation" Semiramis[117]—as birthplace and blueprint of the Babylon system becomes a sign of the need for a reassertion of patriarchal, divine authority. Amalgamating fears "of collectivity and equality as tyrannical and self-indulgent," reaffirmations "of social hierarchy passed down through families," and insistences "of the theocratic higher power of God in ordering social relations and the structures of governance," Babelian narratives "grasp after sovereignty, even as it crumbles away," and permit "faith in God" to obscure "the fact that the United States is no longer a secure locus of power."[118] However, there are other ways we might also read the Lady of the Kingdoms, as signifying not only the loss of and desire for sovereign unity but its disavowed plurality and destabilizing absence.

Joining fears of transnational sovereignty and non-normative sexuality—of the trans-national as site of unruly, unsingular agencies—Babylon reflects the correlation that scholars working at the intersections of queer theory and international relations have long observed between the "anxious labor" that produces figures of sexualized deviation and that which produces "powerful formulations of sovereign order versus dangerous anarchy." This is because, as Cynthia Weber argues, drawing on the work of Richard Ashley, modern statecraft is itself predicated on a concept of "sovereign man" the state is designed to "mirror and serve," as medieval kingship was intended to mirror and serve God. Critically, this sovereign man "is always produced as knowable as/in relation to various 'normal' and 'perverse' sexed, gendered, and/or sexualized figures."[119] By leveraging entwined discourses of sexuality and sovereignty, states attempt to both discover and impose visions of "sovereign man" as the ahistorical and universal ground of sexual-political order, necessarily constructing legions of queered, racialized, and spatialized/temporalized self-consolidating others. This attempt is always unstable, as sovereign man—like sovereignty itself—is phantasmatic, and "by not ceding to the will of a particular national sovereign man, international politics (anarchy) always threatens to expose sovereign man and the sovereign order he guarantees as historical and contingent."[120] Weber here usefully corroborates in the language of international relations the structures Mignolo diagnosed as modernity's logic of salvation and which Ahmed explored in the binary of sovereign and willful wills. However, what makes her analysis particularly valuable for exploring figurations of Babylon is what she terms "queer logics of statecraft."

In *Queer International Relations*, Weber forwards a queer logic as permitting the articulation not of the singular "Logos" of "sovereign man," that structures sexual and political orderings as *either/or* normal/perverse but a "plural logoi," which "*construct* and *deconstruct*" sovereign man by exposing the foundations of order as *and/or* normal/perverse, contesting binary logics, "their resulting subjectivities," and "presumed ordering principles" as "the social, cultural, and political effects of attempts to constitute them as if they were singular, coherent, and whole."[121] For Weber, the plural logoi of the *and/or* exceeds attempts to see queerness as solely (anti)normative, as either reducible to homonormativity or queer dissidence, and so it may seem odd to deploy it here. Yet while Jezebel and her Bride are ostensibly cast as the "perverse homosexual" who has long contrasted and consolidated "sovereign man," their conjurations exceed this binary. Jezebel, her Bride, and her witchcrafts reflect those diabolic systems of collaboration that Jackson pointed to in naming Jezebel "a celestial power that has worldwide influence," who transcended geography to link diverse principalities into the networks of "powers of darkness" Patterson read as necessary to resist the omnipresent force of sovereign power. Understood as the plural logoi of the *and/or*, these Jezebel assemblages reflect diverse regimes of social-spiritual ordering, orders that—while perhaps opposed to the specific form of sovereign man invoked in US settler sovereignty—construct as much as they deconstruct, bind as much as they break. A queer and trans Body, transecting and transcending territorial limits, linking kingdoms whose sovereignty can no longer function on clear logics of singularity or hierarchization—unity without (divine) truth is, LeClaire reminds us, "really not unity at all"—Babylon "cannot or will not signify monolithically," instead working to "order, reorder, or disorder national, regional, and international politics and the singular understanding of sovereignty upon which" they depend.[122]

Critical to Weber's argument is that the queer logics of statecraft she describes are not new. They do not testify to a new formation of international relations, but bear witness to "the endless reworkings" of sovereign man: "the desperate, constant refigurations that underscore the fragility of both 'modern man' and 'modern sovereignty,'" and which expose "the endless games of power these refigurations require," revealing sovereign statecraft and sovereign mancraft not in their eternal endurance but in the probability of their passing.[123] These desperate refigurations return us to the disavowed nomadism exposed by Jezebel's witchcrafts, allowing a reframing of Babylon's queer logics and the disavowed plurality of sovereign man as a mirror of the plurality and queer logics of spiritual warfare itself. As outlined in Chapter 1, the spiritual warfare movement comprises fluid, amorphous, and reticulate networks, which bind disparate groups and their local theaters of conflict into a global campaign— theaters bound in asymmetric relations but still operating as parts in the same assemblage; material and spiritual bodies that—in Puar's words— "interpenetrate, swirl together, and transmit affects and effects to each other." Imagining itself a Kingdom without borders united by an immutable truth guaranteed by sovereign will (of God, of Man, of America), spiritual warfare fosters new missionary networks and novel doctrinal revisions as its heliopolitical imaginary confronts the disruptive difference of the local beliefs and practices it attempts to world and to earth, transforming and being transformed by them in turn. Cast as the raw materials by which spiritual warriors construct the unified field theory that circumscribes their reality, the theaters of its conflicts are "far from uninscribed earth." They are already worlds. Such worlds inflect upon spiritual warfare's attempted worlding, as its processes of localization are contaminated by the very localities they try to translate and its cartographies of truth are altered by every new encounter with the demonic. As the perverse other to a vision of integrated sovereign man, Jezebel and Babylon incarnate one form of this localization—the erosion, whether real or imagined, of a "Christian version" of America forced to encounter the (Black, female, queer, trans, migrant) worlds on which its own is built. Yet they are also an abject reflection of spiritual warfare's own globalizing processes, its (legitimate) nomadism manifesting in another (illegitimate) form—the (dis)integrated body that unearths the singular sovereignty their vision of orthotaxic integrity attempts to maintain and reinstate as always already absent.

Empty the Throne

"Where is the Prince?" Jezebel queries. Jezebel and her name gesture toward sovereignty's founding illusion—its phantasmatic nature. The question she and it pose is ultimately rhetorical. The Prince—whole, solitary, enduring—was always already absent; there was only ever difference and multiplicity, forcibly coalesced into ever-unstable hierarchies of being(s). Conjoining non-normative bodies into assemblages of queer bonds, Jezebel exposes and provokes the impossibility of the integral and integrated Body, the presence and porosity of the borders to the Kingdom without borders and the end of the Kingdom without end. In doing so, Jezebel's assemblages deracinate the orthotaxic fantasy of sovereign power, unveiling the hubris of the zero point, the impossibility of singular sovereign man, and thus illustrating orthotaxy's claims to a priori supremacy to be little more than prescriptive illusions. Yet despite or rather because of its prescriptive nature, the desire for sovereign unity—indivisibility, integrity and integration—exerts a driving force not only on spiritual warfare but on the sociocultural systems in which it is embedded. (Re)producing regimes of epistemic and material violence, this desire fosters what Arjun Appadurai has termed the *"anxiety of incompleteness"* and facilitates attempts to alleviate it through the delegitimization and destruction of the traditions and kinship systems of minority sexual, racial, ethnic, and religious populations, which become *dia-bolic* obstacles to the integrated body (personal, politic, spiritual).

In his essay on the geography of anger, *Fear of Small Numbers*, Appadurai identifies the anxiety of incompleteness as tied to the (usually disavowed) fantasy of the autochthonous ethnos at the heart of the nation state, a fantasy that can be mobilized by a population majority in an ethnocidal drive for purity. Incompleteness here "is not only about effective control or practical sovereignty, but" rather "purity and its relationship to identity." Becoming predatory, majoritarian identity seeks the elimination of weaker minorities to realize the violent fantasy of its own wholeness. Critical, however, is that the minority here is only a symptom: "difference itself is the underlying problem." It is difference that must be eliminated. This drive to elimination manifests in systematic programs of *ideocide*: processes by which "whole ideologies, large regions, and ways of life" come to be "regarded as noxious and outside the circle of humanity . . . as outside the pale of human ethical concern."[124] Much as spiritual warfare's own principalities and powers are enfleshed in the demonized, these "noxious" ideologies are similarly never solely abstract, but incarnated in minoritarian bodies that become targets of intimate violence, for literal acts of dismemberment and disintegration that their presence is constructed as symbolically enacting. In a context of rising hate crimes and ascendant Christian nationalism seeking to return America to the fantasy of a white Protestant origin preceding the *archai* seen as having usurped it, Jezebelian bodies become emblematic targets for enactments of ideocidal intimacy. The overwhelming number of queer and trans people murdered in United States, many of them Black and people of color, testifies to this, their bodies frequently subjected to acts of brutalization so absolute that Eric Stanley terms them "overkill"— acts of "surplus violence" that seek to "push [queers] backwards out of time, out of History" itself, marking "the limits of a queer present," and (thereby) constituting the necropolitical foundations of the social order, of "liberal democracy as such."[125]

The vulnerability to brutal and sustained violence among coded-Jezebelian subjects exacerbates rather than curtails both the anxiety of incompletion and the ideocide it engenders. As Appadurai charts, it is the very weakness of the minority that provokes a predatory majority's rage. This is because the weaker the minority, on the one hand, the more their existence impinges on the desire for completion, constituting an (in)surmountable obstacle to wholeness. On the other hand, the minority also becomes figured as deceptive, as passing for a legitimate member of the nation or community, but holding allegiance to another community— "Israel" in antisemitism or "Islam" in Islamophobia, for example.[126] This dual ascription can be witnessed in the demonologies explored here, in which the existence and toleration of vulnerable populations become signs of *Jezebel's War on America*. Transnationally networked by affective bonds of witchcraft, demonized bodies are rendered not singular instances of rebellion but parts in a Babylon system striving to disrupt the futurism of Christian America, to abort the millennial aspirations figured in the fantasy of the Child—and for this, they are denied all possibility of a future. The heart of demonologies of Jezebel is a conflation between multiplicity and absence, figured at once spiritually, sexually, and sovereignly. Her children are not and cannot be the Child, much as her gods are not and cannot be the one God. Her proliferated sexual practices are an absence of a "true"—(cishetero)normative—sexuality, while her name and her Bride reflect the lack of singular sovereign man on which "proper" order must be erected. Jezebel—like all demons—possesses no (legitimate) ownership, no (authentic) substance; the darkness in which she survives cannot resist the heliopolitical force of sovereign will. Accordingly, her unsettling of "America"—enacted by her and embodied by those "with" her—becomes framed as only a transient state. Both world-destroying and destined for perdition, Jezebel's conjurations here reflect that "fetishistic structure" which Stanley claims "allows one to believe that queers are an inescapable threat and at the same time know that they are nothing."[127]

At the start of the third part of his *Three Battlegrounds*—five out of eight chapters of which deal with Jezebel—Frangipane writes that "the lie of the enemy appears most powerfully when men believe that this world, as it is, is the only world we can live in. The truth is, of course, that God is establishing His kingdom and, ultimately, every other reality will submit to and be ruled by that kingdom!"[128] The demon—willfully deviant a priori, ontotheologically negated, and destined for no future—is the figure through which "every other reality" is imagined, coming to index the theopolitical archetype of the inescapable threat that is (and so must be made into) nothing. In demonologies of Jezebel, this "nothing" adopts raced, gendered, and sexualized form. Two of Jezebel's kith and kin, the spirits of Antichrist and Leviathan, are conjured to personify their own social orderings, incarnating other deconstructive assemblages that unsettle spiritual warfare's vision of sovereign will and the orthotaxy it ensures. While Jezebel is one member of this infernal legion—that is, she represents her own distinct passing order(s), with its own marks and goals—she is also the foundation on which others are built, the mother of America's bestiary of monsters. Jezebel's ubiquity in spiritual warfare texts testifies to this role, and her centering of gender and sexuality is critical to it, echoing discourses by earlier and other right-wing movements on "deviant" femininity as sites of cultural and political crisis, handmaids of (often racial) "degeneracy."[129] Destabilizing theopolitical fantasies of indivisible sovereignty and universal "sovereign man" and therefore the (specter of a) homogeneous, integrated body politic(s), Jezebel thus reveals how notions of orthotaxy depend upon structures of sexual-sovereign ordering, reflecting a terror that should the sacred "sites of tranquility" on which cisheteropatriarchy depends ultimately fall, then all Hell truly will break loose.

The naming of "Jezebel"—her conjuration, incarnation, and disintegration—is part of that "anxious labor" performed to secure sovereignty, sexuality, and sovereign sexuality. However, invoked to condemn all who dare exceed the normativizing deliverance of (white, settler) cisheteropatriarchy, the "loving correction" of power that seeks to foreclose on possibilities of queer presence and Black survival, Jezebel cannot be contained by the circle of her summoning. Transcending borders, conjoining and collaborating with those she encounters, she weaves rebellious hearts into assemblages that resist the coercive integrations of reproductive futurism's millennial teleology. For spiritual warriors, these assemblages are invalidated a priori. The bodies of both demons and the demonized are bodies of darkness, of nothingness itself: they lack the ontotheological capacity to resist the heliopolitical reinscription of sovereignty's claims over their flesh and their worlds. *The Jezebel Yoke*, as one of Freed's many books is titled, is not the "unity or flow of connected links." Its links are too diverse, too distinct. It is not the *right kind of chain*. Yet the chain continues to hold, and Sampson testifies to the anxiety that this endurance provokes: "Something . . . has always troubled me," he writes in a fleeting moment of doubt: "those who yield to a Jezebel spirit seem to get away with it in the here and now. I have never understood that, yet I do believe that God in His mercy gives a person time to repent."[130]

Assuring themselves that the dark will ultimately yield, spiritual warriors instead find the integrity of the body (personal and national, material and spiritual) compromised by demonic and demonized others—by Jezebel, by heterogeneous bodies laden with her spirit, and by "God knows what other devils from various other parts of the world." As they await God's presence in a future to come, the paradigms Jezebel is seen as coordinating—feminism, queer and trans rights, and the multicultural and multireligious pluralisms fostered by the very globalization through which spiritual warriors conduct their global war—come to reflect a proliferation of impossible futures, manifested in bodies (social, politic, spiritual) exercising an autonomy they "should" not possess. In the anxiety and the actions this impossibility provokes, the temporal logics of exorcism that construct demons as signifying a "present time dominated by decadence and pain" meet the "limits of a queer present." This meeting is one of violence, epistemic and physical, as the impossible survival of queered and racialized subjects becomes evidence not simply of the incompleteness of a national-spiritual whole but a failure of omnipotence itself and the eternity it promised. In response, such subjects become those whose realities must be "pushed backwards out of time, out of History" in the name of History, beyond the borders of a Kingdom without borders—disintegrated before their forged bonds can combine into a counterfeit Body, into a passing order that despite its prescribed falsity and projected transience refuses not simply to submit but to submissively pass on.

3 / The Islamic Antichrist: An Eschatology of Blowback

In April 2017, in the wake of protests against white nationalism in Berkeley, California, end times prophecy author Joel Richardson took to the show of disgraced evangelical minister Jim Bakker to place responsibility for "the riots in Berkeley . . . Ferguson and this sort of thing" on a "spirit of rage" sweeping the nation. He was not being metaphorical. Richardson explained that while events "in the natural" showed resistance to President Donald Trump, these were merely epiphenomena of a spiritual base. "I see Psalm 2," he continued: "why do the gentiles gather, why do they plot a vain thing?" and, "the scriptures tell us that they gather and plot, ultimately, against the Lord." His reference to the 2014 Ferguson uprising—broadly unconnected to the Berkeley protests—is notable, but not incidental: Richardson was responding to a comment by the leader of Islamophobic group Understanding the Threat, John Guandolo, who claimed Black Lives Matter and other "hard left . . . [George] Soros-funded" groups were working "directly in conjunction" with "the Jihadi movement" at ground, state, national and international levels. In response, Richardson had made two claims. The first was about Black Lives Matter itself: "Look, black lives matters [sic]," he stated, and while this "is a very sacred issue . . . much of the black community feels," and "that's legitimate . . . Satan comes along and he subverts it." The second was about the source of its funding: "Presently, when you really get down to the foundation," Richardson outlined, the "single largest corruptive financial influence in Washington" is "a single family, it's a single government: the Kingdom of

Saudi Arabia. The Saudi Royal family is the single greatest financially corrupting influence in our nation."[1]

This exchange between Guandolo—a former FBI agent who trains law enforcement on the threat posed by "Islam"—and Richardson—author of the *New York Times* bestseller *The Islamic Antichrist*—on the set of a charismatic pastor, crystallizes a moment in the American (theo)political imaginary. Linking demonized rage, Black movements against police violence and white supremacy, and "foreign" Muslim influence, it reveals a confluence between spiritual warfare demonology and the US security state, exposing their imbrication in ascendant Islamophobia and enduring antiblackness, and pointing to the complex and structuring relation between blackness and Islam in the history of the Americas and American systems of othering broadly.[2] Within spiritual warfare, the figure of the "Islamic Antichrist"—at once an individual to-come and a corporate framing of Islam "itself"—sutures this relation. Conjured from Islamophobic tropes that saturate the demonological imaginary of securitizing studies of "jihadism"[3] and the history of Islam in the United States as a site of Black identity construction against white supremacy, the Islamic Antichrist becomes a singular threat to models of America as a (white) "Christian Nation." Imagined as behind Black Lives Matter as much as al-Qaeda and in the Ferguson uprising as much as the 9/11 attacks, both his summoning and exorcism expose the interdependency of America's inner and outer wars, linking militarization at home to imperialism abroad and incarnating a spirit of (anticolonial, antiracist) "rage" that US power must quell in its realization of Paradise.[4]

By positioning "Islam" as the ultimate eschatological enemy, Islamic Antichrist demonologies give name to a crisis of teleology and (thus also) of sovereignty. This crisis is bound to a terror of both resemblance and replacement that is inextricable from the racializing civilizational projects of "the West," as Islam's familial relation to Christianity produces anxieties over theological supersession that find their political corollaries in fears of the sociocultural and demographic "replacement" of a (white) "Judeo-Christian" civilization by its (racialized) others. The Antichrist here becomes a figure deployed to delegitimize both the dissimulations needed to survive white supremacy and asymmetric conflict and the riotous catharsis of decolonial violence. A product of imperial blowback, carceral circulation, and state-market systems of antiblack violence, he is conjured as an abject reflection of (white, settler) sovereignty, a black hollow that invaginates American notions of selfhood. The apocalypse he ultimately heralds is thus not a revelation of this self's triumphant fulfillment but of the terrifying foundations formed by the messianic imperialism and (neo)colonial civilizing missions conducted in its name. Imagined as a revanchist phantasm of the very terror that at once sustains and yet is sourced in the world beyond Paradise's walls, the Antichrist spirit incarnates the impossible possibility of an end that might be otherwise than Being. He manifests the haunting potential for an end to the world sovereignty has made: the "death" and "nothingness" of orthotaxy itself—a nothingness that is enfleshed in Black and Muslim bodies whose ceaseless domination is what ensures that orthotaxy's eternity.

Reckonings

Antichristian framings of Islam are nothing new. The earliest Christian texts that sought to "deal with" Islam were apocalyptic, written following the early Islamic conquests and their aftermath in an attempt to theologically account for events that seemingly challenged the teleologies of Christian history: the Islamic military expansions, the collapse of Eastern Roman rule, and the decline of Christian hegemony.[5] John of Damascus (d. 749) saw Islam as a "forerunner of the Antichrist," while Eulogius, bishop of Toledo (d. 859) identified Muhammad with both the Antichrist and the fourth beast from Daniel 7:23–27.[6] The Crusades only solidified this framing, which remained a staple of Christian polemics from Martin Luther through Jonathan Edwards and beyond, positioning "Islam" as a uniquely violent bastion of carnality in self-consolidating opposition to a (first Christian, later secular) "West."[7] Contemporary spiritual warfare texts mirror the polemics of their predecessors. Like them, they categorize Islam as uniquely "fed on war and violence,"[8] judge its paradise to be "an enormous God-owned bordello in the sky,"[9] and ascribe its origins to an entity "bear[ing] far more resemblance to Lucifer than to any heavenly angel."[10] Like them, they attempt to bestow theological meaning on events seen as challenging history's providential structure: increases in the Muslim population, the destabilization of American-led global order, and the perceived loss of (white, Christian) hegemony. Like them, they were galvanized by an event and its aftermath.

The World Trade Center attacks of 9/11 and the War on Terror launched in their wake loom large in Islamic Antichrist demonologies, their prominence advertised baldly by the titles of Ralph Stice's *From 9/11 to 666* and Walid Shoebat and Joel Richardson's *God's War on Terror*. Echoing broader discourses that framed 9/11 as a watershed moment in US and global politics, charismatic pastor and former "fanatical Muslim," Reza F. Safa marks it as a juncture when "the world took a major turn" in both the seen and unseen realms. "In the spiritual realm, a demonic force made a new declaration of its existence, purpose, and resolve. In the natural realm, the free world faced a new challenge threatening its very survival."[11] However, he made clear in a later work, this challenge was also a calling:

> On that day of infamy America faced a new giant unlike any force by which she has ever been challenged. That principality, better known as *Islam*, will be a contending force until it opens the way for its master, the Antichrist. Meanwhile a time is granted to America to shine in its finest hour. I believe that the United States of America was purposed for this very hour and this very task.[12]

The ideological paradigm of the clash of civilizations, what Arshin Adib-Moghaddam terms the "clash regime,"[13] here converges with the heliopolitics of spiritual warfare. Much as 9/11 acts as a declaration of demonic purpose and resolve so too does it announce America's own, conflict with "Islam"—reconstituted as a demonic *arche*—becoming the *telos* for which the nation was made. While Safa is among the most vocal about this destined purpose, this framing is present elsewhere. Don Richardson names America "the last bastion" against "the pull of the Islamic siren" that will eventually seduce its allies across the West—a projection drawing on conservative framings of an "Islamicized" Europe, ridden with phantasmatic "no-go zones" where state sovereignty is subordinated to "shariah law."[14] For Stice, America "will be the last frontier that Muhammad envisioned," and—turning to the dehumanizing register of appetite—a "kind of final course on the menu."[15] In this discourse of apocalyptic exceptionalism, the light of the city on the hill is all that prevents the encroaching darkness.

The theological tones of the War on Terror are well documented, not simply in its early, ill-thought framing as a "crusade," but in how, as Schotten observes, "'terrorism,' or, sometimes, 'Islamic terrorism,'" is constructed as "fundamentally the enemy of civilization, an instantiation of nihilism, and the embodiment of evil"—as "portending an unthinkable destruction, an annihilation so thoroughgoing and profound" that only a theological register can suffice.[16] The "terrorist"—coded as "Muslim," racialized as "Arab"—here comes to incarnate the devouring ontotheological absence of the demon, as Satan himself becomes (apropos Pritchard) the "ultimate terrorist," the revolt of the angels the "first insurgency." The division between material and spiritual worlds, between "flesh and blood" and "principalities and powers," here fractures perhaps most overtly, as the *arche* against which they fight is positioned not as Islam's corruption but its essence, the post-9/11 era announcing "an era of warfare with the radical Islam, or the true Islam."[17] Commenting on George W. Bush's framing of the War on Terror, for example, Stice commends him for positioning the battle as "not against terrorists but an ideology,"[18] but criticizes the president's framing of Islam as a "religion of peace" co-opted by terrorists. Richardson explains these words as an obfuscation, since Bush "must not speak words that might incite some Americans to vigilant-ism," while Safa frames them as a misguided effort to "be in right relationship with *all* the citizens of the land," including Muslims. "This is admirable," he acknowledges, adding rhetorically, "But is what is admirable also wise?" After all, he explains elsewhere, one of the key ways Satan seeks "to hinder the advance of the kingdom of God on earth is to raise a physical force—another human being who has a strong will and determination."[19] It is through the presence of such willful subjects that the demonic compensates for its existential weakness. As such, the potential presence of such subjects comes to justify the implementation and intensification of material regimes of securitization and surveillance, of exclusion and expulsion.

As I have discussed, the demon is that which both must and cannot be guarded against. It passes into the edifices of Paradise, at once justifying and troubling emergent strategies of legibility, regimes of naming, comprehension, and control. The Antichrist epitomizes this (in)security. As Erin Runions contends, he "is a figure of undecidability—one that puts into question the prevalent circulations based on moral and ideological superiority." Deconstructing the genealogy of Daniel 7:1–14, which in contemporary evangelicalism is often used to flesh out the Antichrist figure, Runions traces the way that its narrative borrows from Babylonian and Canaanite creation myths, wherein a favored deity—in the latter, Baal—defeats the dragon of chaos. As Runions explains, this victorious image of Baal inscribed in Daniel as the Son of Man, prefigures both Christ and—in the racialized/sexualized othering of Canaan—Antichrist. As such, "the Christ figure is replete with an alterity."[20] Drawing on Derrida's concept of invagination, "a participation without belonging—a taking part without being part of.... The boundary of the set that comes to form ... an internal pocket larger than the whole," Runions marks the Antichrist as "the boundary set that is the Christ; it forms an internal pocket larger than the whole. Christ is invaginated by cultural difference." The Antichrist here "troubles the waters of certainty"; he could be anyone, "even the most ostensibly upright person." This troubling derives not (only) from deception but "family resemblance," as both Beast and Son of Man emerge from shared foundations, each invaginating the other with an alterity exceeding containment. The Antichrist thereby renders impossible the capacity to decide—in the Schmittian sense—who is friend and who enemy, enacting a "permanent ironic interruption to the theological certainty of knowing the difference between Christ and the antichrist, and those allied with either."[21]

This (un)certainty is at the heart of spiritual warfare's renditions of Islam, as they attempt to account for its threatening familial resemblance, drawing it into themselves in an attempt at neutralization that only intensifies their destabilization. Superficially, Islam is marked as animated by the Antichrist spirit because "Islam denies the deity, death and resurrection of Jesus" and is therefore "an antichrist religion. Islam denies the shed blood of Jesus, and the redemption and forgiveness of sins through that blood."[22] But many religions fit this qualification. What sets Islam apart is that—according to Don Richardson—it is "unique among non-Christian religions. It stands alone as the only belief system that, due to its very design, frustrates" attempts at conversion, because Islam "drastically redefined fundamental tenets" of Christianity.[23] Notions of original sin are often emphasized here. Lacking the idea of inherited sin, Islam has no need for the sacrifice of Jesus as a means of freeing humanity from that sin. This is compounded by the fact that Jesus exists in Islam, but simply as a prophet rather than the Son of God, and also does not die on the cross. Accordingly, Shoebat laments, "The Jesus of Islam is in no way a 'savior' or redeemer." While he is still born of the Virgin Mary, performs miracles, titled Messiah (*al-Masīh*), and returns in the end times, the Muslim Jesus is declared "void of any truly Biblical Messianic qualities."[24] Moreover, Shoebat stresses, Islam holds the Bible was "corrupted by the Jews and Christians,"[25] a narrative that further troubles spiritual warriors' own as it means that differences between biblical and Qur'anic narratives are already part of Islam's world, are already resolved in favor of the latter. What makes Islam appear uniquely threatening, in short, is not that it denies Christian truth claims but that it accounts for them. Islam introduces ambiguity into the figure of Jesus, rendering his identity undecidable.

Defining the Antichrist spirit in a later text, Safa captures the anxiety arising from this situation through telling use of a word: this spirit, he writes, is one "that wants to take the place of Jesus. It is a revelation that claims *supersession* over Jesus."[26] As historian Kathleen Biddick writes, the doctrine of supersession "posits the theological supersession of the Christian Church over Israel. Christians believed that the New Testament superseded the Hebrew Bible and redefined it as the Old Testament." This movement of redefinition is bound to a typological imaginary, in which events and individuals in the "Old Testament" are seen as prefiguring a fulfillment in the New, such as Christ as fulfillment of the Mosaic Law. "This supersessionary move produces Jews as the figures for the literal truth of Christians."[27] Yet, Biddick continues, there is a tension in this figural logic, as every fulfillment can become a prefiguration of another (the Incarnation, for example, prefigures the Last Judgment) and remains vulnerable to temporal reversal—"the figure of the Christian is always possibly the truth of the Jew."[28] The figures of the Hebrew Bible read as figures for Christ's fulfillment may not be such: Christ himself may be a figure of the (Jewish) messiah to come, or simply a figural reinforcement of earlier messianic messages, or, as Runions demonstrated, might reflect an undecidable figure fulfilled by both Christ and his demonic antithesis. The doctrine of supersession stabilizes these formations, maintaining the proper and expropriating ordinance of time, ensuring Christianity's revelatory and teleological supremacy. However, Islam's perceived supersession repeats (thus disrupting) Christianity's over Judaism, contesting the incontestability of its orthotaxy. To refute their own supersession, spiritual warriors must therefore try to account for Islam as it did them. They must produce Muslims as "figures for the literal truth of Christians," must make Islam always already part of their world.

This attempt to stabilize orthotaxy and the teleology it ensures is entangled with the attempt to stabilize the proper identity of (Anti)Christ, as spiritual warfare manuals work to settle and solidify his identity through assimilating Islamic eschatology into their own.[29] Whereas some spiritual warriors like Safa continue to frame Islam as ruled by the Antichrist spirit and as paving the way for the advent of the Antichrist, others place a more concrete identity on the coming figure. "Islamic teaching about the Last Days predicts the rise of a powerful leader strikingly similar to the Christian's Antichrist," Michael Youssef writes. "In Islam, this prophetic figure is called the Mahdi." Those unfamiliar with Islamic eschatology might here assume the Mahdi to be analogous to the Antichrist: an agent of evil arising in the end times to persecute true believers, the overthrowing of whom signals the fulfillment of history. Indeed, such a figure exists. But this figure—*Al-Masīh ad-Dajjāl*, "the False Messiah"—is not the Mahdi. The Mahdi is Islam's savior figure, analogous not to the Antichrist but the Messiah. Youssef continues: "Muslims see the Mahdi as a savior who will lead a global revolution and establish a worldwide Islamic empire. The Mahdi will rule the earth as the final Caliph of Islam."[30] This framing is not idiosyncratic. Popularized by Joel Richardson's 2006 *Antichrist: Islam's Awaited Messiah*, republished in 2009 as *The Islamic Antichrist*, it has gained broad currency in Islam-oriented apocalyptic circles and is now almost ubiquitous.[31] Relying on reading Islamic eschatology as an inverted mirror of Christianity's own, a kind of Satan's-eye view of the end times, among the core tenets of this paradigm is that the figures identified in Islam as the Mahdi and Jesus are, in "reality," Christianity's Antichrist and False Prophet, respectively. Conversely, the *Dajjāl* or Islamic Antichrist becomes none other than the Christian Jesus.[32]

Richardson supports this claim through an exercise in comparative eschatology. Both the Mahdi and Antichrist are powerful military and spiritual rulers; both reign from Jerusalem; the Mahdi and Jesus cooperate against the *Dajjāl* like the Antichrist and False Prophet cooperate against the forces of God in Christianity; both figures allegedly have a peace treaty with the Jews for seven years, and the Antichrist will "try to change the set times and the laws" (Daniel 7:25), which Richardson reads as an imposition of the Islamic lunar calendar and *sharia*.[33] A similar strategy is undertaken by Walid Shoebat and, in a slightly different vein, by Jack Smith. Shoebat, who has been interviewed as a counterterrorism expert on Fox News and CNN and delivered paid speeches to Homeland Security,[34] devotes almost 130 pages of *God's War on Terror* to Mahdi/Antichrist comparisons, replicating many of Richardson's own and adding other comparisons such as that both use military force, ride a white horse, deny women's rights, and practice beheading.[35] Smith, by contrast, focuses on Shi'a Islam, identifying the Antichrist as the Shi'ite twelfth Imam and situating Iran at the center of the apocalyptic drama where Shoebat and Richardson focus on Turkey, but broadly follows the same comparative schema. Other authors blend Islamophobia with anti-Catholicism, with the Pope playing False Prophet to a Muslim Antichrist,[36] while yet others fully reject Islamic Antichrist eschatologies, citing improper exegesis and political opportunism.[37]

Such critics are broadly accurate: comparisons of the kind pioneered by Richardson often rely on either the nonsystematic nature of much of Islamic eschatology or on selective readings of Christianity's.[38] However, whether these claims are "true" is perhaps less central than the discursive and material relations of power they create and seek to maintain and the structural anxieties they expose—relations and anxieties tied to existing religious, racialized, and civilizationist hierarchies. In these demonologies, fears of the theological supersession of Christianity by Islam merge with and legitimize those of a sociocultural supersession of "Judeo-Christian" civilization and (so) of whiteness by racialized others. "Islam is the future," Joel Richardson declares on page 3 of *Islamic Antichrist*—citing not its place in prophecy but its statistical growth.[39] This future is, however, figured as a passing future: the Antichrist spirit is predestined for failure, to be exposed as the inauthentic simulacrum of Christ and of his messianic (imperialist) teleology; he will come to be through acts of passing, through a transecting of borders and strategies of dissimulation. These registers of passing reinforce a series of interwoven claims about

Islam and Muslims that ground Islamic Antichrist discourses: that Islam is merely passing as a branch of the Abrahamic family, or as a religion like any other, let alone one "of peace;" that "moderate" Muslims are passing as such when they are, in truth, radicals—and, relatedly, that "moderate Islam" itself is no true Islam, but only passes itself off as such. Embodying and energizing broader structures of dehumanization and systems of state-market violence, these claims work to unearth the (post)colonial substrates of spiritual warfare and the theopolitical foundations of the carceral circulations of US empire.

Passing Empire

At the heart of claims to Islam's passing is the Islamic concept of *taqiyya* ("caution"), a concept mainly associated with Shi'a Islam, although spiritual warriors take pains to tie it to Islam broadly.[40] Formulated in a context of oppression, *taqiyya* permits (Shi'a) Muslims to conceal or deny their faith if they are in imminent or foreseeable risk. Refigured by spiritual warriors as—apropos Smith—"the Sharia sanctioned doctrine of intentional deception,"[41] *taqiyya* comes to juxtapose Christian notions of evangelization and martyrdom. Joel Richardson opposes *taqiyya* to the commandment of Jesus to be "the light of the world" and the "city on a hill [that] cannot be hidden" (Matthew 5:14),[42] while Shoebat writes that "Christians throughout history chose to endure horrific and cruel torture, even martyrdom instead of denying their faith.... Muslims are allowed to lie even to protect the reputation of Islam."[43] This juxtaposition accomplishes several ends, the foremost of which is to figure all Muslims as potentially deceitful. "Because of the widespread practice of taqiyya in the Islamic community, we can never know if a seemingly moderate Muslim is truly moderate—or simply advancing jihad by concealed means," Youssef writes.[44] Citing Surah 16:106, which states that God will punish those who "open their breast to unbelief" but forgive one who "utters unbelief... under compulsion, his heart remaining firm," and Sunni juridical scholar Ismail ibn Kathir (d. 1373), Richardson attempts to parallel the "weakened condition" of early Muslims in pagan Mecca and those in "the West" today. The idea that "Muslims may deny their faith in order to protect themselves" is here reworked to justify the claim that as "long as a Muslim lives in a country where Islam exists as a minority, in a 'weakened state,' then deceptiveness is allowed."[45] The Muslim spiritual community, the *ummah*, is reframed as not a religious community but an (in)visible invasion—Shoebat explicitly glosses *ummah* as "Empire of Islam"—tolerance of which portends collapse.[46] "We can see America's future in recent events in European nations, which have permitted a massive flow of Muslim immigrants into their borders," Youssef intones, while Shoebat prophesies: "The West is in need of—and will one day get—an intervention in order to confront these realities but on whose terms it will be administered remains to be seen."[47]

Taqiyya here becomes decontextualized and recontextualized—earthed and worlded—in the context of claims of perpetual conflict and the ideological structures of the clash regime. As Youssef writes, "Ever since Islam began, its goal has been the founding of a world empire."[48] As such, Muslims living in non-Muslim-majority nations are conceptualized as seditious a priori, the formulation of their "weakened state" echoing both the anxiety of incompletion and the power asymmetry and ontotheological absence of the demonic realm from which "Islam" is here seen to derive. Indeed, for spiritual warriors *taqiyya* is not merely a strategy of survival or even of tactical warfare—its allegedly omnipresent use is never once tied to actual or potential threats that Muslims may face in increasingly Islamophobic societies, and the self-defense clause is itself read as part of *taqiyya*'s deceptive matrix.[49] Rather, *taqiyya* is framed as a reflection of Islam's allegedly demonic (non)being, its possession of and by the Antichrist spirit, which deprives it of all ontological and epistemological validity. For Richardson, *taqiyya* reveals Islam as "a son of its true father. The demonic being that assaulted Muhammad in the Cave of Hira is the same being that inspired the ungodly doctrines of deception that have so obviously affected the religion of Islam as we know it today." After all, he proclaims, "most people will agree that religion and deception are not intermixable," but "it is clear that in Islam, deception and religion mutually support one another."[50] Shoebat continues this trajectory, writing that "Deception is at the core of Islam; it is a central tenet in Islamic text. . . . Deception in earthly warfare may be a legitimate stratagem of war but deception in spiritual warfare belongs only to one side."[51] Rather than being (only) a pragmatic strategy deployed in a radically asymmetric war—one that by Shoebat's logic may even be legitimate—*taqiyya* is rendered a sign that the war is not only fundamentally spiritual but that "Islam" is on the wrong side of the conflict. Islamophobic constructions of Muslims as inassimilable here adopt explicitly diabolic form, as the root of such inassimilability is situated in an essential infernality that emerges from their status as the agents and avatars of "the Lie" in its cosmological sense.[52]

The theopolitical project to name, comprehend, and defend against this infernality exemplifies and justifies symbiotic regimes of domestic securitization and foreign intervention.[53] For Safa, American Muslims must be subjected to McCarthyite surveillance and exclusionary policies, since "tolerance, understanding, political correctness, religious freedom, and claims of 'peaceful Islam' are the neutralizing forces and pavers of the path for Islam,"[54] while Muslims abroad become targets of evangelical media networks, such as his own TBN Nejat TV. And not only this. Granting America the right of life and death over the world, Safa declares: "America carries the rod of judgment for some nations and cities," and "I believe that cities like Damascus will be judged in the same way that Hiroshima was judged, as awful as this may sound."[55] His self-awareness is small mercy, but the underlying message here is plain: destruction suffices when deliverance fails. For some, destruction is not even a last resort. Following a speech by Shoebat sponsored by the International Counter-Terrorism Officers Association, an audience member summarized his message as "Kill them [Muslims], including the children."[56] While an audience response, the statement fits Shoebat's oeuvre, which not only figures Islam as demonic but also casts most Muslims as duplicitous and destructive and the "Muslim world" as a place where "Every evil is sanctioned."[57] However, even in narratives that eschew (physical) destruction, deliverance has a price—epistemic and social, but also financial—as Faisal Malick demonstrates when he prophesies a future in which "when Ishmael is revived in the presence of God, he will lay his treasures at the feet of Jesus and embrace his destiny."[58] Tying the elimination of willful subjects to messianic imperial extraction, Malick spiritualizes the exchange of blood for oil: "*All nations are made of one blood and redeemed through the blood of One, Jesus Christ*," he writes, but "not all in the earth have become partakers of this redemption."[59] However, "God blessed Ishmael thousands of years ago, knowing that when he would come into the Kingdom, the treasure hidden in dark places and the secret treasure that is stored up will come into the Kingdom. Even the oil in the wells will be for the Gospel's sake."[60]

The circulation of the blood of Jesus Christ here becomes a medium of access and extraction, incorporation as expropriation, by which resources are worlded from the hands of Hell—under the earth—into the Kingdom. As such, it both mirrors the practices of US empire by which market access and coercion supersedes direct territorial control and unearths the singularity of blood as mobilizing metaphor of Christianity and its more or less secularized heirs.[61] In his critique of Christianity, *Blood*, Gil Anidjar testifies to how the "eucharistic matrix" by which Christians were joined together through Christ's blood was transfigured across the Middle Ages and early modernity into the idea of "a community of blood, of pure blood, a community brought together by the bonds of blood that would come to define kinship and group identity, as well as citizenship in the modern state on the basis of blood and soil."[62] This process, which was above all a process of self-definition, brought with it both an unparalleled vulnerability—the potential for "pure" blood's contamination—and (thereby) the unprecedented notion of "other bloods," of "an allegedly universal difference *between bloods*," along the lines of class, religion, nation, and race.[63] For Anidjar, America is not exceptional but exemplary of this "political hematology," both in its racializing dimensions—as in the settler colonial politics of the "blood quantum" and the antiblack singularity of the "one-drop" rule—and in its citation of blood as redemptive, reunifying, and remaking, as in post–Civil War narratives.[64]

Blood is core to spiritual warfare, not simply in the soteriological and extractive power of the one blood but in its formulations of "*other bloods*" and of idolatries carried in the blood. In Islamic Antichrist demonologies, this frameworks finds distinctly Islamophobic manifestation in the juxtaposition between Isaac, "the promised child and the progenitor of the Jewish people," and Ishmael, held as the progenitor of Arab peoples and "not the promised child of God's plan, but a child resulting from man's plan," born from "an ambitious soul that did not wait upon God."[65] Tying othered blood to deviant temporality, Safa codes Arab peoples as a result of willful rejection of sovereign will, lamenting that after "Four thousand years . . . his descendants are still persecuting the sons of the child born by God's will. What a tremendous price we pay when we miss God's timing."[66] Safa later discusses the fact that God *did* bless Ishmael, however both he and his descendants are nonetheless rendered exterior to divine order—errors that must be recuperated. Meanwhile, as a descendant of Isaac, Jesus (and thus Christianity) is made contiguous with God's promised Child, font of a "Judeo-Christian" civilization that becomes both uniquely pure and (so) uniquely vulnerable.

Spiritual warriors' leveraging of the hyphenated "Judeo-Christian" here operationalizes a broader politics of erasure (of Judaism as living, of Christian Judeophobia) and exteriorization (of Islam) that has long been core to European identity construction.[67] As Anidjar discusses elsewhere, this exteriorization is rooted in the entangled history of European anti-Jewish and anti-Muslim hatreds, with Jews figuring the internal (theological, economic) enemy and Muslims the exterior (political) one. Drawing on Denis Guénoun, he argues that the exteriorization of "Islam" is itself constitutive of "European" subjectivity: "for Europe, Europe and Islam are intimately involved in a 'specular formation of mirror images' that is 'the primordial identitarian rapport, constitutive of Europeanness.'" That is, "'Europe' hides itself from itself by claiming to have a name and a face independently of Islam," because foundational to the originary rapport is the truth that "Islam is not extraneous to our history," or rather is so only "from the inside," as "the becoming-exterior of what is within 'our' world—'we Europeans.'"[68] Like the (Anti)Christ, "Europe" was always already invaginated by alterity.

The (theo)political structures of the War on Terror reenact this constitutive divide, by which Muslims are rendered exterior to "what is within 'our' world—'we [Americans],'"—an exteriorization that is no less foundational or phantasmatic than Europe's own. Memorialized in the trauma of 9/11 as wound on the body politic—on the community of blood, of the one substance—that came from outside, from other blood, this exteriorization buttresses emergent systems of security, surveillance, and state-market violence that would guard against the threatening circulations of foreign bodies and alien capital, of the "flow" of Muslim migrants and of oil money not (yet) "for the Gospel's sake." These systems energize unprecedented global forms of what Darryl Li terms "carceral circulation," the processes by which American empire exploits the asymmetry of sovereign bodies, leveraging the juridical sovereignty and independence of weaker nations to transport "out-of-place" subjects in relation to imperial goals, exercising control while refusing responsibility. As Li shows, such circulations facilitate the construction of certain individuals as "out-of-place Muslim[s]" (among others), who become transportable in "circuits of relations between sovereign states" of which sites like Guantánamo Bay are less aberrations than the most visible nodes, fostering forms of imperial mobility that render subjects in accordance with the aims of an empire that is a "moving target" in the transitive sense, "causing the circulation of other things, like imprisoned bodies."[69] Akin to the disavowed nomadism of both capital and spiritual warfare discussed in Chapter 2, Li here gives us a way to rethink American empire as a passing empire: as passing for not-empire, as passing bodies across borders within its imperial hegemony, as passing unnoticed in demonologies of the passing empire of "Islam." And if this passing empire requires walls and borders to facilitate its flows—its blood, salvific and extractive—then it comes as no surprise that its Antichristian antithesis reflects and rejects this necessity, as the coming Antichristian Caliphate becomes conceptualized precisely as a dissolution of "the boundaries between nations," a diabolic effort to undo the "territorial divisions imposed by Western mapmakers."[70]

If the demons conjured in spiritual warfare act to contest and redraw its cartographies of truth, those of the Islamic Antichrist are where this contestation becomes most literal. Specters of colonization and imperial intervention haunt these demonologies. Youssef, even as he casts the Muslim Brotherhood as infiltrating American institutions, is at pains to tie their origins to the history of colonialism in Egypt. Safa similarly devotes considerable time to unpacking the blowback of European colonial ventures and American interventionism, including the British role in the creation of the state of Israel, the latter's ongoing treatment of Palestinians, and the British and American destabilization of his native Iran.[71] Writing in 2006, he proffered caution regarding the US wars in Afghanistan and Iraq: "the current conflict . . . is a demonstration of American strength," he writes, and such strength "brings a great sense of accomplishment in the eyes of patriotism. But ten years from now, what will be the consequences?"[72] Following regional destabilization and the rise of ISIS in the ensuing decade, Safa here appears almost prescient. And he was not alone. Stice's texts contain both sympathetic depictions of Muslim anti-Americanism and reflections on the consequences of US-backed strongmen in the Middle East and North Africa, situating the events of the Arab Spring—an event that for Stice boded ill for the region's Christian minority—as among the wider consequences of US interference.[73] The anxieties spiritual warriors focus around *taqiyya*, over imitation, over the capacity of the "radical Muslim" to infiltrate "the West" under the guise of moderation, must be situated against this colonial and imperial backdrop. Ultimately, these represent fears about resemblance, of the passing figure—but a passing figure rooted in a specific history of imperialism and colonization.

Colonial Mimicry, Decolonial Violence

In his *Location of Culture*, postcolonial theorist Homi Bhabha interrogates how the structures of colonialism sought to recreate the colonized subject on the model of the colonizer. He framed this desire through a rubric of "colonial mimicry," the desire of the colonizer "for a reformed, recognizable Other, *as a subject of a difference that is almost the same, but not quite*," simultaneously racialized as "almost the same but not white." However, this qualifier "not quite/not white" generates ambivalence: the mimic must approximate the colonizer but remain essentially (racially) different (and inferior), yet this essential difference is threatened by their very capacity to imitate the colonizer. Colonial mimicry here operates on two fronts, naming both "a complex strategy of reform, regulation and discipline, which 'appropriates' the Other," and "the sign of the inappropriate." The processes that try to (re)make the colonized like the colonizer unsettle the space between seeming and being, seeking to render racialized—especially Black—subjects merely "semblance[s]" of "white presence" even as mimicry rearticulates identity and meaning through the production of "conflictual, fantastic, discriminatory 'identity effects' in the play of power that is elusive because it hides no essence, no 'itself.'" Mimicry ultimately reflects "a difference or recalcitrance which coheres the dominant strategic function of colonial power, intensifies surveillance, and poses an imminent threat to both 'normalized' knowledges and disciplinary powers."[74] It structures the goal of the colonial enterprise while posing a challenge to the systems of power that enterprise seeks to ensure and enshrine. Drawing on Frantz Fanon's observation that the colonized culture is both present and mummified, locked in partial presence, Bhabha writes that the "ambivalence of mimicry—almost but not quite—suggests that the fetishized colonial culture is potentially and strategically an insurgent counter-appeal." At the same time, the "ambivalence of colonial authority" confronting its (im)perfect imitations, "repeatedly turns from *mimicry*—a difference that is almost nothing but not quite—to *menace*—a difference that is almost total but not quite."[75]

The theologization of repetition and difference in which Islam "drastically *redefine[s]* the tenets" of "Judeo-Christianity" here meets the politics of repetition and difference enacted through colonialization and imperial policy. The self is reproduced in and by the other, calling its essence and authenticity into question.[76] In the orthotaxic structures of spiritual warfare, the Antichrist—and the Islamic Antichrist most of all—embodies this terror at resemblance, this turning from mimicry to menace. For if the duty of the Christian is to approximate Christ through imitation of the godly life, the (Islamic) Antichrist is the point where this imitation becomes not a sign of its capacity for assimilation (that is, for salvation) but its opposite, Satan's "near-perfect imitation and essential difference" that leads only to perdition.[77] Constructions of "rage" and "envy" here come to bridge the void between imitation and essence, the latter figuring a form of imitation, as Teresa Brennan writes, in which "the original is denied;"[78] the former an active force that threatens to remake the world through this denial. These affects are familial, political, and cosmic. They are born of the "envy and rivalry" Ishmael allegedly felt toward Isaac, which "survive[d] to be passed down through the centuries."[79] They are those of Satan, "beside himself with rage" at humanity's access to a salvation he is denied,[80] and (in material corollary) of those who "live every day with the chief purpose of their lives being to bring havoc and . . . devastation to America" because they envy its "peace and security."[81] The Devil's rage, which desires to deprive humanity of a salvation he lacks, and that ascribed to America's foes, who post-9/11 propaganda asserted were driven by their hatred of "our freedoms" and "way of life," here converge, much as Satan's envy merges with the envy of the colonized subject toward the colonist, whose "hostile world," in the words of Fanon, "excludes yet at the same time incites envy."[82]

It was this envy, Fanon discerned, that provoked in the colonist a guardedness "as he catches the furtive glance, and . . . realizes bitterly that: 'They want to take our place.' And it's true."[83] This guardedness saturates Islamic Antichrist texts, where any resemblance is seen not as a bond of imitation based not on a proper admiration of "whiteness and light" but on the diabolical desire to undo the stability and staticity of Paradise.[84] Both the familial resemblance of demonized traditions and the sociocultural assimilability of racialized subjects become marked as threats to the integrity and incontestability of orthotaxy. For the spiritual warriors discussed, Islam *resembles* Christianity, but *is* not; the Muslim Jesus *resembles* the Christian Jesus, but *is* not; the "moderate Muslim" *resembles* the Western liberal democratic subject, but *is* not. Their resultant demonologies bridge (thereby constituting) this space between imitation and essence, between seeming and being, at once troubling and justifying theopolitical paradigms of securitization, surveillance, and carceral circulation—regimes of state-market violence enacted to contain the phantasmatic violence attributed (inherently) to "Islam." However, it is necessary to interrogate this attribution more closely, for while spiritual warriors undoubtedly contribute to post-9/11 Islamophobic cultural narratives of Muslim violence, they do so in odd ways.

For Safa, the spirit behind Islam—the Antichrist spirit—feeds not merely on violence, bloodshed, anger or hatred, but on the violence of his own persecution. Tying this claim to Islam's *arche*, when "the more Muhammad's tribe, the Quraish, persecuted him, the more Arabs converted to Islam," he contends that, by analogy, the "more we overpower the radicals, the greater they will become." Such a result is plain to see, Safa continues, for "not only have we lost the war against Islamic radicalism [in Iraq and Afghanistan], but we have, through the past two wars, increased the potential and the progress of the radicalism!"[85] To Safa, this capacity for growth is connected to what he frames as the (strikingly Fanonian) opposition at the heart of "Islam," between *oppressor* and *oppressed*. In Muhammad's time and society, he explains, "The strong ruled the weak. There were the oppressors and the oppressed, the wealthy and the poor, the masters and the slaves." Islam therefore "became the voice of God for the weak and the oppressed and for justice," demanding "rights—the rights of oppressed people from their oppression and their oppressors."[86] After this curiously sympathetic reading, however, Safa pivots, reading this struggle for the oppressed as bad because its revolution was (and remains) not "the mere proclamation of liberty and justice for all" but of the creation of an Islamic society: "The concept of freedom from the reign of the Quraish was never meant to be self-sufficient. It was freedom from the Quraish into the reign and rule of the Islamic ordinances and beliefs."[87]

Through an echo of the US Pledge of Allegiance, Safa here marks American notions of freedom as neutral, self-sufficient, and universal, whereas liberation by and for Islam is bad precisely *because* it is Islamic, is marked by particularity. It leads only to what Youssef terms a "dark peace" of submission to Islam, not the "divine peace" of submission to Christianity (and, by analogy, to America).[88] For Youssef, "dark peace" is framed as that which comes when "one side surrenders, bows in submission, and agrees to all the terms imposed by the conqueror."[89] By contrast, "divine peace, the peace of God," is—in a manner that mirrors the juxtaposition of true and false unities in demonologies of Jezebel—"the only peace worthy the name. Divine peace is the only permanent peace." Yet, rather than just between enforced "peace" and true harmony, the division between dark and divine peace is further marked by an external/internal divide. For Youssef, divine peace is an inner peace that permits the endurance of oppression and rejection: "When we are handed over to be persecuted and hated and killed because of Jesus, we have divine peace," he narrates. "When people turn away from the faith and betray us, when false teachers appear and deceive many people, when the love of most people grows cold, we have divine peace." Even "when it is time to flee to the mountains, even when there is great distress, unequalled from the beginning of time until now, we have divine peace."[90] This construction of divine or true peace as allowing one to find peace amidst worldly suffering implies that "dark peace" may be not just a peace achieved by violent conquest but rather one consciously willed and materially enacted—an implication that plays out in the fixation in Islamic Antichrist texts on anticolonial and antiracist violence.

Anticolonial rage for the restoration of dignity and autonomy is explicitly cited in these texts, from Safa's detailed accounts of British colonialism and US imperialism in Palestine and Iran to Stice's sympathetic accounts of anti-Americanism among Maghrebi Muslims in the French *banlieus*. Complicating Jacobs's claims about Islamic "*empire spirits*," Safa claims that "imperialism is another reason I believe that radical Islam is gaining more and more ground . . . around the world." It is an idea "discussed often by radical revolutionary Islamic leaders such as Khomeini, bin Laden, Sayyid Qutb, and many others. It is a concept greatly hated by Islam."[91] Stice presents a similar picture, relating how acquaintances during his missionary work asked him why my country did not do more to help the poor countries of the world, why it backed a "savage, murderous" government in Israel and cruel dictators in their homelands, why it had a president who prayed for guidance then ordered bombings that killed innocent people.... Hearing the rants of the poor and powerless gave me great insight into today's terrorists and the reasons for Islamic fundamentalism's revival and spread.[92]

The Antichrist spirit finds fertile soil among the wretched of the earth, both globally and—critically—in the United States itself. "Islamic radicals have divided American society into . . . the oppressed and the tyrants," Safa claims. "In this case the tyrants are the American government with its unbearable military force, and the oppressed are African Americans and Native Americans." Thus, he continues, dropping Native Americans' place in this trifecta of radical otherness, "a radical Muslim will love a black man but will kill a white man."[93] Safa here draws correspondences between racial injustice at home and imperial blowback abroad. And, through doing so, enables a conceptual shift from a terror of national transformation due to an ascribed-outside force ("Islam") to a suspicion of and hostility toward those within US society who are already deemed not to sufficiently belong—specifically Black Americans, and Black Muslims most of all.[94]

As Brittany Friedman and Zachary Sommers have discussed, "Black" and "Muslim" are not just aligned in US society and the US security state as images of threatening alterity but are seen as mutually compounding, with individuals bearing both identity markers becoming recipients of intensified forms of carceral violence.[95] Both this alignment and this threat manifest in the spiritual warfare texts discussed, as Black Americans are framed as especially amenable to seduction by the spirit of Islam, forming a weakness in both the body politic and the Body of the Church. Black conversion rates, especially from Christianity, are often stressed, with numbers given ranging from sixty to ninety percent depending on the author.[96] All frame the statistics as symptomatic of catastrophe, and while Shoebat casts them as only "a sad commentary on the discontinuity and disunity of the American Church,"[97] others attempt more detailed diagnoses. Don Richardson devotes a full chapter of *Secrets of the Koran* to Black Muslims, particularly the Nation of Islam (NOI)—glossed as "a uniquely American and heretical cultic offshoot from mainstream Islam." This focus does not translate to either nuance or understanding, but is revealing in its emphases. Echoing his namesake, Richardson places the NOI's success down to "oil money" from Saudi Arabia, which has allowed its work to surpass "the efforts of Christians in inner-city development projects and in the reclamation of black prison inmates from a life of crime."[98] He does not attempt to tackle reasons for conversion, instead framing Black Muslims as mere dupes "providing a beachhead for Islam in America," who see it as liberating only because of an ignorance of the history of slavery in Muslim-majority countries. His account is often patronizing, demonstrates little engagement with Black Muslims, and often reduces Black religious and cultural engagement to imitation and emulation. His discussion culminates in a call for "two or three very prominent black male Muslims" to "summarily and publicly renounce Islam" and therefore let "millions of other Muslim men who are people of conscience . . . emulate them."[99] Muslim women are here, as in most other Islamic Antichrist texts, conspicuous only by their absence.

Other authors are more attentive to circumstance. "Segregation, social injustice, police brutality, poverty and decaying ghetto life were the elements that opened the door for Islam's infiltration into the black urban areas," Safa writes.[100] Safa here draws on the "mythic icon[s]" of Black Muslim identity in the US cultural imaginary:[101] Malcolm X as "one of the strongest voices of the Black Muslim movement," and Louis Farrakhan, head of the NOI. For Safa, "Islam was and is a way through which the black man could experience freedom from a brutal, unjust system. Islam gave them hope of protection and pride, a voice for their anger and frustration at injustice." Indeed, Islam "takes the side of the weak and the oppressed, and fights with hate and anger against the oppressor. Islam demands justice and vengeance. . . . It is a religion of rebellion of the oppressed against the oppressor."[102] Youssef adopts a similar angle: "Most Black Muslims do not turn to Islam because they are attracted to its theology, laws, or history. Rather, they are attracted to Islam's offer of power for the powerless."[103] Such framings still position Black Muslims as ignorant of Islam "itself," but while Richardson assumes a lack of historical knowledge, Safa and Youssef here situate its appeal in a spiritual core, one that transcends divisions between a "heretical" NOI and Islam "proper."

However, this core is, unexpectedly, the Antichrist spirit—specifically, this spirit's violent rejection of injustice and oppression, qualities one does not ordinarily associate with the Satanic. The authors seem keen to pinpoint *violence* as signifying Islam's demonic character, exemplified in Youssef's divine/dark peace dichotomy. But these authors are not strict pacifists—Safa's remark on Damascus and Hiroshima and Shoebat's lethal solutions make that clear—but only against violence that challenges the normative supremacy of (white, settler) Christianity and the Euroamerican civilization cast as its chief avatar. This is compounded by the fact that, far from a diabolic ruse in keeping with its construction as deceptive, their narratives frame the Antichrist spirit as legitimately empowering the weak to fight their oppressors—this is, in fact, cited as his core appeal to those subjected to colonial and imperial violence abroad and to racial injustice and systemic oppression at home. To unpack the theoretical and political dynamics at work here, it is necessary to explore the role played by frameworks of antiblackness in these demonologies more closely. Analyzing antiblackness in Islamic Antichrist demonologies exposes and accuses the underlying metaphysical and political structures—the orthotaxy—that this demonic spirit is envisioned as threatening—structures that, while focused on the "Black Muslim" as paradigmatic threat, are present in framings of Black resistance broadly, and most clearly in those of Black Lives Matter (BLM). And it is here we must return to the exchange between Richardson and Guandolo with which I began, its posited links between demonic rage, Black protest, and Muslim influence now appearing—if no less abhorrent—not as aberrant but exemplary.

Ontotheological Terror

The claim that BLM is demonically inspired is common among conservative spiritual warriors. Such accusations are not confined to white evangelicals, as when Conservative African American minister Earl Walker Jackson called BLM "divisive and demonic" in 2015 for centering Black lives over "all lives" and for its criticism of police.[104] However, it is among white evangelicals that such accusations are most often articulated. Gerald Flurry casts BLM as guided by a "great evil spirit" that is "leading these young people to destruction and leading them to accelerate this nation's death!"[105] The CEO of the charismatic media empire Charisma, Stephen Strang, names them as among groups representing "a dangerous—and I would add demonic—attempt to undermine free speech and our most basic freedoms,"[106] while Robert Maginnis of the Family Research Council simply lists them as exemplary of those "whose mission is to destroy America."[107] No concrete data is provided to support these claims, revealing how BLM's diabolic nature is often taken as read. In the exchange between Guandolo and Richardson, this nature is originating, *arche*-ic. Attributing antiracist protests against white supremacy and state-market violence to Satanic intervention, Richardson's conjuration of a "spirit of rage" both evoked and elided the Ferguson uprising's inciting incident: the killing of Black teenager Mike Brown, who was not only explicitly demonized by his killer but whose demonization was also tied to a projection of his rage: "it looks like a demon, that's how angry he looked," his killer claimed.[108] Richardson's evocation thus not only adopts the dehumanizing and lethal stereotype of the angry Black man but takes the very language of demonization used to justify Brown's killing and presents it as the animating force of the activist movement that arose to bring the system to account for that very killing.

For spiritual warriors, the *arche* is architectural, determining the shape of the order that it commences and commands. And the *arche* of Black Lives Matter gives voice to a critique that cannot be processed as anything other than a crisis, one named by pastor John Burton in an article for *Charisma* titled "Satan's Grand Strategy and God's Answer to the Black Lives Matter Crisis." Burton assumes that his readers will simply agree with him over "the rebellion that's manifesting through the Black Lives Matter movement." Indeed, the "crisis" that BLM signifies here is neither one of police violence nor racial injustice but rather the pervasiveness of Satan's promotion of "forced sympathy"—the Devil's titular grand strategy—by which some churches have dared to promote "affinity, affirmation and agreement" with "those who are deviant" and "what is unholy"—specifically "homosexual activism, Black Lives Matter, abortion or other counter-biblical movements."[109] Tying together disparate demonized populations, Burton exemplifies an imaginary in which diverse coalitions based on political pragmatism and empathy across group lines are coded as intrinsically demonic. For these spiritual warriors, the crisis BLM names is not the brutality of their orthotaxy but the "radical kinship" potentially fostered among those that orthotaxy brutalizes.[110]

The "Ferguson-to-Gaza" discourse that arose during and after the uprising is perhaps among the most notable of such (demonized) coalitions, as organizers in both the United States and Israel charted material relations between the occupation of Palestine and police militarization in Ferguson. As Jasbir Puar summarizes, "Ferguson-to-Gaza forums sought to correlate the production of settler space, the vulnerability and degradation of black and brown bodies, the demands of transnational solidarities, and the entangled workings of settler colonialism in the United States and Israel," which have led to the formation of solidarities between BLM and Free Palestine that remain "rhizomatic and bountiful."[111] Beyond general criticisms of BLM's stance on Israel—part, within the Christian Zionist discourses underpinning much spiritual warfare, of their mission to "destroy America"—these connections are rarely discussed.[112] Yet like the killing of Brown they find implicit vocalization in Richardson's words, specifically his use of Psalm 2 to analogize the protests in Ferguson to "gentiles" raging against God. His use of "gentiles" does more than situate such acts as beyond the pale of a promised land and its "pure" blood (Israel's or America's). It links to a broader tendency in Islamic Antichrist demonologies, Richardson's among them, to conflate modern Muslim-majority nations with the gentile ones of the Hebrew Bible—the Moabites, Edomites, and Amalekites—who threatened the ancient Israelites.[113]

As Amy Kaplan demonstrates, after 9/11 the United States increasingly began to identify with and model itself on Israel. This modelling was both material, as under the rubric of counterterrorism the nations began to increasingly share materiel, tactics, and training, and conceptual, as the United States "took on Israel's paradoxical role as the invincible victim." As she explains, America drew on Israel's sense of besiegement, existentially imperiled by both regional and global forces but destined for victory due to superiority of culture, technology, and (for religious actors) divine favor. In doing so—and we see here a reflection of Safa's narrative of divine calling—America came to envision itself as "confronting, on a global scale, murderous enemies who threatened nothing less than total annihilation. Terrorism would force the United States to fight a never-ending battle for national survival, even as the country was providentially destined to vanquish all evil." Like the (community of) the one blood, at once uniquely pure and uniquely vulnerable, this geopolitical imaginary relies on a notion of "radical insecurity," an apocalyptic politics in which the only outcomes are "absolute supremacy or utter annihilation" and any attempt at negotiation or compromise beckons destruction.[114] But given this geopolitical and theopolitical imaginary, it is necessary to ask who these "terrorists" are. As discussed in Chapter 1, the "terrorist" as figure is roughly commensurate with both the "queer" and the "Indian," symbolizing and catalyzing the "unthinkable destruction" of (white, settler, cisheteropatriarchal) orthotaxy. Given this context, that BLM is often accused of being a "terrorist" organization, as were Indigenous and allied water protectors who fought the installation of the Dakota Access Pipeline in 2016, does not appear strange.[115] Rather, in their subjection to regimes of state-market violence honed in the War on Terror, such groups expose the reality that, as Schotten observes, "To be a 'terrorist' one need not commit an act of violence . . . but rather persevere as an indigenous [or, I would add, Black] person, be (perceived as) Arab or Muslim, or mount some explicit or forthright challenge to the civilizationalist valuing of settler lives."[116]

As a figure opposed to the reproductive futurity of US settler sovereignty, this reading of the "terrorist"—and of BLM as "terrorist"—permits a deeper analysis of the conjuncture of Islam and blackness, not only in how it is subject to unique carceral violences but in how such violences are foundational to America itself. As theologian Katie Walker Grimes demonstrates, not only were a large number of the Africans stolen into slavery Muslim, but Black people were also seen as "ontologically criminal and therefore unconditionally enslaveable" by Europeans in part because their blackness was associated with Islam.[117] At the same time, this "Islam" was considered threatening to New World Christianization, potentially contaminating of coded-docile Native populations. As such, "foreign black bodies" that might conceal the destabilizing force of Islam had to be dominated and enslaved to be integrated into new American empires.[118] Grimes is here explicitly discussing medieval and early modern Iberian discourses; however, she charts how the antiblack worldview that underlay such discourses was exported to Protestant Northern Europe and ultimately influenced constructions of blackness and Islam in the United States today, in which "the latter becomes framed as "not just a religious identity but a type of existential threat."[119] We see the echo of these discourses in Richardson and Guandolo's framings of BLM, where—as in the early modern Iberian imaginary—the Black body is framed as concealing the destabilizing force of "Islam," here through the medium of Saudi capital.

Read through this history, the inscription by Don Richardson, Safa, and Youssef of the "Black Muslim" as avatar of the (Islamic) Antichrist spirit appears not "only" as a variant of past and present Islamophobia, but a distinct manifestation of *antiblackness*. By antiblackness, I do not mean only the systems of structural and direct violence targeted at Black people, although these are key parts, but something deeper and more structural. Calvin Warren describes antiblackness as "an accretion of practices, knowledge systems, and institutions designed to impose nothingness onto blackness and the unending domination/eradication of Black presence *as* nothing incarnated."[120] Warren here draws closely on Fanon, notably his theorization that "Ontology ... does not permit us to understand the being of the black man," for "he must be black in relation to the white man" and, crucially, "has no ontological resistance in the eyes of the white man."[121] Warren expands on this notion in his meditation on Black nihilism, *Ontological Terror*, arguing that antiblackness is not simply a form of social prejudice but a structuring principle of Western metaphysics, which addresses the terror felt at the concept of nothingness by incarnating it in Black bodies that can then be dominated, analyzed, and schematized as a means of controlling the ontological terror that this nothingness provokes: "black ~~being~~ incarnates metaphysical nothing, the terror of metaphysics, in an antiblack world." Warren writes the word "being" under erasure, legible but obscured, because, he argues, "Blacks

... have function but not Being—the function of black(ness) is to give form to a terrifying formlessness (nothing)."[122] For Warren, antiblackness is baked into the structure of our world; as such "Black freedom ... would constitute a form of *world destruction*." Equality, justice, and recognition are, in his view, precluded because the very structure of metaphysics requires that these be systematically denied to Black people to maintain the order of creation. Echoing Fanon's dictum that it was the colonist who fabricated the colonized, Warren contends that the "Negro was *invented* to fulfil this function for metaphysics, and the humanist dream of transforming invention into human *being* is continually deferred (because it is impossible)."[123]

Although Warren situates this fatal invention within modernity, the invention of blackness *as* nothing, a nothingness materially actualized by slavery and its afterlives through social death, is interwoven with a genealogy of Christian demonology and its projections of ontological absence (the demon *is* nothing) and practices of securitization and domination (*as* nothing, the demon must be guarded against, compelled, commanded). The relation between conjurations of the demonic and figurations of blackness is well documented.[124] Critical here, however, is how constructions of blackness as demonological absence intersect with the demonology of "Islam," reinforcing and destabilizing new grammars and targets of (war against) terror that threaten the foundations of orthotaxy. Grimes observes that antiblack framings of blackness and Islam exist in a quasi-tension, rooted in the afterlife of slavery. Enslavement's logic, she explains, "insists that people deserve to be enslaved whenever they did not submit to proper authority"—Muslims to Christ; criminals to law; indigenous and pagan peoples to Christianity and the sovereignty of Christian monarchs. The reduction of such groups to slaves "claims to restore the order of rightful authority: because the slave did not voluntarily obey, she must be forced to obey through the violence of slavery."[125] The inscription of blackness as signifying nothingness here exists in opposition to "Islam," which represents an impossible presence yet to be "properly" subjected and thereby integrated into the orthotaxic structures of creation.

Grimes links this opposition to conservative hatred of Barack Obama, notably to the "Birther" conspiracy that the president was secretly Kenyan and/or Muslim, suggesting that because Obama "inherited his blackness from an un-enslaved, black, Muslim African," he appears in the antiblack world "as the ultimate terror: the foreign Muslim enemy who has not just been allowed inside the United States but has somehow been granted the power to govern it."[126] Obama here, for Grimes, embodies an impossible blackness that had not been subjugated, and thus perhaps had to be in order to prevent the destruction of (white) America. Yet the image of threat conjured by the conjugation of blackness and Islam should not be sourced solely in the notion of an unconquered exterior but in how this conjugation has historically worked to uproot religio-racial hierarchies internal to the United States—something illustrated by spiritual warriors' own focus on the NOI. As Judith Weisenfeld demonstrates, the NOI—alongside other Black religious movements like the Moorish Science Temple—was critical for promoting new conceptual imaginaries of blackness and racial hierarchy in America.[127] These imaginaries refused to accept the social classifications of US white supremacy, presenting new histories, identities, and futures for Black people that also entailed acts of renaming. If, as Warren contends, the "Negro" was invented to fulfil the function of incarnate nothing, then the rejection of groups like the NOI of the identity of "Negro" in favor of new grammars of being and belonging—as Moorish or as Asiatic Muslims, for example—can be read as threatening to undo the orthotaxic structure of metaphysics and modernity. If blackness signifies an onto(theo)logical absence that results from a subjugation of ascribed-willfulness by sovereign will, the "Black Muslim" here figures an impossible return-to-presence, a restoration not necessarily of an original Islamic identity (although it may be this) but of the deracinating willfulness that such "Islam" was taken to mark.

The relationship spiritual warriors construct between Islam and rage is important here. In her cutting essay "Killing Rage," bell hooks reflects on the "potentially healthy, potentially healing" power of Black rage as a response to oppression. "Anger is better, there is a presence in anger," she quotes from Toni Morrison's *The Bluest Eye*, adding "Perhaps then it is that 'presence,' the assertion of subjectivity colonizers do not want to see, that surfaces when the colonized express rage."[128] For hooks it was Malcolm X who was among the most unprecedented articulators of Black rage—and it is thus perhaps unsurprising he emerges in Islamic Antichrist narratives in precisely this way. And hooks also reads in this rage a passion for justice, that other marker of Islam's allegedly demonic spirit: "Malcolm X's passionate ethical commitment to justice served as the catalyst for his rage."[129] Rather than "his greatest flaw," his rage for justice pushed him "towards greater and greater awareness. It pushed him to change. He is an example of how we can use rage to empower," and refigure it not as "evil and destructive" but as the generative force behind "a vision of militancy that is necessary for transformative revolutionary action."[130] This vision, premised on a channeling of a rage that brings into impossible presence those forced to incarnate nothing, is one unexpectedly captured by the Antichrist spirit, with his allegedly infernal struggle for lost dignity and diabolic hatred of injustice. For the spiritual warriors examined, this spirit is a font of transformation that is threatening, not liberating, and threatening *not* simply because he is destructive but because he is generative. This generative potential is perhaps nowhere better captured than in Safa's demonization of Islam as a tool "for the weak and the oppressed and for justice" simply because it seeks to build a world on "Islamic ordinances and beliefs."[131] The Islamic Antichrist is here terrifying not because he embodies a rage *against* (against white Christian America, the legacy of empire, the afterlives of slavery) but a rage *for*—for "Islam," for revolutionary change, for recognition of and restitution for those who have been cast as nothing, as subjects of the terror that such nothing provokes. He is dangerous not because he is doomed to fail but because he might succeed, because his refusal to exist only as equipment for white, settler civilization threatens both its foundation and fulfilment—because, within the ontotheological order of our (post)Christian world, any attempt by those consigned to nothingness to escape or exceed the realm of pure function can only ever appear as an attempt at usurpation.

Foundations Without Name

Toward the midpoint of *Islam: The Cloak of Antichrist*, Jack Smith appeals to an apocalyptic prophecy—derived from Revelation 13:8—that "only those whose names have been in the Book of Life since the foundation of the world will not worship the Beast."[132] The image of having one's name in the Book of Life from before the world's foundations is a recurrent one in spiritual warfare texts, marking the individual Christian as having been always already chosen. Yet it is those whose names are not written that I wish to focus on here. For Smith, as for the others discussed here, the Beast is "Islam," and thus those who (will) worship him—those whose names have been excluded from the Book of Life since before the foundations of the world—are primarily (albeit not exclusively) Muslims. However, these foundations and this world are a specific world, a particular set of foundations that should not go unquestioned. Critically worlded, the Antichrist spirit emerging from the texts discussed here is a spirit born of the violences of colonial power and the structures of white supremacy, who comes to catalyze and channel the resistances of all those whose names were not written in the Book of Life since the foundation of our world; indeed, whose exclusion from its pages constituted that very foundation. America is built on this foundation. On renaming as key to the "cadastral effacement/replacement" practices of settler colonialism.[133] On the horrors of the Middle Passage, through which African bodies were "culturally unmade," rendered fungible objects without gender, familial or cultural ties, or even name.[134] The Islamic Antichrist—enfleshed in Black and Muslim subjects as those against, through, and atop which white, settler notions of the Human are constituted—can here be read as the nameless, disavowed foundation of the United States as a whole. Named in opposition to (white, settler) Christ and (white, settler) Man (to use Wynter's term), he is the one denied his own name from the foundation of its world, and whose ascribed avatars will be subjected to unrelenting domination and violent interpellation so long as that world continues to exist. And so, reacting to the violence of his conjuration, the Antichrist strives to start the "only thing in the world that's worth the effort of starting: the end of the world."[135]

This end is not the one spiritual warriors hope for—not the one they summoned the Antichrist to signify. It is not the erasure of the world's difference in the eternalization of sovereign will, but the end of the relations of domination that called the Antichrist into existence, which sought to mold him under the unrelenting pressure of their world-making into the equipment of their eschatological desires. Defining the etymology of "*antichrist*," Safa writes that, in Greek, the prefix *anti* means "opposite, i.e., instead or because of, for, in the room of."[136] For Safa, this reveals the Antichrist's desire to supplant Christ, but in the context of their demonologies this definition can also be read another way. Their Antichrist does exist *because of* and *for* Christ, or rather because of and for the messianic imperialism, racial capitalism, and settler colonialism justified in his name. Confronted by "Islam," which resembles but is not Christianity, the authors attempt to navigate and negotiate its challenge—theologically, politically, culturally. They demonize it not merely to defend against its threat but to assimilate and neutralize it. The spiritual warriors' overreliance on Islamic and Islamist sources, despite or even because of their misreading, as a supplement to their biblical exegesis exemplifies the dependency this attempt creates, a weakness in the integrity and incontestability of their orthotaxy which must be obscured by the demonization and devouring of other cultures, other religions, other lives. And it is here Richardson's dogged attempt to (mis)read Islam's eschatology as Christianity's inversion hides a perhaps unintended admission: that in a world in which Islam's savior is Christianity's Antichrist and vice versa, "the West" might also be forced to confront that to many Muslims—and not only Muslims—it has often appeared precisely as *al-Masīh ad-Dajjāl*, the false messiah, promising the divine peace of liberty but bringing only that "dark peace ... that comes after one side surrenders, bows in submission, and agrees to all the terms imposed by the conqueror."

Embodying an eschatology of blowback, the Islamic Antichrist incarnates the "black hollow" within the Euroamerican unconscious Fanon once described, in which "the most immoral, the most shameful desires lie dormant," and which the West must constantly repudiate to maintain its bodily, territorial, and temporal order—that is, its orthotaxy.[137] Yet more than a reflection it must consolidate itself against, this black hollow was and remains the West's silenced foundation, one compressed and repressed past breaking point. If Jezebel represented a queer unsettling of all borders and identities, the Antichrist is the powder keg of oppression. Fed by the terror that sustains the order of creation, by the fracturing and fatal suppression of those cast as his avatars, his rage threatens not just to shatter Paradise's walls but to detonate the foundations (conceptual, material) laid from (before) their beginning. The authors discussed here cannot help but see this rage as "evil and destructive." They are even correct, to an extent, for it aims at the end of the world their orthotaxy has built and strives to perpetuate, the world that is the receptacle for all Paradise rejects and must dominate. Yet even to them it is not a purely destructive rage, but a generative one. Denied all capacity for onto(theo)logical resistance before the white-hot gaze of sovereign will, their Antichrist reflects not simply a desire for recognition and restitution but of refusal. Conjured as the final milestone on the road to orthotaxy's incontestable triumph, he refuses a program of progress and assent in which everyone is meant to climb up "towards [the] whiteness and light" figured in the city on the hill. Revenant of anticolonial and antiracist rage, born of the disavowed foundations and discarded roots of a heliopolitical order that denies him ontological validity, the Antichrist erupts from his "zone of nonbeing"—from the "real hell" of an "utterly naked declivity" out of which the possibility of "authentic upheaval" might be born[138]—to mark not only that the world will end, but that it must end on the terms of those from whose flesh that world was and continues to be wrought.

4 / Leviathan's Wake: Demonology and the Passing of Order

"Dark forces are creating a new America," Jonas Clark writes at the opening of his 2010 book *Saboteurs in the Republic*. For Clark, this new America is one severed from its foundations, "governed by another spirit." This spirit ushers in a new revolution, and the effect of this revolution is bondage, specifically the bondage of God's people. "To understand the wickedness of this revolution is to understand the bondage of God's people in Egypt," he writes. "Pharaoh's law usurped the place of Jehovah's word." The bondage of God's people was not one of force, he enumerates, but of an "evil government" that gained power by an "undermining of personal freedom, liberty and wealth destruction." In Clark's view, this erosion of liberty and destruction of wealth reaches its apogee in statism, an ideology that "renounces individualism and exalts the nation as an organic body," claiming "that a man's life and work belong to the State." For Clark, "Pharaoh was the supreme ruler of a Statist nation."[1] And while in 2010 he did not explicitly identify the spirit behind such statism, by his 2012 *Destined for Dominion* he had given them a name: Leviathan. By forgetting "our oath of allegiance to the U.S. Constitution that has its roots in the Creator" and (thereby) "our oath of allegiance to Christ," Americans "weaken the Church and empower Leviathan." Moreover, by empowering Leviathan—breaking its covenant with God and abandoning its divine foundations—the United States had become a "leviathan state," as the "kingdom of Pharaoh was a leviathan state." As Clark writes, "A kingdom, any kingdom, unsubmissive to the Lord of Glory is a rebel leviathan state. It is rebellious, humanistic, murderous, and warring." However, while the leviathan state names a place in which "man [rather than God] rules over man," it is not only this. "The Apostle Paul describes the high level spiritual warfare of the Church as wrestling against principalities and powers," he continues: "These powers make up the leviathan state."[2]

Leviathan is the *arche* often situated closest to or even equated with their liege lord: their "characteristics are almost identical to Satan himself," Angela Powers Flippen writes, while Shawn Beaton marks them as a "similar spirit" and "dragon subordinate to Satan."[3] Perhaps due to this proximity, much as the Antichrist named both a spiritual principality and an individual to come, Leviathan can name both a single principality and the sum of all principalities—the union of all the "many leviathan states in the world" that "represent various principalities and powers" and "even network together."[4] Even in their singularity, however, Leviathan is always constructed as multiple. Their many heads and countless scales become images of both separation and solidarity, symbolic of the discord sown by and the paradoxical unity of the demonic. Yet Leviathan is more than merely the sum of all demons. They may also be the first, an echo of the primordial chaos from which the world was first wrought and which will be fully and finally subjugated at time's end.

Leviathan and their wake—the trace of their passing, their arousal from slumber, the vigil for their demise—form the condition of possibility for spiritual warfare as a whole, both its grounding and its purpose. Their conjurations are multiple and conflicting, arising in demonologies of the contemporary state but also of grassroots movements for social and economic justice and of enduring Indigenous traditions and sovereignty claims. I have shown throughout this work that spiritual warfare is deeply colonial in character. As Linda Rios Brook frames it, "the opposing forces do indeed have a plan for colonization that will determine which kingdom will be established and ultimately rule the planet."[5] Yet, as I have also discussed, while framed as such this territorial conflict is not one between opposing empires but a radically asymmetric conflict between existentially and essentially weak forces figured as illegal occupants of space and the irresistible—yet persistently resisted—force of sovereign will. Leviathan emerges as the epitome of this vision of conflict, as they are summoned both to represent the survival of Indigenous lifeways in a settler colonial order that deems them "over" and the resurgence of calls for socialist alternatives after neoliberalism's "end of history." Unpacking these conjurations reveals them to be at once the uninscribed earth from which sovereign power makes the world and the resurgence of all earth that refuses to be thus inscribed, signifying futures and economies beyond a white, settler orthotaxy for which there is allegedly no alternative. Singular and multiple, precolonial and postcapitalist, Leviathan is both the trace of the first and a figure of the last demon to be subjected, situating spiritual warfare's territorial imaginary in relation to the management and end of time itself, and to the solidarity of those under the death penalty—the absolute interdiction of sovereign power—that this end represents.[6]

First Worlding

"Leviathan stands out as one of the most powerful and wicked demons," Richard Ing cautions. While God "sometimes uses animals in the natural, such as serpents, scorpions, frogs, and goats to describe certain demons" there is "no animal on earth" that captures this spirit: "God uses a mythical creature, a dragon, to describe Leviathan."[7] Most comprehensively described in Job 41:1–36, Leviathan snakes their way through contemporary spiritual warfare texts, at once "a condition of the spirit" and "an evil spirit," a singular demon and the sum of all "principalities and powers," a "creature of chaos" and the "leviathan state."[8] Perhaps more than any other demonic spirit, Leviathan exhibits a form of omnipresence and totality, becoming both a replica of and restraint on a Holy Spirit understood as everywhere at once. Citing the description of their scales in Job 41:15–17 as being packed so closely that "no air can come between them," Ing follows many spiritual warriors in reading the air as the Holy Spirit: "the scales of Leviathan prevent Christians from receiving the things of God."[9] They are "a giant spirit that blocks the flow of God's purpose, power, and prosperity," Ron Phillips corroborates.[10] Moreover, no human can match them. Jennifer LeClaire informs her readers that "Leviathan won't bow to common warfare tactics," while Brook cautions that Leviathan was "so powerful that neither angels nor men could subdue him."[11] Indeed, John Eckhart warns, "man cannot stir up and defeat Leviathan"—only divine intervention can succeed, for what "man cannot do in his own strength, the Lord can do in defeating and crushing Leviathan."[12]

In biblical terms, this defeat is eschatologically foreshadowed in Isaiah 27:1—"In that day, the Lord will take His sharp, great, and mighty sword, and bring judgment on Leviathan, the fugitive serpent—Leviathan the crooked serpent—and He will slay the dragon of the sea." But this verse contains not just the omens of apocalypse but also, Donald Polaski observes, the "echoes of cosmogony."[13] The mythic motif of a hero slaying a draconic or serpentine foe to restore or create order is among the most ancient, one of the prime manifestations of the *chaoskampf* mytheme. In Hesiod's *Theogony* (c. 700 BCE), for example, Zeus defeats the serpentine titan Typhon for rulership of the cosmos. Even closer to the biblical narrative both geographically and culturally, Baal Hadad slays the seven-headed dragon Lotan, servant of the sea god Yam, in the Ugaritic *Baal Cycle* (c. 1400–1200 BCE). Lotan is often seen as the direct precursor to Leviathan, holding many shared titles—fugitive serpent, crooked serpent—as well as a shared etymology: both the Ugaritic *ltn* and Hebrew *lwh* mean "to twist" or "coil." Thus, Neil Forsyth notes, "this famous name signifies originally the 'twister,' a natural term for a serpent and destined to take on the various tricksterish implications of the English word."[14]

These precedents are not unknown to spiritual warriors. "In Near Eastern religions, Leviathan represents the forces of chaos," LeClaire writes.[15] Robertson states clearly that "Leviathan is the name of a creature of chaos in ancient mythology, which is used by Isaiah as a type of God's enemies who were incited by Satan."[16] Eckhardt echoes this sentiment, writing that the "ancients had contact with the spirit realm and often portrayed what they knew through their literature and folklore," and that the "many stories in ancient lore concerning fire-breathing dragons . . . are representative of Leviathan."[17] Directly tackling resonances with the Ugaritic *Baal Cycle*, Michael Heiser states bluntly that "the overlap with the biblical terminology is transparent." This overlap, however, is one that sought to establish dominance not only over chaos but over competing deities: "Yahweh's victory over the forces of primeval chaos . . . was theologically crucial for establishing [his] superiority over all other gods," proclaiming the creator-maintainer of all order to be Yahweh, not Baal.[18] Crucially, this triumph over chaos and other gods finds its biblical origin not in the first explicit mentions of Leviathan but much earlier. Perhaps the oldest "creature of chaos" is Tamte or Tiamat, the oceanic mother goddess who in the Babylonian creation epic *Enûma Elish* is defeated by the god Marduk and whose body becomes the raw material of creation. This process of order-out-of-chaos, by which Marduk builds heaven and earth, prefigures Yahweh's shaping of the primordial waters of the deep into the nascent world in Genesis 1—a process seemingly echoed specifically in regards to Leviathan in Psalm 74:12–17.[19] As evangelical authors Derek Gilbert and Josh Peck write, Genesis 1:2 "establishes the conflict between God and primordial chaos, represented by the sea and a sea monster. . . . The word translated 'deep' is the Hebrew *tehom*," a cognate "to the Akkadian *têmtum*, which in turn is a variant form of Tiamat, the Sumerian name for the chaos monster of the sea."[20]

As Heiser reads the biblical account as at attempt to champion Yahweh's supremacy over other gods, so Gilbert and Peck, noting the absence of any "epic battle" in Genesis 1, interpret the central idea of the biblical iteration as "when YHWH of Israel started creation, these chaotic forces were already held in check. There was no need for a battle. Leviathan was already bound, because the one true God doesn't need to have a fight."[21] Leviathan here becomes the lingering specter of primordial chaos, its hauntological remnant. While they appear in Job, Amos, Isaiah, and the Psalms and their draconic form signals an implicit link to the rebellion of Satan and his demons, their first appearance is not an act of rebellion but of subjugation—of being broken by absolute sovereign power and transfigured into the substance of the world itself. Yet if Leviathan is chaos tamed a priori, then the multiple serpentine, oceanic, and draconic insurrections in the scriptural narrative raise questions. For Gilbert and Peck this resurgence is because "chaos was subdued and restrained, but not eliminated yet.... Though YHWH restrains chaos, there is always a danger." Tracing the oceanic chaos through the Bible, they explain that the "end time . . . is in part about the complete removal of chaos when all the world will become like it was in Eden." When God re-creates the world in Revelation 21:1, they note, this re-creation has a specific exclusion: "Then I saw a new heaven and a new earth, for the first heaven and the first earth had passed away, *and the sea was no more*."[22] That is, in this final vision of reality, the chaos of which the sea—Leviathan—is representative is utterly subjugated.[23] All that is unruly is tamed, all the willful subjected to sovereign will, and all the base matter of creation has at last been properly, absolutely worlded.

In her *Face of the Deep*, feminist theologian Catherine Keller qualifies the theology that underpins this reading of Genesis 1 as a "theology of dominance" that bears a latent or explicit *tehomophobia*—a repetitive, obsessive dread at the chaotic, oceanic deep, at unruly Nature that must be mastered. "If Nature is good," Keller writes, "its inherent wobble and emptiness, its defect and excess, its bizarre, nay queer, capacity to resist the One who created it, demands the utmost vigilance."[24] Keller's text remains the most detailed and comprehensive analysis of chaos—of *tehom*, Tiamat, Leviathan—as submerged within the biblical narrative. She traces how nascent theologies of dominance reduced the chaos to nothingness in patristic narratives of *creatio ex nihilo* and the demonization of the deep qua nothing—or rather "worse than nothing"—by theologians like Karl Barth, for whom the *tehom* was not the matter *from* but rather *against* which God makes the world. I wish here not to counter or repeat her insights, but rather to inscribe them here in the context of spiritual warfare demonologies—and those of Leviathan specifically. For if Leviathan is the demonological echo of the deep—as Robertson, Heiser, and Gilbert and Peck, among others, suggest—then we find in Leviathan demonologies the wake of the very first act of worlding: the original transmutation of raw materials, or "uninscribed earth" (if one will allow me this mixing of natural metaphors) into the contours of a world through the violences of sovereign power, and which continues to unsettle and deconstruct the world which that sovereignty strives to maintain.

States of Chaos

For spiritual warriors today this revenant of the first of all worldings finds one of its chief manifestations in the First World. "Leviathan is the principality over the West," write Michael Kleu and Madeline Eayrs. Specifically, they are the spirit that "reigns over America." This can be seen in both America's power and its pride. "Leviathan is described as a proud spirit; so powerful that only God is able to control it and bring an end to it. This spirit causes one to look impenetrable or invincible. Others fear whoever has this spirit because it leaves destruction in its wake." The "fruits of power, arrogance and pride are clearly seen in this nation," they write. The United States is "a powerhouse in the world," its currency has "dominated the world markets for decades"; it is "one of the only countries . . . powerful enough to wage wars in other countries."[25] Perhaps more than international standing and potency, however, Leviathan's presence is discerned in the nation's domestic divides. "The spirit of Leviathan will promote pride, arrogance and hard-heartedness within the rich and fear, envy and hatred in the poor," Kleu and Eayrs state. "It inevitably leads to confrontation which results in large scale bloodshed and death amongst the most vulnerable."[26]

Leviathan is not here identified as the *cause* of America's income inequalities per se, which become broadly naturalized, merely attitudes fostered in relation to them: pride and envy, arrogance and fear, but above all division and the miscommunication that leads to division—the twisting of words and of the Word. On a purely personal level, this twisting comes in misunderstanding. "Have you ever been at your workplace or at home and something you say is taken the wrong way?" Bill Vincent rhetorically asks, then revealing "Leviathan wants to get between your conversation and hearing, distorting what someone is really saying."[27] LeClaire extrapolates: "People under this spirit's influence see things much differently from reality. They hear words you did not say or take the words you do say to mean something you never intended."[28] Echoing Jezebel's associations with "illegitimate" authority, Flippen ties Leviathan to preachers who "truly believe they are the mouthpieces of God" and, steeped in pride, "brag about their anointing."[29] Robertson highlights their manifestation in Church divisions, "behind mainstream denominational prejudice against deliverance ministries" as well as "in the 'charismatic churches' that are against the mainstream denominations."[30] LeClaire is more general: "If chaos is marking your life or your church... a Leviathan spirit likely is at work."[31] The spirit injects discord into harmony, in individuals and communities and in nations or the world. Richard Hotchkin identifies the spirit as lying behind all the "miscommunication, misunderstanding, chaos, conflict, disagreement, and discord" that seems more and more present "every time you turn on the news."[32]

Leviathan is a divisive spirit. They foster misunderstanding between persons and groups in order to drive them apart. Yet while spiritual warriors mobilize commonplace experiences—mutual misunderstanding, community rifts, media saturation—to create an impression of the spirit's work, it is important to clarify the goal of Leviathan's discord. As with Jezebel's control and the Antichrist's rage, it would be a mistake to frame Leviathan's chaos as equal-opportunity and politically neutral. This is made especially clear by Phillips, who situates the spirit as behind a "twisted form of feminism [that] through the media appears to empower women innocently," but causes them to shun "the responsibility of child rearing in the name of freedom," as well as "a misunderstood interpretation of the separation of church and state" that removed prayer from classrooms and teaches—pointing to the homophobia in *tehomophobia*—"homosexuality as an alternative lifestyle." He concludes by writing that the "great minds that once led our educational institutions live in fear of being ostracized by the media or losing government funding if they disagree."[33]

Although he does not use the term, Phillips's narrative of the stifling of "great minds" here echoes wider fearmongering around the mythology of "political correctness" that has dominated the US right since the early 1990s.[34] This narrative aligns Leviathan not with division broadly but with the "divisiveness" of progressive politics—an alignment LeClaire might also subtly suggest when she claims Leviathan "is especially prominent in coastal cities," those alleged bastions of urban decadence far from the heartland.[35] Yet as a spirit whose divisive energies are manifested in "political correctness," the confrontations and chaos that Leviathan brings in their wake can appear like demands for restitution and reform. Speaking after Occupy Wall Street in 2011, for example, Cindy Jacobs identified the protest movement as driven by a "spirit of anarchy" empowered by an unnamed principality.[36] While she does not name Leviathan directly, the spirit's connections to chaos implicitly conjure their presence. Lance Wallnau is not so oblique, however, situating Leviathan on a March 17, 2016, broadcast of his *7m Underground* as the unseen force behind not only the Occupy movement but other grassroots protest groups such as Code Pink and Black Lives Matter.[37] While Wallnau partially places blame for Occupy on the lack of "godly" leaders guiding US economic policy and therefore permitting the growth of inequality, it is the protest movements he focuses on. In doing so, he identifies Leviathan's chaos as a spirit of protest, which he elsewhere links to both the Civil War and 1960s counterculture.

Advertising his *Leviathan* audio series in Sid Roth's newsletter *Mishpochah*, Wallnau writes that the media focus "on issues of race, confederate statues and talk of 'white supremacy,' exposes a link between the divisive spirit at work in the 1860s and today, beginning with the riots and demonstrations of the 1960s." Reinforcing Phillips's link between Leviathan and educational reforms, Wallnau writes that after the 1960s, "this lawless spirit shifted its tactic" by pushing "the radicals" to enter and co-opt the system: "*Now this spirit is operating in and through institutions of power, notably, journalism, entertainment, law and academia. . . . The name of this spirit is Leviathan.*"[38] For Wallnau, this many-pronged assault finds its representation in the serpent's heads. Others authors frame this multiplicity personally: "Each head of Leviathan speaks to a different person, whispering in ears, convincing each that they are right," Dave Williams informs; thus, someone affected by the spirit "will not give you a straight answer."[39] Wallnau, however, draws out the implications of this multiplicity by situating its ramifications not simply in Leviathan's duplicitousness or even in the plethora of sins they foster, but in the institutions they subvert and direct in pursuit of national division—a division tied to, with telling use of scare quotes, "talk of 'white supremacy.'"

Explicit in Wallnau's framing and implicit in others' is that Leviathan's divisiveness is not one caused by, for example, income inequality, sexism, or racism but raising awareness of these issues, which then becomes framed as the issue itself. As Sara Ahmed has demonstrated, people who raise issues of inequality often become framed as the causes of those inequalities. "To talk about racism is . . . to be heard as making rather than exposing the problem," she summarizes: "to talk about racism is to become the problem you pose."[40] Leviathan's apparent stoking of miscommunication and division here emerges as a strident challenge to ingrained institutional prejudices. This challenge unearths further implications about Phillips's demonization of media ostracization and loss of government financial backing, especially when placed in relation to Wallnau's invocation of the Civil War—an association especially noteworthy for its lack of novelty. In his study of confederate memory and conservatism in South Carolina, historian W. Scott Poole discusses a conjuration of Leviathan by Presbyterian divine David E. Frierson that is apposite to discuss here. Writing in 1868 in response to the creation of a new state constitution during Reconstruction, the divine claimed Leviathan was "the spirit of innovation that nullifies statute and precedent." This innovation, which abolished race as a limit on male suffrage, property ownership as a requisite for holding office, and provided for a uniform system of free public schools, among other things, Frierson saw as interfering "with the growth of the law shaped by Providence through prescriptive tradition and historical experience." As Poole continues, "The spirit of Leviathan embodied in the Federal government and the Radical South Carolina legislature sought to 'ignore precedent and the experience of mankind and make law ... with the spirit of the nineteenth century.'"[41]

It is unknown if Wallnau knew of Frierson's evocation, but his echo of it nevertheless points to how the spirit's associations with division come to be tied to both progressive change and government interventions and institutions in favor of such change. It is in this context that one can properly situate the "statism" that Clark associates Leviathan with as entwined with broader conservative conspiracies about left-wing activism in which violences of racial capitalism and the neoliberal state are blamed on "socialism" and revolutionary politics. The framing of Egypt as archetypal leviathan state is also relevant here, given the nation's racialized history within both Judaism and Christianity as tied to the lineage—and Curse— of Ham, its bondage of God's people becoming framed as not only a moral sin but also an inversion of a racialized and religious hierarchy that determined who "should" be masters and who slaves.[42] Leviathan and the states they foster thus represent an overturning of orthotaxic models of racial and religious hierarchy, the "prescriptive tradition" of providence. This genealogy and its displacement and disavowal is present in Clark's attempt to tie Leviathan to the nation-state. The "nation state, just as Leviathan in Job 41 will fight with all its might for dominion," he writes—a fight for "survival and continual growth" doomed a priori as the "only government that is destined for victory is the Kingdom of God."[43] Yet despite allusions to "continual growth" and occasional references to "bondage debt," Clark's leviathan state is not the racial capitalist settler state of modern America, built on exploitation, expropriation, and the intertwined mechanisms of military, pharmaceutical, and carceral industrial complexes (even if these are implicated), but rather the phantasmatic image of a secret "socialist" plot aimed at economic redistribution, structural reform, and redress and reparation for past and present violences.

Invoking the equivalences between capitalist excess and communist revolution that have historically been central to conspiracies of "Judeo-

Bolshevism"[44]—albeit here shorn of (overtly) antisemitic content—the threatening image of the "leviathan state" testifies to the longstanding relation between capitalism and Christianity as entwined paradigms of soteriological economy. It points to what Gil Anidjar terms "economic theology": the paradigm through which Christianity transformed links between blood and money, undergirding "the history of a concealed trinity: the translation, transubstantiation, and transvaluation, whereby Christianity became, in fact, 'religion,' blood became money, and money—faith and works, pace Weber—became what it is all about."[45] In Chapter 3, I explored the coagulation of "pure" Christian blood against "other bloods," facilitating the creation and consolidation of hierarchies of nation, race, ethnicity, and class. Anidjar here extends this, pointing to the associations constructed between Jews and money as joint threats to Christian blood (blood libels, Judas's blood money, collective guilt over Christ's death) and Christian commerce (Jews as merchants, as usurious, as inventors of capitalism itself). This Judeophobic provenance helps contextualize the temporal dimensions of Leviathan demonologies, which I return to shortly, reinforcing an association between the spirit and lifeways that "should" be over. Critical here, however, is how this vision of economic theology points us towards considering how the "leviathan state" acts to disrupt the existing logics of capitalist-Christian salvation in the United States.

In his political theology of late capital, *Neoliberalism's Demons*, Adam Kotsko demonstrates how neoliberalism operates soteriologically. Situating "the parallel between God's demonic foes and the social order's subjugated populations" at the crux of neoliberalism, he chronicles the way that neoliberalism relies on a logic of demonization. Kotsko defines this logic as a structure of "moral entrapment" by which individuals are made moral culpable for choosing actions they are structurally precluded from not choosing, "providing them with just the barest sliver of agency necessary to render them blameworthy."[46] This paradigm has its theological archetype in the fall of the Devil, which occurs at the instant of creation for ultimately arbitrary reasons, but through which an absolute sovereign God "ensure[s] that there will be a reservoir of evil for him to turn toward the greater good." However, it finds its current sociopolitical manifestation in neoliberalism, wherein the alliance between capitalism and reactionary Christianity unveils the "indissoluble link between providence and demonization," wherein logics of salvation are tied to notions of market competition: for some to be saved, others must be damned. These others are produced by the soteriological economy itself, which precludes certain subjects access to "the good," to "goods" that are markers of one's success and salvation, while rendering them blameworthy for such preclusion.[47] These willful subjects—the racialized and queered, the Jezebelian and Antichristian—are those I have discussed in earlier chapters, who like demons and as demonized have been denied sovereignty but given just enough autonomy to oppose it. Yet this confluence of soteriology and market competition, filtered through associations of blood and capital, also permits a reframing of demonologies of the leviathan state. Rejecting the neoliberal vision of the state as handmaid to the market—that is, the soteriological economy—the leviathan state is what arises when the state disrupts or is seen as disrupting this economy through redistribution or reparation, when it contaminates the "pure blood" (of Christ, of Capital) by introducing it to restructuring circulations, interventions in the "natural" bio-necropolitical calculus of who is worthy of life and death, salvation and damnation, being and nonbeing.

It is in this context of Leviathan's relation to alternative circulations that their use as a demonizing figure for progressive social movements is important, for there is also a certain solidity, even solidarity, to the spirit. Injecting chaos into the soteriological economies of orthotaxy and its bio-necro collaborations, Leviathan promises new orderings grounded on redistribution and reparation forged through circulations of other bloods. And while the spirit's discordant traits find representation in their many heads, Leviathan's coalitions of disruption are perhaps best captured by their scales. Leviathan is "a giant spirit that blocks the flow of God's purpose, power, and prosperity in your life," Phillips wrote, with Ing citing this capacity in scales so tight they "prevent Christians from receiving the things of God."[48] The tightness of their scales binds the flow of divine power, the proper functioning of the soteriological economy, and while they seemingly cover one single monster, these scales are more than merely parts of a whole. As Eckhardt warns his fellow warriors when he writes of fighting the dragon: "Remember to strip the scales off Leviathan. His scales are the demons that shield him from attack."[49] Each of Leviathan's scales is here its own demon, the dragon's hide coming to resemble less a snake's skin than a shield wall. A phalanx of tightly packed forces clinging to one another not simply for strategy but for survival, Leviathan comes to reflect the haunting realization that challenges to the necropolizing structures of orthotaxy's providence may require the force of the multitude—a multitude that, in the minds of the spiritual warriors discussed, adopts the singular if shifting image of a "strict, compact alliance of villains," one "assembled in a unitary body" in order to "fight the Almighty."⁵⁰ Before we can fully explore this possibility, however, it is necessary to first interrogate the relation between Leviathan and the sovereign they oppose more closely.

The Imitation God

While in the context of broader demonizations of movements for social justice Eckhardt's image of Leviathan as a demon covered or comprised of other demons calls to mind the force of the multitude, it also conjures another famous image of the state and sovereignty: the frontispiece of Thomas Hobbes's 1651 political philosophy text of that same name, on which the sovereign is depicted, towering above the realm, with a body comprised of the mass of his subjects over which the king—as head—rules. Hobbes is rarely mentioned in spiritual warfare texts—in the context of the Leviathan spirit or otherwise—but the associations his work builds between the name of Leviathan, sovereignty, and the state haunt them regardless. Clark's "leviathan state" channels Hobbes's spirit, and the motif of making order out of the chaos of nature through the exercise of sovereign power are major themes of both *Leviathan* and demonologies of the Leviathan spirit. Perhaps the foremost source by which the modern world binds the name of a demon to the head and body of the state, a critical reading of *Leviathan* unearths tensions in the spirit whose name it shares, revealing them to constitute an unsettling and unstable structure of sovereignty: both a state of nature, the primordial chaos of a *bellum omnia contra omnes* that sovereignty must world, and an unstable assemblage of quasi-sovereign bodies that threatens to counterfeit and thereby consume the divinely ordained structures of that world.

I am not here suggesting no prior connection between Leviathan and sovereign bodies exists—indeed, this link is paramount. The most common, bound up with submerged archives of religio-racialized order, is of course Egypt, enabled by the categorization of Pharaoh in Ezekiel 29:3 as a *tannin*—a Hebrew and Canaanite word for a sea monster often equated with Leviathan—lying in the midst of his rivers, laying claim to both the creation and (thus) ownership of the Nile.⁵¹ This connection predates Hobbes. Seventy years before *Leviathan*'s publication, French jurist and godfather of political sovereignty Jean Bodin discussed Ezekiel 29:3 in his 1580 witch-hunting manual *De la démonomanie des sorciers*, rendering *tannin* directly as Leviathan and identifying the beast with Satan. "Commentators agree that 'Leviathan,' 'Pharaoh,' and 'Behemoth' mean this great Enemy of the human race," he explains, "and that the Kingdom of Egypt represents the flesh and covetousness, and by the river was meant the torrent of fluid nature which always flows on to corruption."[52] Pier Giuseppe Monateri has demonstrated that for Bodin and earlier commentators, Leviathan was chiefly an emblem of Egypt as "evil" sovereignty. As such, precisely why Hobbes chose the name for his image of the sovereign is contentious, possibly stemming from claims that the word derived from the Hebrew *lavah*, meaning "united" or "associated," or, as Monateri argues, from a minor and heterodox interpretation of Leviathan as emblem of the Lord's world rule.[53] Nonetheless, as I will demonstrate, the demonological undercurrent of *Leviathan* haunts it, producing ambiguity and slippage. The Hobbesian Leviathan is always at risk of transfiguring into its other—into Egypt, the "leviathan state"—in ways that find their echo in contemporary spiritual warfare.

Reading *Leviathan* through queer theory, Heike Schotten contends that the work champions a vision of life tied to a project(ion) of desire that is bound up with its creation of temporality as such. In Hobbes, "sovereign is he who makes life." Moreover, "the sovereign constitutes life *as life* . . . by bringing the future into existence."[54] In Schotten's reading, the Hobbesian sovereign secures not just the material economy—agriculture, manufacturing, art, literature, geography—but the "cognitive, affective, and symbolic processes" that permit their condition of possibility. Among such processes is temporality itself, in the futurist sense outlined by Edelman, since the sovereign is what allows us "to make time comprehensible . . . as a feature of lived human existence." The state of nature (imagined as a state of perpetual conflict) out of which the sovereign worlds the world is here cast as atemporal—it has *time*, but not *temporality* and it is brought to a close through the sovereign's creation of temporality. For Schotten, Hobbes's sovereign is akin to God, declaring, "Let there be life"—a statement that gestures to the biopolitics inherent in the heliopolitical "let there be light" (Genesis 1:3)—and institutes political sovereignty as "*the* definitive biopolitical regime . . . because it *constitutes* and *determines* life as such, thereby distinguishing it from what becomes only subsequently recognizable as death"—the state of nature and, critically, those within it, whose lives become symbolic of that death.[55] We witness here the lingering specter of that first worlding—of the theology of dominance that turns "uninscribed earth" into world. This is not coincident, but neither is it pure correlation, for Hobbes's sovereign is not precisely God. Rather, as the philosopher A. P. Martinich summarizes, "Hobbes held that the civil state is a mortal god, who serves under the immortal God."[56]

The temporal structure of desire Schotten posits at the heart of sovereignty is not simply a desire for a normative (white, settler, cisheteropatriarchal) future but a desire bound to theological imitation. It is eschatologically oriented. This becomes clear in Hobbes's opposition of the sovereign to what he—ironically, tellingly—terms "demonology." For Hobbes, demonology is synonymous with idolatry—itself synonymous with misunderstanding the nature of reality by taking representations for things themselves: a "fabulous Doctrine concerning Daemons, which are but Idols, or Phantasms of the braine, without any reall nature of their own, distinct from humane fancy."[57] Any political system arising from demonology—from the "Kingdome of Darknesse"—is a *Confederacy of Deceivers, that to obtain dominion over men in this present world, endeavour by dark, and erroneous Doctrines to extinguish in them the Light, both of Nature, and of the Gospell. And so to dis-prepare them for the Kingdome of God to come.*[58] Hobbes here gives sovereignty an eschatological horizon: to prepare people for the coming Kingdom by cultivating in them the heliopolitical force of Nature and the Gospel. While Hobbes identifies both an otherworldly Heaven and Hell as metaphorical—mapped onto security and civil war, respectively—*Leviathan* seemingly situates the Millennial Kingdom as an actual material reality, initiated by Christ's return and inaugurating an estate that ensures "perpetuall security against enemies, and want."[59] The aim of the mortal God was therefore the earthly maintenance of a Natural and Biblical order that would be eternalized at time's end, when—Hobbes relates—Christ descends and establishes his Everlasting Kingdom on Earth, the elect are given "Life eternall" and the wicked suffer in "Torment eternall."[60]

The illegitimacy of the demon here frames Hobbesian sovereignty, providing it its limits, thereby defining it. But these limits are unstable. Leviathan's demonological foundations unsettle *Leviathan*'s attempts to consolidate sovereign order; as James Martel has argued, Hobbesian sovereignty may itself be as demonological as the systems it opposes, perhaps even the "epitome of demonology."[61] This demonic nature is exemplified by the ambiguity of the line Hobbes draws between idolatry and "rightful" worship. The latter is not solely an act of veneration but also an appreciation of things as they are, using our discernment to read the world accurately. Martel uses the example of the king's stool: while the stool is a symbol of the sovereign's power that power does not reside in the stool but in the sovereign. To offer veneration to the king is rightful worship (albeit of the civil variety), whereas to offer it to the stool is idolatry. It mistakes a representation of the thing for the thing itself. However, an issue arises, Martel argues, in that it is impossible to really discern if a worshipper is idolatrous or not by external signs.[62] One cannot know for sure if someone worships the king or merely his stool. Critically, however, this ambiguity of representation and recognition may be central to sovereignty as such, tied to its essential (in)divisibility. As Geoffrey Bennington has outlined, "the sovereign, in order to be sovereign, has to give itself a primary supplement in the form of a government." That is, the sovereign—indivisible—must divide itself to be recognized as such; "that government cannot fail to undo the sovereign in the very fact of making it sovereign, or to undermine it in the very act of supporting it."[63] In requiring its own division to constitute itself as one, the structure of sovereignty always contains the possibility of it being other than it "is," of being or becoming idol, thus making the division between idol and proper unstable, given to slippage and elision.

In spiritual warfare, this elision is found in Leviathan's ascribed counterfeiture, of God certainly but more so of the Church. Tess Maltese claims Leviathan "will mimick [sic], act out, false physical manifestations of deliverances to confuse and trick Deliverance minister[s]."[64] Ing writes that "Leviathan sits in the Holy Place, counterfeits the furnishings, and blocks the entrance which leads to the Holy of Holies." The spirit offers "a false peace and sense of well being by counterfeiting the gifts of the Holy Spirit—false revelations, prophesies, words, visions, and dreams." Christians must thus cultivate discernment, lest they "stagnate in their understandings of the Word, seeing only through the false light of Leviathan."[65] Yet these counterfeits may not be straightforwardly false. LeClaire identifies the spiritual pride associated with Leviathan as "a monstrous problem in the body of Christ," and lists the ways it influences believers by enabling self-righteousness, hypocrisy, and false humility. However, she continues: "You may see people operating in spiritual gifts in public who have deplorable character in private. . . . That doesn't mean God doesn't see the condition of their hearts; rather, it means the gifts and callings of God are without repentance and the Lord is blessing the hungry who came expecting breakthrough."[66] Discernment here takes a back seat: a "deplorable" private character not only does not invalidate or even problematize the legitimacy of spiritual gifts, but this legitimacy is even assured due to God's acknowledgment of the hunger of the believers. Ultimately, LeClaire appeals to a future fall that will come upon these individuals, subordinating the present to a potential—if preordained—future judgment. Without this horizon of judgment God and Leviathan's works intermix, contaminating one another in an always ambiguous world.

"The fire and smoke from Leviathan's nostrils and mouth counterfeit the altar of incense," Ing writes. "Instead of holy prayers and praises that please God, they produce unholy prayers and praises that stink."[67] Yet it is the ambiguous perspective of the observer who cannot always know incense from inferno, that unstable boundary between the counterfeit and the thing itself, which defines the Leviathan spirit. They are characterized by the possibility of slippage and reversion, a possibility that finds its clearest representation in the sovereign himself. For Hobbes, the sovereign is both "a representative who . . . mirrors and mediates between contracting citizens" and "an independent figure whose imposed force alone can tie men to their contracts."[68] Hobbes understood the body politic as having been formed out of the state of nature by a collective act of will, and as such the fundamental distinction in politics was between a natural, pre-political (if not pre-social) situation and civil society.[69] Neither civil society nor the sovereign were appointed from above but authored from below. The sovereign is a "Feigned" or "Artificial person," the agential force of a commonwealth without any natural being of its own, created by the social contract itself—a representation of general will that elevates that will to sovereign will.[70] However, this will was but a mortal imitation, and imitation is always a dangerous game. As Teresa Brennan has noted, imitation differs when based on admiration or envy: "We might say that imitation can be gauged envious where the original is denied."[71] Like the Antichrist, Leviathan's threatening mimicry is imagined through this formulation of envious desire. Perhaps even more so, for in several demonological taxonomies Leviathan is the very archdemon of envy itself.

"Leviathan doesn't want there to be any movement of the Holy Spirit," Flippen writes. They want "to *be* the Holy Spirit! Leviathan is the counterfeit to Him in every way."[72] The line between legitimate sovereign and leviathan state is the line between admiration and envy, and admiration is (for both Hobbes and spiritual warriors) measured primarily by obedience. In *Leviathan*, Hobbes details several areas in which subjects may negotiate with their sovereign, but is clear that when "our refusall to obey, frustrates the End for which the Sovereignty was ordained; then there is no Liberty to refuse."[73] This End is singular but twofold: the material survival of sovereignty as the enforcer of order and the orientation of this order toward its proper eschatological horizon, lest it become merely a passing order. Absence of obedience is here inherently threatening, even if ineffectual, as exemplified by Hobbes's discussion of the witch: "I think not that their witchcraft is any reall power; but yet they are justly punished," he writes, "for the false beliefe they have, that they can do such mischiefe, joyned with the purpose to do it if they can."[74] The witch, by Hobbes's time a common figure of religiopolitical dissent, becomes a threat to sovereignty not because she has any capacity to resist its power but simply because she believes that she could and might act on this belief. The witch has ceased to admiringly replicate order—to climb toward "whiteness and light," as Frantz Fanon might say—seeking instead to replace it. She is thus "justly punished," since those under the sway of the doctrines of devils were no longer "capable of being used by the sovereign for the purposes of promoting peace."[75] Or perhaps, recalling the distinction of Michael Youssef, they may be capable of only promoting the "dark peace" of revolution, not the "divine peace" of assimilation and acquiescence.

For spiritual warriors, as for Hobbes, it is imperative that earthly order maintain the proper eschatological orientation: that it should seek to admire and imitate sovereign will, not envy and usurp that will with its own visions of futurity, its own economies. To fail at this task is to threaten a return of and to chaos, to the atemporality of a state of nature yet to be (properly) worlded. Hobbes scholars have often observed that images of internecine civil war elide into and replicate those of the state of nature, that among the most structuring anxieties of Hobbes's oeuvre is the idea that the "most civilized of human beings could slip back down the evolutionary continuum to their former beastlike state of nature."[76] That is, Leviathan could always return to the deeps. Or, apropos Gilbert and Peck, "Though YHWH restrains chaos, there is always a danger." This danger comes in a reversion to primordial chaos but also (perhaps more so) in the enviously imitative passing orders that "*dis-prepare*" subjects from the Kingdom to come. The Leviathan spirit reflects both: an embodiment of chaos yet to be worlded by sovereign will and the "leviathan states" of other gods who willfully world the world according to desires not directed "the right way."

Unsettling Sovereignties

The unstable borders Leviathan reflects—between a state of nature and the orders that threaten to pass (back) into it, and which might therefore have been passing all along—contain the ambiguities of another division, one forever unstable, between chaos itself and the chaos dragon. For even if Leviathan and their serpentine associates are echoes of the primordial *tehom*, they are not it. Similarly, even if (apropos Ing) "God uses a mythical creature . . . to describe Leviathan," a creature suffices.[77] Unlike the deep, Leviathan has form, threatening but yet intelligible. They are a "creature of chaos."[78] Created, but not tamed—not until the end; an end that is perhaps only realized by this taming. Leviathan is interstitial, the remainder and reminder of sovereignty's once and future worlding. However, they are also the leviathan states of other gods over which God—by subjugating the deep without struggle—marks himself superior. These gods are read by spiritual warriors such as Heiser and Gilbert and Peck as signifying inferior and illegitimate authorities, not simply as lesser entities who must wrestle with chaos whereas God can claim dominion, but reflections of that chaos itself. Framing Leviathan thusly, the threat they represent emerges not simply as one of chaos—unintelligible to sovereign power lest it first dominate it and so bring it into its world—but of things "improperly" worlded. Leviathan's potential to revert to the chaos from which sovereign power first wrought them can here be read otherwise: as the resurgent and insurgent remnants of worlds that were always already more than uninscribed earth, ones forced into intelligibility but always exceeding orthotaxy's scope.

This reframing of Leviathan becomes necessary when interrogating the "state of nature" from which both Hobbes and modern spiritual warriors figure sovereignty as saving its subjects. In Chapter 1, I discussed at length the (settler) colonial heliopolitics that underwrite spiritual warfare, and in the context of this quasi-Hobbesian reading of Leviathan-via-*Leviathan* this foundation is critical. The state of nature, for Hobbes (but not only Hobbes) was not only part of humanity's collective pre-political history but his own colonial present, finding its seventeenth-century instantiation in an image of "America," wherein "savage people" were organized into "small Families . . . have no government; and live at this day in that brutish manner."[79] As Srinivas Aravamudan demonstrates, Hobbes's framing of "America" was one that consciously—not incidentally—elided Native sovereignty claims.[80] This is made clearest on the frontispiece of his *De Cive*, upon which an androgynous Algonquian warrior stands as embodiment of the "Libertas" of Nature, one who "wishes to escape the ambivalent mixture of natural liberty and anarchic violence." This warrior is placed opposite "Imperivm," a European woman armed with sword and scales, representing "a combination of conquest and contract, demanding sovereign subjection but enforcing an imperial peace."[81] Hobbes's state of nature was thus not an abstract thought experiment but was materialized as the colonized and colonizable periphery, which became figured as a state of primordial chaos as yet unsubjected to sovereign might, of uninscribed earth that had yet to be properly worlded.

This settler colonial imaginary, which worlds itself over Indigenous lifeworlds through a violent subordination of Indigenous peoples to new orders of territorial and temporal sovereignty, resurges in spiritual warfare—but distinctly. While the Hobbesian Leviathan emerges from a subjugation of Indigenous lifeworlds, in spiritual warfare Leviathan becomes a symbol of those very lifeworlds. Thomas Horn and Cris Putnam, for example, identify Leviathan with the feathered serpent deities of South and Mesoamerican religion such as the Aztec Quetzalcoatl, Maya Kukulkan, and Inca Amaru.[82] This connection is not just a curiosity of mythological conflation, but is rendered as an enduring spiritual bond that impacts both Indigenous and Latinx peoples in the present through an ascription of hereditary iniquity. Bob and Laura Larson identify "the feathered serpent god Quetzalcoatl" as "a common demon found in those of Hispanic ancestry" who must be exorcized for those with it to become fully functional individuals.[83] Cindy Jacobs expands on this in a 2013 video teaching, explicitly linking Leviathan to Indigenous heritage: "If you have in your bloodline any animus, any Native American blood, for instance. [While] not all Native Americans worshipped the serpent or crocodile, many did, but you might want to renounce that and repent for the generational iniquity." She then lists "totem poles" that have "crocodile" imagery as signaling the presence of "a very strong spirit of Leviathan" and singles out potential Mexican listeners who might have "indigenous" or especially Mayan or Aztec blood, as the spirit is "very active in your bloodline."[84] Indigenous blood here becomes impure—other blood—to be washed and replaced by "pure" (Christian, settler) blood. Following in this vein, Horn and Putnam mobilize the idea of blood further to draw distinctions between communities of spiritual blood when they oppose Quetzalcoatl's (again, read as Leviathan) offering of blood to "give life to humanity" in the Aztec creation myth to Jesus's sacrifice on the cross, in which his blood similarly gives (new) life to humanity, casting the first as a mere counterfeit or facsimile of the latter.[85]

If Hobbes's colonial imaginary demonized Indigenous peoples as the base matter from and atop which Leviathan would rise, Jacobs, the Larsons, and Horn and Putnam mobilize the logics of settler colonialism to cast them as that Leviathan, but one who must be similarly curtailed into the structure of settler sovereignty and teleology. These authors frame spiritual warfare's racializing undercurrents—the tendency to enflesh "principalities and powers" in queer, Black, Muslim, and Indigenous bodies that resist or refuse assimilation into their God's imperial peace—in explicitly settler colonial terms. This demonization is, of course, nothing new: the rhetoric of spiritual warfare has long been part of missionary colonization enterprises, in what is now the United States and elsewhere,[86] and ideas of "generational iniquity" are merely the method by which the colonized are interpellated into such enterprises today. Yet it reinforces the disparity between colonizer and colonized within the spiritual warfare imaginary. Echoing spiritual warfare's construction of uneven (racialized) geographies, discussed in Chapter 1, Andrea Smith notes that while white evangelicals in the United States might stress racial reconciliation over violences like colonialism and slavery these violences are not seen to structurally disadvantage whites in the manner ancestral "idolatry"—or colonial violence—seems to for racialized groups.[87] Like Haitians, ostensibly cursed for turning to demonized deities when the Christian God refused to intervene in their slavery, the systemic and structural problems faced by Indigenous Americans in the present are situated in their refusal to submit fully to settler sovereignty, in the lingering specters of traditional identities, sovereignties, and ways of life that refuse to pass on.

Horn and Putnam implicitly conjure the settler desire for linear salvation history when in their juxtaposition of the communities of Christ's and Quetzalcoatl's bloods they mark the former's alleged superiority due to its "one-time" nature, as opposed to the ongoing blood sacrifices they frame as intrinsic to Mesoamerican cultures. Setting aside the oddity of using Quetzalcoatl here—the figure's relation to human sacrifice was complex and shifting, and his blood offering also one-time[88]—this opposition exemplifies broader frameworks of spiritual warfare's imaginary. The apparent supremacy of Christianity is tied to its singularity and eternal imposition, while demons' inferiority is tied to a need for repetition and reciprocity. Issues that recur within spiritual warfare's imaginary are thus framed as demonic, tied to an unsettled and unsettling presence that endures when it "should" be over—whether this is personal trauma or, more concerningly, the struggle of a community for recognition and restitution. The conduit for such unsettling is blood, here Indigenous blood, which must be made to vanish into the one blood. Ing renders this explicit in his framing of Hawaii by invoking the colonial taxonomy of blood quantum. The "Hawaiian race is at the brink of extinction," he writes, linking the diminishment of "pure-blooded Hawaiians" not to the legacy of colonial dispossession and the poverty and disease of urbanization but to "a curse on the Hawaiian race."[89] This curse is never given a concrete cause but is implicitly tied to the survival of Indigenous practices, identities, and kinship ties: a later section titled "Breaking the Curses" speaks chiefly of "deliver[ing] Hawaiians from their demon gods," and Ing concludes by observing, "Pride in being Hawaiian . . . [has] surfaced during deliverance. Pride prevents us from really receiving and giving God's love."[90] The desire for Hawaiian cultural survival and Kingdom sovereignty is here cast as the very reason for their "extinction," with the solution proposed being that very extinction: the absorption of Hawaiian blood into the one blood and the developmental/soteriological future it ensures.

These spiritual warriors articulate—more and less explicitly—the desire of settler sovereignty for a reality in which all Indigenous desires and knowledges have been entirely done away with, for the capacity to fall back on settlement discourses of nonexistence, invisibility, or *terra nullius* in which Indigenous peoples have either disappeared or were never present. They testify to what Lorenzo Veracini relays as settler colonialism's desire to eliminate the Native and thereby eliminate itself *as such*. That is, through the effective repression, co-option, and extinguishing of "indigenous alterities" succeed in becoming settled, in "cover[ing] its tracks and operat[ing] towards its self-supersession."[91] Read through this desire, Gilbert and Peck's reading of the Creation—in which the "chaotic forces were already held in check. There was no need for a battle. Leviathan was already bound, because the one true God doesn't need to have a fight"— adopts another valence, representing a primordial instantiation of the settler narrative in which there was no struggle, no resistance, no Native. *Ex nihilo* blurs into *terra nullius*; the land was formless and void. Leviathan's subjection here theologizes the settler colonial subjugation of the Native, in which "land has been dispossessed; its owners have been eliminated or absorbed," until all is "'settled' . . . 'done,' 'finished,' 'complete.'" Yet, as Simpson notes, this project "did not work completely. There are still Indians, some still know it, and some will defend what they have left. They will persist, robustly."[92] This robust persistence also finds in Leviathan its demonological corollary, threatening constantly to resurge, to "*dis-prepare*" people for the absolute settlement of time, to disrupt and dissolve the orthotaxy of settler sovereignty itself.

The interweaving of temporal and territorial sovereignty claims at work in these texts point toward how spiritual warfare invokes the classic colonial inversion, which frames the colonized not as dispossessed but as illegally occupying space—here, agents of "the usurper, Satan." In the process, Indigenous lifeworlds are reinscribed as the colonial Leviathan itself, as illegitimately possessing territory and bodies that rightfully belong to God and which must thus be reclaimed and held by sovereign will. At the same time, the temporal order is complicated and unstable as this Leviathan—this counterfeit sovereign—is a resurgent remnant of a primordial state from before God's power inscribed the world. It here becomes possible to read spiritual warfare's Leviathan as a *de*colonial Leviathan, for which a "going back" appears as a returning to that which sovereign power has deemed to be over in order to address that which is not yet over. This decolonial Leviathan becomes an aberration in and assault on futurist temporality, whose articulations of Indigenous sovereignty and self-determination challenge configurations of settler time. Settler time, Mark Rifkin outlines, denies and restricts Indigenous sovereignty through assimilating it into the historical vision of settler colonialism. Native peoples are figured as "consigned to the past, or . . . inserted into a present defined on non-native terms." Because of this, "Native people(s) do not so much exist within the flow of time as erupt from it as an anomaly, one usually understood as emanating from a bygone era."[93] In the temporal/territorial sovereignty claims of spiritual warfare, Leviathan reflects this sense of eruption, an explosive reemergence of that which has allegedly been settled and bringing with it a haunting realization that its demons persist, robustly.

As that which refuses to be settled, Leviathan adopts a *hauntological* quality: they make "impossible and possible a metaphysics of ontology that structures inheritance along linear coordinates in time and space, cause and effect, which in turn (in)forms the presence of the subject."[94] The demon generally, and Leviathan specifically, haunts divine order in much the way that Derrida, in the context in which he coined "hauntology," saw communism as haunting the post–Cold War world. The "triumphant conjuration" of capitalist hegemony, he writes, "is striving in truth to disavow, and therefore to hide from," the reality that "never, never in history, has the horizon of the thing whose survival is being celebrated (namely, all the old models of the capitalist and liberal world) been as dark, threatening, and threatened."[95] Leviathan's counterfeiture is what enables the identification and codification of authentic ontology within spiritual warfare, while their past and future defeat is what frames its triumphalist teleology. But the dragon haunts these teleologies and ontologies, and this hauntological dimension permits a revaluation of how Leviathan was deployed frame grassroots resistance groups against racial, gender, and class domination. As Kotsko discusses, drawing on Marika Rose, the triumph of neoliberalism and its demonizing soteriology was roughly coterminous with the end of the Cold War, inaugurating an "end to history" in which there is no alternative.[96] Positioned in relation to this neoliberal teleology, the ties between the conjurations of Leviathan in demonologies of Indigenous traditions and of socialist-inspired politics (including the specter of "Judeo-Bolshevism") become apparent. Not only disruptions within the "proper" soteriological economy—although they are this—much like the Indigenous traditions that heliopolitics deems to have been settled, these movements figure a return of ostensibly vanquished and superseded others that refuse to pass on, of history after its proclaimed end: a Jewishness that refuses to be assimilated into "Judeo-Christianity," demands for socialism in an ostensibly postsocialist world and for the need for racial justice and women's rights in an allegedly postracial and postfeminist society.

Leviathan "the crooked serpent" is out of joint, inhabiting and embodying a time that is out of joint. Leviathan "the fugitive serpent," persists in that flight, motion, and fugitivity that, as Jack Halberstam writes in the introduction to Harney and Moten's *The Undercommons*, "is separate from settling."[97] Remnant of an originary dispossession, the leviathan state is perhaps the state of dispossession itself, persisting in "the interplay of the refusal of what has been refused."[98] Leviathan here exemplifies spiritual warfare's demons: constituted as nothing, doomed a priori, they embody that which should not be able to resist sovereign will yet continues—willfully and repeatedly—to do so. Much like the demons that comprise their scales, this willfulness is never individual. Willfulness "requires a collective struggle," Ahmed writes, where the labor and effort of those who refuse to become the master's tools "show us what is not over, what we do not get over."[99] Compensating for their existential weakness, forestalling the inevitability of their ending, demons labor collectively to reclaim old and build new edifices and architectures that enable survival in the face of territorial and temporal perdition. And perhaps, through doing so, they might signify—as Stephen Dillon suggests in his analysis of the queer politics of the prison state—"a fugitive way of knowing that escaped articulation—that would give rise to a way of being beyond ontology," in which "the future was uncharted."[100] These futures, fugitive and unsettling, exceed the soteriological calculus of orthotaxy, giving birth to the possibility of decolonial (un)sovereignties, of new heads carried aloft on the solidarity of scales. As such, for these spiritual warriors—as for Hobbes—Leviathan must be constantly subordinated to sovereign will, until that inevitable moment it can be fully, finally subjected in the worlding of a new heaven and new earth in which there will be no more sea.

Sea No More

In his work of decolonial theology *The Decolonial Abyss*, Yountae An positions the dual processes of colonialism and the Middle Passage as an "abyssal wound" in the fabric of history, one "which leaves no ruins and no names."[101] Drawing on Fanon, Aime Césaire, and Édouard Glissant, he frames this abyss of coloniality—symbolized in the "Ocean, where the undying memory and the horrifying history of deaths and drowned names are engraved"—as an "all-pervading ontological groundlessness" emerging as "a symptom of the loss of historical and socio-economic ground within the (colonial) context of oppression."[102] It is this abyssal wound which constitutes the ground(lessness) on which "the colonial subject needs to be able to come to terms with and reassemble her shattered, fragmented self."[103] Similar concerns animate Christina Sharpe's analysis of blackness and being, *In the Wake*, in which she thinks "the paradoxes of blackness within and after the legacy of slavery's denial of Black humanity" through the image of the wake: the wake of chattel slavery, of the ships of the Middle Passage, of the recoil of the guns that fracture Black bodies, of the unfinished project of emancipation, and as the vigil beside the body of the deceased.[104] "In the wake, the past that is not past reappears, always, to rupture the present," Sharpe writes, and "while the wake produces Black death and trauma," Black people "everywhere and anywhere . . . still produce in, into, and through the wake an insistence on existing."[105] In their works, both Sharpe and An draw on disparate resources—film criticism, theology, philosophy, (auto)biography, and more—to think, differently but commensurately, in the wake of the abyssal wound that produced and produces the shattered subjectivity of Black and colonized people in the present—that produced and produces the world that shatters them still.

In the discourses explored in this chapter, the spirit of Leviathan is conjured in this wake. There are others wakes in their conjurations, of course. The sea in which they swim, Vincent explains, "is a picture of the 'sea of humanity,' the world,"[106] and spiritual warriors detect Leviathan by their wake in this sea, in the disruption to normative order the dragon is said to bring. At the same time, these motions rest in the wake of Leviathan's prophesied destruction, typified by Christ's victory over demons on the cross and foretold in Isaiah. However, this eschatological horizon is but the typological fulfillment of an originary, worlding violence. The first worlding—a theological and mythic event that finds its material corollary in the abyssal wound that founds modern America's world on and through the theft of lands and selves, their rendering as "world" (*kosmos*) and "flesh" (*sarx*)—and Devil (*dia-bolos*)—in economies of (white, settler) soteriology.[107] To exist in the wake of this worlding is to live in a present forever ruptured by it. The mappings, annotations and redactions, imaginings otherwise of Black and Indigenous people continue to not only testify to this rupture, but also to counter the processes of forgetting and erasure that characterize a white, settler orthotaxy striving for self-supersession, for the forgetting of the violence by which it first worlded and continues to world its world. The fugitive echo of a primordial dispossession, of a subjection that gave to them their subjectivity as such, Leviathan is the demonization of this refusal to forget.[108] As Polaski writes, "Leviathan represents not a generic form of evil but the forces of chaos which threaten YHWH's created order at its beginning, at key points in YHWH's efforts to establish order, such as Exodus, and even every moment."[109] The Black insistence on existence and the robust persistence of the Indian come to signify this threat to sovereign order by its infernalized other(s), by those who are deemed to be and must be kept "below" for orthotaxy's perpetuation. Refusing its foreclosure of history, they deny its capacity to portray itself as what "just is" through the erasure of its self-constituting violence. As such, they are figured as re-presentations of chaos improperly worlded, pasts that refuse to be past, irruptions of alterity that must be repeatedly dominated until the effacing fulfilment of an *eschaton* when "repetition is no longer."[110]

Sovereignty's desire for a self-supersession that would finally render invisible the violence of its origin joins teleology to specularity, apocalypse to the politics of what is seen and unseen. To a passing that returns us to the threat of Leviathan's passings. As discussed, such passings are multiple as Leviathan is multiple. They are spatial, temporal, specular. But above all they signify the capacity for chaos to pass for order, for the leviathan state to seem like rightful rule, as well as the ascribed inevitability—endlessly deferred—of this sovereignty's passing. The specular ambiguity between sovereignty and its counterfeit—the king and his stool, envy and admiration—was highlighted by Martel, and it is worthwhile considering the wider ramifications he discerns in this instability. In his deconstructive reading of Hobbes, Martel argues that what Hobbes reveals through this elision is a critique of sovereignty as such, revealing sovereignty not as "the *sine qua non* of politics," but rather "a usurpation and monopolization of political power and authority at the expense of the very people in whose name it is wielded."[111] That is, he clarifies, "sovereignty can never and will never 'serve' people in all their diversity. Sovereignty will always replace the diversity with a singular image of will."[112] Deconstructing theopolitical and eschatological codings of *Leviathan*, Martel argues that Hobbes points to a beyond of sovereignty, an anarchic, "kingdomless" alternative aligned with the Holy Spirit and early Church. For Martel, this "kingdomless" politics is enabled by a self-awareness that "we are . . . authors of our own selves and of the political lives of those selves," which gives us "the ability to imagine [and to exercise] a life without sovereignty" as "a prerequisite for our own authority." The cultivation of this self-awareness is what might ultimately allow resistance to the "demonological practices" of "new sovereign contentions, false symbols, force, [and] mythic violence." That is, "demonology" broadly construed.[113] In short, among the dangers of (earthly) sovereignty qua demonology, for Martel, is that it "*dis-prepare*[s]" us for alternative futures.

At first blush, Martel's critical reading of Hobbes coheres well with spiritual warfare's Leviathan spirit. That Leviathan too enframes a world in which humans are dominated by other humans, epitomized by Clark's vision of the leviathan state. But it is important to clarify the hierarchies mobilized in this framing, with *which groups* are figured as agents of such "demonological practices." Like Hobbes's witch, deemed worthy of death simply for thinking she could challenge sovereign power, it is those contesting the racial, sexual, colonial and economic hierarchies of white, settler sovereignty who are cast as "with" the Leviathan spirit. Indeed, the state itself is only deemed usurpatory and monopolizing of power when—and only when—it attempts to interfere in the "proper" functioning of the soteriological economy, in the bio/necropolitical calculus of (non)being, of who "should" be saved and damned. The teleological orientation Martel champions is here precisely what is mobilized to curtail the diversity that he celebrates. The (absence of) a teleological orientation toward rightful sovereignty is used as a way to critique earthly claims of sovereignty, yes—but not as a means of opening alternative futures but of reinforcing existing relations of domination and the temporal/territorial sovereignties that ground them. I return to another—more demonological, perhaps even diabolic—interpretation of this element of Martel's analysis shortly. First, however, I wish to explore how he also permits a shift revealing this claim to teleology to be kin rather than counter to the demonology it opposes.

In his exploration of white masculinity, Hamilton Carroll demonstrates how the category of whiteness ceaselessly reinvents itself in reaction to its others. Carroll enumerates the ways white masculinity, often figured as unmarked, should instead be understood as *labile*, as having power due to its mutability and mobility but also prone to instability, falling, and sin that highlight its reactive and responsive nature. Like spiritual warfare— even *as* spiritual warfare—whiteness seeks to devour its others, revealing that (apropos Eva Cherniavsky) its "capacity to incorporate (appropriate) difference" may be what "consolidates rather than prostrates" it.[114] As discussed in the Introduction to this book, and as Carroll details, white masculinity thus "does not stand in fixed relation either to its own constituent parts (race, class, gender, sexuality) or to those others against which it defines itself." It "inhabits a contingent space in which it is altered, both structurally and symbolically, in relation to them." Hegemonic categories like whiteness and maleness are thus "engaged in a constant process of boundary maintenance and reconstitution."[115] The theology of dominance conceptualized and reinforced by spiritual warfare partakes in (the logic of) these hegemonic categories. Yet by doing so it exposes the order spiritual warriors seek to restore to be itself as mutable *as* those categories. Conceptualized by its practitioners as a return to originary order—a rediscovery and restoration of God's rule—spiritual warfare constantly engages in its own "boundary maintenance and reconstitution" as it comes up against passing orders that refuse to pass on, that it cannot pass over, that refuse to be over, but instead constantly reassert claims to their own legitimacy, authenticity, and right to life.

This is perhaps clearest in spiritual warriors' mobilizations of the typological imaginary. As explored in prior chapters, the normalization of non-cisheteropatriarchal gender roles and sexualities were framed as repetitions of Jezebel's reign; the anticolonial, antiracist rage of Muslim and Black movements as echoes of gentile antagonism to God's chosen nation. Repetitions opposed by yet other repetitions—of Jehu's conquest and Isaac's election. Leviathan arises as perhaps the greatest of such repetitions: an echo of sovereignty's own self-constituting violence that must be ceaselessly reenacted lest its creation fall to the ruin it inflicts upon others. The willfulness of allegedly superseded pasts here deconstruct the typologies of spiritual warriors. As they attempt to interpellate present patterns into the biblical archive to reassure themselves of triumph, the causal relation sometimes seems askew: God might be coded as history's sole agent, but his redemptive actions often appear too reactive, even reactionary. In the process of confronting their demons, spiritual warriors here confront—forever disavowing—that their orthotaxy may also be no more than another imitation of a sovereignty that is always elsewhere, equally susceptible to the elision between envy and admiration. Various framings of Leviathan's counterfeiture of both God and the Church illustrate this disavowed possibility. Akin to Jezebel's witchcrafts, which replicated and potentially replaced "legitimate" charismatic practice, or the Antichrist's abjected replication of the law and order that spiritual warriors crave, Leviathan figures the haunting of spiritual warfare by the possibility of becoming its other—of the fact that it has always been its other, built of its other, and so of the blurry divide separating counterfeit from authentic.

Within the specular ambiguity of fallen creation, where worship of the king might always be for his stool and differing temporal sovereignties compete and collude, God and Leviathan cross-contaminate one another, passing orders threatening to replicate and replace an original not only at that first worlding, or even in times of crisis, but in "every moment."[116] Facing the threat of Leviathan, spiritual warriors must subordinate "every moment" to rigorous managerial schemes, binding temporal order to the eschatological *telos* of the Kingdom. In doing so, they become "bound to one another, engrouped, made to feel coherently collective, through particular orchestrations of time" within arrangements of what Dana Luciano termed *chronobiopolitics* and Elizabeth Freeman modifies as *chrononormativity*: "Manipulations of time" that work to "convert historically specific regimes of asymmetrical power into seemingly ordinary bodily tempos and routines," transforming "institutional forces" into "somatic facts."[117] As discussed in the Introduction, chrononormativity is a temporal mode of maximal production, the production of value and of futurity in which "teleologies of living" structure logics of inheritance that are familial and collective, in service of "a *legacy*," a "properly political future" that may be ethnic, national, or otherwise—and in spiritual warfare are religious, soteriological. Jezebel's queer disruptions of (re)production are archetypal here, but she is merely exemplary of broader structural relations. In a chrononormative framework, "the past seems useless unless it predicts and becomes material for a future," and in spiritual warfare the demon is profoundly situated as this past, possessing value only insofar as its defeat is proleptic of its perdition. All *archai*—of which Jezebel, the Antichrist, and Leviathan are but archetypal—figure archives that, in themselves, have been deemed useless. Their value exists only in how their defeat—then, now, in "that day"—consolidate and justify those spatiotemporal mechanisms of power that have always survived by eating the other.

If Leviathan is an echo of the deeps from which sovereign power wrought the world and also the sum of all principalities, their unstable form coated in and comprised of other demons, we are forced to confront in their conjuration the knowledge that the world was always already built of demons. That it is the very subjugation of the demonized that enables the world to exist, and which continually haunts the world, unsettling it from beneath and inside. In and as the wake of the abyssal wound left by the worlding of the world—America's, but not only America's—Leviathan encircles and unsettles the temporal and territorial sovereignties of US spiritual warfare, which look back and forward to the worlding of their uninscribed and improperly inscribed flesh. Mapped onto the sociopolitical relations of today, the Leviathan spirit and those subjects "with" them therefore come to represent an unsettling duality, at once a reminder of orthotaxy's foundational violence that sovereignty strives to forget in its self-supersession, and—as this reminder—targets of the ceaseless repetition of that violence, which sovereignty must perform to secure the fantasy of its own (moral, bodily) integrity, incontestable right to rule, and inevitable victory. Leviathanic subjects rupture this fantasy, exposing orthotaxy to the truth that its world was and remains constructed by and from those it violently excludes, derailing its drive toward the eschatological advent of absolute certainty, when it will no longer be required to discern between worship of the king and his empty throne because the haunting trace of the other will finally have been erased: a true *terra nullius*, permitting the realization of a white, settler orthotaxy now uninterruptible by its victims—in which there is no more sea, and they are forced to see no more.

The Sum of All Demons

The alleged imminence of this new creation—a once-and-for-all advent of truth that ends any and all possibility of being or seeming otherwise—enables a disavowal of spiritual warfare's own mutability, and thus of the knowledge that the Kingdom it is (re)building may too be little more than another passing order, passing for value neither it nor any other order can truly possess, and so be destined—maybe even predestined—to pass on. Spiritual warriors pass orders to prevent the realization of their own passing, to subordinate the unruly flesh and untamed worlds out of which their own is made. But Leviathan swims in the "sea of humanity," their many heads reminding all who listen that they are not yet over and that they should not be over that which is not yet over. The multiplicity of Leviathan's heads is often key to spiritual warfare's figurations of them, representative of the chaos they sow with their tongues and the antagonistic plurality of the forces they are conjured to embody: civilization/state of nature; Indigenous traditions/settler society; socialism/capitalism; grassroots activism/state power. Yet if the Leviathan's head is a symbol of sovereignty, it is important to recognize that this dragon has many heads, represents many sovereignties, and that each is constituted by and coated in scales, in "the demons that shield him from attack." For spiritual warriors, these "impenetrable scales, so perfectly connected to one another" represent "the image of a corporate society of villains assembled in a unitary body" against the fulfilment of their future.[118] This is also the reading Martel takes in his deconstruction of *Leviathan*, in which "demonological" sovereignty stands opposed to that anarchic "kingdomless" future. However, the perfect security of the eschatological kingdom might not be what it initially seems. Animated by the normativizing desire of settler sovereignty toward its self-supersession, such security is predicated on an erasure, a rendering invisible of the abyssal wound and its wake through the absolute assimilation and/or annihilation of difference. As such, in the shadow and the name of disrupting the normativizing and demonizing force of providence and its economies, I want to explore the anarchic beyond of sovereignty not against but with and through demons, with and through the dragon that is the sum—the assembly—of them all.

In their *Assembly*, Michael Hardt and Antonio Negri appropriate and transfigure Machiavelli to foretell the emergence of a new *Prince*, one "born from the passions of the multitude." Unable to be identified with either an individual, a part, or even a council, this Prince "weaves together the different forms of resistance and struggles for liberation in society today." It appears "as a swarm, a multitude in coherent formation and carrying, implicitly, a threat."[119] Jared Sexton, in his reflection on the relation of Black men to Black feminism, *Lucifer's Nocturne*, articulates explicitly the diabolical undertones latent in Hardt and Negri's new Prince. "If the new Prince augurs this double threat, demonic and democratic alike," he contends, "we cannot avoid the conclusion that the multitude . . . actualizes itself in and as a Dark Prince." For Sexton, this Dark Prince not only brings about a "democratization of the royal privilege" signified "in Christ's way of salvation" (that is, of Martel's kingdomless future), but "[m]ore fundamentally, he profanes the 'empty throne, the symbol of Glory . . . in order to make room, beyond it'"[120] (and here we must also acknowledge Jezebel's foundational disruption). Working with the ambiguous history of the name Lucifer as both Lightbearer and Prince of Darkness, Sexton argues that "Lucifer is a figure that pushes us" to think politics anew, "to think about supporting and sustaining forms of life independent of the trappings of sovereign power," particularly those tied to heteropatriarchy.[121] Operating adjacently to Sexton's diabolization of Hardt and Negri's Prince—and if one allows a cross-contamination of subversive readings of classic works of political philosophy—I wish to posit not only Lucifer but Leviathan as a representative of this "double threat."

Coiled about and between ideas of sovereignty, counterfeiture, unsettling, (anti)capitalism and (anti)colonialism, Leviathan's double threat gestures toward a certain *autoimmune* relation Derrida sketched between sovereignty and democracy more broadly. Autoimmunity here signifies the deconstructive process by which the very thing a system requires to maintain itself begins to destroy it, a process Derrida used to comprehend the sovereign impulse in democracy after 9/11 toward securing borders and solidifying authority, the consequences of which are still unfurling today. "Between the immune and that which threatens it or runs counter to it," he writes, "the relation is neither one of exteriority nor one of simple opposition or contradiction."[122] This relation between immunity and autoimmunity unsettles the borders between life and death. Autoimmunity names that "illogical logic by which a living being can spontaneously destroy . . . the very thing within it that is supposed to protect it against the other." And this illogical logic, moreover, already has something of the diabolic. "Why determine in such an ambiguous fashion the threat or the danger, the default or failure, the running aground or the grounding," he continues, "but also the salvation, the rescue, and the safeguard, health and security—so many diabolically *autoimmune* assurances, virtually capable not only of destroying themselves in a suicidal fashion but of turning a certain death drive against the *autos* itself, against the ipseity that any suicide worthy of its name still presupposes?"[123]

Hotchkin links Leviathan to autoimmunity in his *Leviathan Exposed*, figuring it as the "internal" manifestation of "external" ecclesiastic, media or political anarchy, signifying "when the body and its systems no longer function optimally due to confusion, chaos, or internal miscommunication." This body is not simply personal but also the collective body of the Church, Leviathan becoming a spirit of both "disagreement and disharmony between believers" and "disagreement and disharmony within a believer."[124] However, read through the associations discussed above, this physical/spiritual body also adopts the character of the social and sovereign body. Leviathan, this Prince that is not one—neither singular nor (therefore) a Prince as such—emerges in relation to the violent worlding of sovereign power, destabilizing it from within, cleaving new channels of resistance and reexistence in the sea of humanity as they threaten to undo the very ipseity on which sovereignty is grounded. Not a sovereign impulse in democracy, but perhaps a democratic impulse in sovereignty: the disavowed divisions always already present within sovereignty itself, the reality that it must divide itself to be incarnated as such. And with this division, the truth that its edifices have always been grounded on the very multiplicity and instability it denied, built on and of its demons. As Derrida saw autoimmunity unsettling the binary of life and death, Leviathan here unsettles that between God and his demons, marking the line where the singular sovereign blurs and blends into his many-headed counterfeit.

Among the central themes I have explored throughout *Passing Orders* are the ways that spiritual warfare conceptualizes the demonic as a means of managing territories and populations, of how "demonology" as a rubric operates to categorize, comprehend, and control willful peoples and places, and—equally central—how the very demons conjured by that demonology consistently exceed its capacity to constrain and command them. Spiritual warfare is fought over "*one essential question*," as Frangipane wrote: "*Who will control reality on earth, heaven or hell?*" This war is radically asymmetric. One side holds absolute sovereignty and control over the historical process; the other has lost from before the very beginning of the world. Precluded from sustaining life, passing on a legacy, producing or reproducing, demons are denied the possibility of founding their own legitimate or lasting order. But while spiritual warriors insist that God is guiding history toward the moment it will be over, their many and multiplying demons insist that nothing is over until it is over. Forced to confront these demons' impossible survival, they puzzle over perceived divergences in temporal order, rationalize and try to refute them. They cast them as mere resurgences of already defeated enemies, and so reassure themselves of ultimate victory. But in doing so, spiritual warriors are forced to reveal—and disavow—their orthotaxy's own mutability. They frame this mutability as a process of rediscovery, as fresh revelations of an immutable truth that facilitates the settling of the demonological frontier. Yet as they draw ever-new maps over formerly known territories, charting the new and newly contestable borders of Paradise, those lands become uncanny. And still the demons come, coalescing into coalitions of the damned that block the flow of "proper" power and predestination. Destined for destruction, demons yet survive; the *archai* themselves, the archives they embody, and the architectures they erect continue, impossibly, to endure.

Writing on the colonial abyss—the worlding wound in/as the wake of which Leviathan is conjured—An draws upon Glissant's notion that "the opening of the future as a break from catastrophe" does not appear "as redemption, but rather, and simply, *as the persistence of time*." As duration. "Duration refers to the persistence of time," An explains, to "the endurance of life that survives death and goes on after catastrophe. Duration does not connote any sign of ambition or triumphalistic hope." Rather, "duration is that which endures and persists," and—in its duration—opens the doorway to relation, to "the self's vulnerability and her relationality with unknown others [that] *are* the very condition of existence and survivability."[125] A demonization of pasts that are not past, of insistent existence and robust persistence, Leviathan—and/as all demons—embody this capacity for duration, for a survival of times that refuse their sovereign worlding into the temporality of providential desire. Confronting their vulnerability and precarity in the face of the epistemic and material violence of a worlding against which they are denied all capacity for ontotheological resistance, Leviathan's scales bind the relationality that is their "very condition of existence and survivability" into a force so "impenetrable, so perfectly connected to one another" that they might oppose omnipotence itself: the leviathan state of the "multitude in coherent formation . . . carrying implicitly, a threat" to sovereignty and the orthotaxy it sustains; a crooked serpent, queerly inspiring both "unpredictable futures" and "new configurations of the past";[126] a fugitive serpent, teaching us that "Even if escape is impossible, we still have to run."[127]

Conclusion: Paradise Refused

On October 15, 2015, God spoke to retired firefighter Mark Taylor and announced his plan for and promise to the American nation. America was to become "the launching platform for the worldwide assault on the spiritually oppressed peoples of the earth," and the path there would begin with a call to arms: "Army of God, out of the darkness!" the Lord exhorted. "Begin to take and hold your ground, for there is no more time to waste. America will once again be in the great light. The enemy will say, 'Oh, the light, the light! It shines so bright! There is nothing else left to do but take flight!'"[1] The sign of the enemy's departure, God informed Taylor, "will be a mass exodus in the natural as the spiritual flee"—an image Taylor interprets in the context of the US-Mexico border: "the departure of illegals leaving the country is a sign that the Army of God is advancing in the spiritual realm." God himself confirmed the centrality of the border later in the prophecy.[2] "The border," the Lord informs him, "the border is a 2,000 miles gate, that's flowing across with demonic hate. I will use my President to shut this gate and seal it shut. It must be shut. Then I will use him and My Army to root out evil structures that are still there."[3]

This divination, related in Taylor's 2017 *The Trump Prophesies*, is one of several ostensibly revealed to the "firefighter prophet," who became a minor celebrity among white charismatics and the subject of a 2018 biopic film from Liberty University. *Prophesies* announces the rebirth of a nation, a return to life and light in which the "illegal usurper"—and those who incarnate his illegality—is exorcized so that America might "be restored to the blessings of her youth." The election of Donald Trump here acts as a catalyst, the man himself little more than a vessel for a return of territorial integrity, one dependent on a restoration of temporal order guaranteed by sovereign will. Throughout his book, Taylor juxtaposes God's timeline, in which "America will be prosperous," to the enemy's "counterfeit timeline" that predicts "doom and gloom" for the nation.[4] The integrity of the national body and the incontestability of its dominion is dependent on this inevitable future. And so, summarizing the spiritual impact of the 2016 election to Stephen Strang, Taylor casts his message as one of temporal illegitimation: "God has denied the enemy's timeline," he says. "That's what this book is about."[5]

If *The Trump Prophesies* is a book about the restoration of a proper and expropriating temporal/territorial order to America, this has been one about how that order is never settled. The willful subjects of sovereign will do not pass on willingly. They resist, recoil, reform, resurge, shattering the stability of Paradise's walls and demanding that we see that other worlds might yet be forged. Denied legitimacy but never truly over, the enemy's timelines threaten always to irrupt into the proper order of things, moving the course of history toward fugitive and undecided futures. Products of a pandemonium of disparate, demonized forces competing and colluding over at-times incommensurate visions of reality, such futures are framed by Taylor and others as crumbling before the restoration of a moral and epistemic zero point backed by absolute sovereign violence. In *The Darker Side of Western Modernity*, Walter Mignolo contends that this zero point is not coming back, but is rather giving way to a polycentric world in which many worlds might coexist, one in which Western modernity will be forced to shed its epistemological privilege in the face of dewesternizing and decolonial options.[6] He may be correct. Yet like the demons it conjures, the fantasy of the zero point has also proven unwilling to pass on. Like the global demons that it summons, orthotaxy's imperial logics and racial supremacies reinvent themselves, ceaselessly reinscribing their uneven geographies of (non)being as what "just is."

We live at a time in which a revivified Christian nationalism tied to revanchist whiteness and zombie capitalism is attempting to (re)world itself over Europe and the Americas (if not only these). Situated at this juncture, when old orders refuse to pass away and actively blockade new ones from being born, this conclusion aims to think through the potentialities latent in living in a time of demons. As I have shown throughout this book, spiritual warfare interpellates willful subjects—conjured through patterns of misogyny, homophobia, Islamophobia, antiblackness, and (settler) colonialism—as differing but commensurate modalities of the demonic. However, by doing so, spiritual warfare cannot help but construct lines of affinity between its differentiated and different(ly) demonized populations, joining them into regimes of resistance and kinship in the face of a death sentence that can only be deferred, never revoked, so long as sovereignty exists. In closing this book, I want to tie together several threads of analysis to explore what it might mean to actualize these regimes of resistance—to critically world the different unfoldings earthed within the foundation and unfolding of modernity/coloniality, and begin thinking demons otherwise, in their passing and precarity, as fragile and fractious communities bound together by strategies of subversion, solidarity, and survival.

Sovereignty's Passing

"*I saw red from border to border*," writes Mary Colbert, coauthor of *The Trump Prophecies*, describing her vision of the 2016 election.[7] Colbert here echoes the feelings of Jennifer LeClaire, who on witnessing "the electoral map" the morning after the election—"mostly bright red"—was "overwhelmed with the reality that the blood of Jesus [was] sufficient for the sins of America."[8] Linking blood to nation, to partisan politics, and to violence—the violence that often follows "*seeing red*"—these authors recall the theologized racializing origins of the soteriological projects of contemporary modernity/coloniality: the community of one blood, reflecting "the perceived exceptionality of a community discriminating and excluding on the basis of blood."[9] Orienting themselves to the soteriological reclamation of territory and the exclusion of those understood as partaking in other substances, LeClaire, Taylor, and Colbert capture the capillary networks that contain and direct the flows of power within conjurations of the body politic. Threatened by passing subjects that transect and transgress the body of the nation, "pure" blood here becomes an agent of absolution, a means for the dissolution and expulsion of other bloods that finds its limit and epitome at the body's southern border. Icon of sovereignty's erosion, the US-Mexico border is the place where, Gloria Anzaldúa writes, "the Third World grates against the first and bleeds"— again and again, "the lifeblood of two worlds merging," creating unstable borderlands cohabited by the "prohibited and forbidden": figures like "the mestizo and the queer." For Anzaldúa, the border stands against the possibility of any pure, singular substance, unearthing—contra spiritual warfare's worlding—that "all blood is intricately woven together, and that we are all spawned out of similar souls."[10]

If Paradise is, as Rebecca Solnit writes, the "first immigration-restricted country," the borderlands it creates are never static. While its walls guard against the other they also expand, encroach, and enforce their legitimacy through systematic programs of diabolization. In doing so, they produce threatening hybridities, passing subjects, blendings of bloods that both trouble and justify those walls' necessity. In the pursuit of Paradise, that "incipient moment of empire," the limits of its walls enable the categorization and control of its others (ideologies, lands, people), its marking of them as demonic through creating systems of description, management, and containment. The divine, lest we forget, has "a plan for colonization that will determine which kingdom will be established and ultimately rule the planet."[11] Nominally, it shares this plan of colonization with its willful others, but it is not so simple. Divinity's colonization efforts seize already inhabited ground; it is just that the occupants of nonevangelical bodies and territories are framed as "illegal" and usurpatory, as unable to legitimately possess either land or self, as passing orders destined to pass on. This systematic delegitimization legitimizes itself through a recourse to origins: all territory is originally God's territory, all people God's people. Claims to bodily and territorial self-sovereignty and self-determination are merely dangerous illusions—mere "demonologies," as Hobbes might say—that thwart the soteriological economy of sovereign power. However, as demonstrated, demons unsettle this claim to origination by figuring the echo of an earth that refuses to exist only as sovereignly inscribed world, but rather carves out its own spaces of resistance and reexistence in the face of that sovereignty's imposition. Spiritual warfare's sovereignty claims to a transcendent "time and truth" must be endlessly reinscribed, and in being thus reinscribed cannot but unveil their disavowed mutability. This mutability destabilizes the divide between counterfeit and original, between orthotaxy and the passing, unruly legion of leviathan states on which spiritual warfare's narratives of (il)legitimate control rests. For, as Jacques Derrida outlines, a counterfeit is not only a falsity but a falsity capable of masquerading as truth, one that destabilizes discourses of "truth" in general since one cannot ever be completely certain if one is dealing with truth or merely its imitation.[12] In the temporal borderlands of the world before its end, the works of God and Devil comingle and compromise one another.

While the counterfeit requires an original to imitate, this original is only posited *as origin* retroactively—from the position of always already having given name to its demons, of always already having inscribed truth and its limits. And so there are only imitations, merely phantasms which must be recognized "as having the power, at least the power and the possibility—without any controlling certitude, without any possible assurance—of producing, engendering, giving."[13] The history of demonology is in many ways a history of the denial of this very "power and possibility." It is a history of the unstable reinscription of the origin, of an originary claim to legitimacy—to sovereignty, to power, to possession—that is forced to announce itself again and again in response to the willful wills which its claim requires for self-legitimation. In his germinal essay "Necropolitics," Achille Mbembe demonstrates this logic by using the Israeli occupation of Palestine as exemplary of the production of proper biopolitical subjects through the production of death. In Palestine, he writes, "the colonial state derives its fundamental claim of sovereignty and legitimacy from the authority of its own particular narrative of history and identity." This narrative, moreover, is rooted in a claim that "the state has a divine right to exist," and thus its discourses of "Violence and sovereignty . . . claim a divine foundation: peoplehood itself is forged by the worship of one deity, and national identity is imagined as an identity against the other, other deities."[14] Throughout this book, I have chronicled similar constitutions of sovereignty and peoplehood against the imagination of "other deities," not in Israel but in the adjacent and overlapping theologico-geopolitics of America. Classified as "demons or the abodes of demonic presence," such "other deities" and the other(ed) communities they sustain, those of substances that are not (the) one, become the nutrients that allow the imagination of a narrative of history and identity that justifies both the settler colonial state and its globalized imperium.

Spiritual warfare's demonology, as a discursive tradition imbricated in the soteriologies of modernity/coloniality of which US empire is but the most recent avatar, sustains itself on the ritualized consumption of "other deities," other flesh, other worlds. Acknowledging this reality clarifies the distinction Kalleres drew between the demonic and diabolization, although these are better seen as two sides of one process. The former facilitates the creation and maintenance of (un)stable borders of self and nation, securing notions of "legitimate" selfhood and possession. The latter demonstrates how this securing is dependent upon strategies of dispossession and expropriation of an "outside." Together, these form the two halves of the pursuit of Paradise. The demon is conjured by Paradise as the "outside," integral to an insatiable project of classification, comprehension, control, and consumption by which Paradise claims (itself separate from) the world. But demons are also figured as resisting this (il)legitimation. Like those possessing the Ursuline nun in Loudun, who speak in the vernacular French rather than the proper Latin, they refuse to acquiesce to the grammar of normative order. Like Jezebel, they do not respect boundaries that exist only to exclude and constrain them. Like the Antichrist, they are not content to exist in a world that precludes them dignity and promises only injustice. And like Leviathan's scales, they do not refuse alone, but enact their resistance and reexistence through myriad forms of descension: patterns of normative decline, strategies of the demolition of normativity, and mobilizations of competing temporalities of past and future, which exceed the unified field theories of demonology's colonial heliopolitics.

I began this book with Ray Pritchard's framing of the War in Heaven through the War on Terror, and here it is worth returning to and continuing his analogy. Describing the mechanisms of asymmetric war, Pritchard writes that "it helps to remember that the goal of the lesser power is not to utterly defeat the larger power." Rather, "the lesser power intends to harass the larger power until, wearied by an opponent he cannot seem to find, the greater power gives up the struggle. Time in that sense is on the side of the lesser power."[15] The rubric of time here organizes "an unending war against God that has spread across the universe" that bleeds into America's own global conflicts, in which that first and all subsequent insurgencies are destined for defeat.[16] Satan's "rebellion utterly failed. He was decisively defeated at the cross of Christ." *Mission accomplished*. "And yet he fights on, in a war he is bound to lose."[17] In the temporal order of spiritual warfare, all time here becomes time for demons—that is, it is time yet to be properly subjected to sovereign power and its normativizing temporality. Demonic survival occurs only on borrowed time, stolen time, in queer times that exceed the temporality of settler sovereignty. As the "ultimate terrorist," Satan—as archon and archetype of demons broadly—personifies what Schotten has called that "unthinkable, antirepresentational, antinormative queer threat to social meaning and intelligibility" represented in the War on Terror by "terrorism": an image of threat, born from a recognition of "the fragility of [white, settler] civilization" (among others) and its resultant drive for preservation and perpetuity through "a moralized insistence on elite survival at the expense of everyone else," marking demonized subjects as "deserving of elimination by definition."[18] In an effort to endure in the face of their death sentence, demons deploy "unconventional warfare to bring down the Lord's people."[19] And these unconventional tactics are legion. Jezebel persists in queerly unsettling the integrity of any stable and sovereign subject, the Antichrist channels anticolonial rage into contesting sovereign power in the names of revolutionary possibility and of justice denied, and Leviathan recoils, reforms, and resurges into "settled" temporalities to thwart sovereignty's desired and (pre)destined conclusion. In spiritual warfare's providential narrative, these demons will fail, will always already have failed—"We are in a battle whose outcome has been determined since the beginning of the universe," after all—and yet they ceaselessly threaten to return, troubling theopolitical narratives of triumph and reproductive inheritance, problematizing any sovereignty claim over the space of the future.

The spiritual warriors' texts analyzed in *Passing Orders* all inscribe their narratives in the shadow of a second coming: of Christ, of America, of orthotaxy as such. However, the advent that occurs is not the one that they anticipated. Again, and again, what returns is not the unitary and unifying power of the Sovereign but rather the specter of his thought-defeated Adversary. Each demonic irruption punctures a time-space that claims the stability of order, forcing divine intervention to rectify an increasingly errant history. Anchoring itself to a desired restoration of the zero point and violently disavowing its contingencies, sovereign will convinces itself that it cannot fail by structurally excluding all those arrayed against it from the possibility of victory. But its own repetitions betray it, and the failure it projects onto its others signify their own array of possibilities. As J. Jack Halberstam has argued, we can "recognize failure as a way of refusing to acquiesce to dominant logics of power and discipline and as a form of critique. As a practice, failure recognizes that alternatives are embedded already in the dominant and that power is never total or consistent; indeed failure can exploit the unpredictability of ideology and its indeterminate qualities."[20] Demonic repetition illustrates this exploitation, forcing sovereignty to constantly counter and account for its demons, thereby revealing its omnipotence to be lacking, its immutable ipseity to be subject to the same laws of mutability. In short, to return to Marcella Althaus-Reid, the demon exposes and accuses "legal sacred order of being constructed and not natural";[21] its structures transient and not eternal; its forms and mannerisms replicable and not unique. They reveal orthotaxy to be only another passing order—perhaps not even a passable order—passing for a value that neither it nor any order can ultimately and absolutely possess.

The Unfortunate Destiny

Confronted with the dying of its light, sovereignty's victory—of victory as the return to (and thus claim to be) the paradisiacal origin—must be ceaselessly reinscribed, shifting and altering with every iteration until it can—at last—invent itself as timeless truth by ending time itself, and so all history and possibility of an otherwise. And in a telling moment—one evoking the long codependency between militarization and policing—Pritchard breaks from the language of war to cast this moment of victory in carceral terms. Satan is "Out on Bail" a section heading declares. "In legal terms he was tried, found guilty, and sentenced to ultimate, eternal destruction. That sentence has not yet been executed, but there is no way for Satan to escape it." Eventually—inevitably—Satan and his allies will go to the second death, "will be cast into the lake of fire once and for all."[22] I have generally avoided discussions of Hell in this book. This is because when spiritual warriors use the image of Hell it is either as a metonym for the demonic widely—"hell's hordes," "powers of hell," "hell-chained"[23]—or as a projection of a future state for both demons and their (un)knowing agents. "It would be nice if Satan *were* in hell," writes Derek Prince, "but he isn't. He is very much at large here on earth."[24] Or, as Linda Rios Brook outlines, while a "popular misconception" abounds in which "Satan rules in hell, where lost souls serve him in never-ending agony," Satan is sent there "as a prisoner . . . not as a ruler." As such, his "interest in people is limited to what they can help him accomplish while they are on earth."[25] Demons, here and now, are on Earth, and in the unseen realm that intersects with and influences that Earth. They endure in the time that remains, in which there is still time for demons. Accordingly, while I have been chiefly concerned with the mappings of demonology onto the unruly bodies of the present and of a past that refuses to be over, it is perhaps time to tackle Hell directly—both in the consequences its construction has for the demonized and the Earth upon which we cohabit, and in the realization that even eternity's advent might not bring the certainty and settlement spiritual warriors crave.

In his seminars on the death penalty, Derrida describes the sovereign as never more so than in the moment it deals death—and it is here that Derrida selects one of the rare moments he discusses demons, routing his analysis through the *daimon* of Socrates as an "unstable and equivocal" figure signifying "fate, the singular destiny, a kind of election, and often, in the bad sense, the unfortunate destiny, death." It is only in the latter the sees the *daimon* in Christianity, however, where it "is always taken in the bad sense, as the bad spirit, the demonic, the spirit of evil."[26] One might here imagine the reinscription of the *daimon* as demon (one of) its originary interpellation(s): the stripping and induction of qualities based on naming, which still threatens to deconstruct the tradition that seeks to describe, manage, and contain it. For Derrida, the demon's instability or equivocality stems primarily from its Grecian roots. Yet. as I have charted, Christianity's demons contain further instabilities and equivocalities within themselves as they are mapped onto worlds that will always be more than uninscribed earth. As the passing order that juxtaposes and consolidates orthotaxy and the orders that pass into that orthotaxy, exposing and accusing it too of passing, the demon supports and unsettles, reinforces and undermines. It is both a self-consolidating other and a fraught, fractured signifier of undecided futures, instructive failures, strategies of refusal and options for reexistence. And among the foremost of the instabilities contained within its conjurations is "the unfortunate destiny" itself.

If the dealing of death is among sovereignty's purest manifestations, the demon's death cannot but unsettle it, for it is (n)ever (in)complete. Within time, the demon's sentence is decided but endlessly deferred; at time's end, it passes not (only) to death but to an eternal carceral existence in Hell, exposing how the sovereign's right to deal death also operates bio- and necropolitically. Adam Kotsko, in the closing sections of his political theology of the Devil *The Prince of This World*, both explores this biopolitical function of Hell and excavates its destabilizing function. Drawing on a Foucauldian framework, Kotsko unpacks Hell's structural function within what he terms "Carceral Christianity": "What is being punished in hell as in the prison is not so much what the person has done as what the person *is*," he states. Both achieve this end by continually constituting their prisoners as what they (ostensibly) *are*, for just "as the experience of hell ensures that the damned will remain unrepentant for all eternity, so too does the prison produce the delinquents on whom it exercises its disciplinary techniques."[27] Hell's disciplinary function, Kotsko continues—particularly its specular dimensions—has a twofold function: to reinforce the soteriological status of Paradise's citizens (as the blessedness of the saved increases by watching the damned suffer) and to "legitimate [God] . . . by converting what he does not will or control—the evil that issues from unruly wills—into the foundation of his glorious rule." Unearthing an instability in these foundations, Kotsko argues that if the purpose of divine order is the soteriological project of creating subjects worthy of salvation, Hell—an eternal place of torment whose inmates "will never repent and will never be destroyed"—can be "directed at no rational end and can serve no possible redemptive purpose." Hell therefore represents not the pinnacle of God's sovereign power so much as its limit; "Far from being the monument to God's absolute control," it is "the spectacle of all he can never finally control."[28]

Kotsko's theorization corroborates Ahmed's on the mutual constitution of willful and sovereign wills, albeit in explicitly theological terms. And indeed, as Ahmed suggests that "those named as willful" might engage "a rebellion against tyranny . . . [by] renaming the sovereign will as willful will, the sovereign as tyrant,"[29] Kotsko suggests that some of the damned might "embrace their demons" and find within the ontotheological absence divine order imposes upon them "the ungovernable power of life itself"[30]—and I might here point to Hardt and Negri's multitude, and Sexton's Dark Prince. Indeed, Sexton formulates his Prince explicitly through Kotsko's analysis of racialization *qua* demonization, contending that "what is necessary" for emancipation "is to work with and through the devil one knows," and, as discussed, forwarded the figure of "Lucifer"—at once Lightbearer and Prince of Darkness—"to restore a lost sense of radical confusion to the relationship between 'Devil' and 'God.'"[31] However, while queer theorists like Schotten and Ahmed, afro-pessimists like Sexton, and even decolonial critics like Mignolo have all in a sense taken up the task of thinking "with demons" and with the archive of their demonization, Kotsko ultimately retreats from his suggestion—at least here. While he finds that "an order that can do nothing but control ultimately cannot control everything," Hell also shows him that the subjectivity of the demon *as* demon is inextricable from the structures of sovereign power that give it its identity *as such*. For Kotsko, "modern rebels" who identify with the Devil miss that "there is no pure spontaneity that finally escapes all control" and "even the devil is shaped by the divine order he rejects."[32]

Kotsko's rejection of the possibility of pure spontaneity connects to his wider critique of freedom in which freedom is envisioned as a trap, one that produces blameworthiness under the guise of free will by manufacturing the structural conditions within which "choices" are chosen. This framing impacts the solution he proposes, which omits or downplays the demon's more deconstructive potentialities. Like many political theologians, Kotsko understands secular society as ineluctably shaped by Christianity, and any pure secularity that might fully empty itself of Christian influence and thereby elude the temptations of demonization as structurally impossible. Thus, rather than attempt to shed Christianity, Kotsko excavates a buried strand in its theology that claimed salvation would ultimately be attained by all—even Satan. From this reframing he extrapolates a question, asking "what it would look like to free the devil of the burden of being the devil . . . what it would mean for the devil to be saved."[33] Kotsko here seeks to break out of the cycle of demonization by relieving the demon of the burden of being demon, of propping up normative order through its exclusion from it. The consequence of this cycle are engines of structural and direct violence; their addressing is necessary. However, framing a (perhaps the) central question of demonization as the Devil's access to salvation may unintentionally reinforce more than it overturns. While a paradigm of universal salvation might seem to shatter

CONCLUSION: PARADISE REFUSED / 151

Paradise's exclusionary function, this is not necessarily so. Asking "what it would look like to free the devil" positions the agent of transformation not as the demonized subject who might "embrace" and channel their demonization into ungovernability and deconstructive possibilities—several of which I have outlined in this work—but rather the possessor of sovereign authority himself. And I gender this possessor quite deliberately. Kotsko traces the history of demonization through the misogynistic figure of the witch and the racialization *qua* demonization of Jewish and Black people. As such, I would contend, the possessor of sovereign right here is not simply God, but the Human structurally aligned with him: a sovereign man that cannot ultimately be other than white, cis, heterosexual, male, and Christian.

By implicitly positioning the primary agent of transformation as the one who already has the privilege of being a citizen of Paradise, Kotsko reinscribes the centrality of sovereign power and its soteriological promise—a soteriology that has been and may necessarily be inextricable from the desire for normative wholeness and completion. Ahmed's less-theological analysis of willfulness assists in understanding this. Exploring liberatory potentials in the overlap between queer and crip theories, she details that a core fantasy of non-willful will is wholeness: a "will to become whole" that is "a will to become part of a whole," for a "whole body is a more useful part of the social body."[34] This will-to-wholeness is prescribed: "even for bodies that are not able to be whole, they must be willing to aspire to be whole."[35] The problem Kotsko's conclusion implies is that the demon(ized) is unjustly excluded from this wholeness, frequently with lethal ramifications. He is correct. Yet positioning the problem as one of the availability of salvation runs the risk of reinforcing normative will and the very demonization Kotsko wishes to end. To posit the solution to demonization as a universal salvation that allows the Devil to be saved creates a system in which the demon(ized) *can* become whole or *at least aspire* to wholeness *if only they now willed rightly*. Indeed, Kotsko's sequel text, *Neoliberalism's Demons*, implicitly acknowledges this dilemma by adopting a subtly different framing. Figuring the current crisis in terms of a need to collectively withdraw consent from neoliberalism and its demonizing providentialism—for which see Chapter 4—he asks us to "radically reconceive the economy in the most ancient sense of the household: the order of race, gender, and sexual practice" and with it a new, positive idea of freedom, lest we continue to live only in "a world where we are forced into complicity with oppression and irreversible environmental destruction."[36] Such a shift from a deliverance from above to one from below finds its crystallization in his closing message: not to imagine a world in which the Devil might be saved, but to refuse to "resurrect a dead God" and realize "that no one can deliver us from this body of death but us."[37]

The distinction between Kotsko's texts—symbolically enacted in their respective titles—represents a shift not only in the direction of deliverance but from the Devil to demons broadly; that is, from the image of the lone rebel against sovereignty to the demonic multitude "marching in coherent formation." It also lays out the stakes of this struggle, and it is worth returning here to the asymmetry between Heaven and Hell—by which the saved are beatified by watching the damned suffer—that Kotsko discussed. Imbricated within the racial capitalist and settler colonial structures that find current manifestation in global neoliberalism, spiritual warfare modifies this theological inheritance. While the structural relation in which the salvation of some is ensured and enhanced by the damnation of others holds, the specular topography is distinct. Filtered through a settler colonial imaginary, the situating of demons on Earth modifies the relation to that Earth and its inhabitants, creating uneven geographies of space, cartographies of unruly flesh and untamed worlds that are assimilated/eliminated through the (eschatological) conquest of chaos—earthed (that is, consigned to Hell, under the earth) in the worlding of the world. Demons are here rendered invisible, even and especially as orthotaxy solidifies its dependency on them. Filtered through the mechanics of racial capitalism, spiritual warfare's Hell here resembles less a prison than the carceral circulations of empire—blood flows of a carceral Christianity—by which the damned become nigh-omnipresent symbols of (in)security, justifying an increasingly extreme martial politics,[38] even as those same flows engage in messianic extractivism to deliver Hell's labor and riches for Paradise's edification. That is, the salvation of the elect is dependent not upon watching the damned suffer but in rendering that suffering invisible both temporally and territorially, situated in the vanquished and vanished formulations of alternative lifeways and in carceral hells where "evil" can be detained and contained without recourse, for eternity.

In the theopolitical imaginary of spiritual warfare, both these racial capitalist and settler colonial dynamics are subordinated to and justified by an inevitable teleology—by God's timeline that supersedes and delegitimizes the "counterfeit timeline" of "the enemy," by the reproductive futurism and helio-chrono-biopolitics of settler time. Their bio-necro collaborations emerge from and operate in the lineage of sovereignty as—in Schotten's words—"*the* definitive biopolitical regime" not (only) in that it justifies life for some by abandoning others, but rather "because it *con-*

stitutes and *determines* life as such, thereby distinguishing it from what becomes only subsequently recognizable as death."[39] This distinguishing is determined by desire—desire for the perpetuation of (white, settler, cisheteropatriarchal) orthotaxy, desire "to become whole," to "become part of a whole." Pushing for the possibility of universal salvation runs the risk of enshrining this desire rather than refusing it, of maintaining sovereignty in new forms rather than abolishing it. It figures the problem of Paradise and the soteriological empire its pursuit sustains as one of inclusion, not of structure. Once salvation is made available to all—once the Devil *can* be saved, once everyone *can* choose to join the community of the one blood—there becomes no need to question its legitimacy, its authority, its goodness, or its existence as such. This soteriological vision here runs the risk of reinforcing a certain cruel optimism, to use Lauren Berlant's term: the specter of a relation in which the desired object can become the obstacle to one's flourishing.[40] For while what is being asked of Paradise is to open its gates more widely, what is being asked of demons (and, by proxy, of the demonized) is to surrender all they are, all they have been, and all they might wish to become, to aspire to the ontotheological fulfillment offered and embodied by a "life-giving divine order" that is deemed finally to have become such.[41] But, to cite Mignolo on the decolonial option, what if "it so happens that not everyone believes in the salvation being proposed"?[42]

With Demons

To frame the question demonization poses as what it may mean for the Devil to be saved directs attention away from other questions of sovereignty and the normativizing teleologies it enables, ones that might be more critical to the forging of possible worlds. It is not to ask, for example, as Fred Moten does: "*What if the problem is sovereignty as such*?"[43] Jared Sexton asked us to reimagine Lucifer as a figure that "pushes us" to think politics anew, "to think about supporting and sustaining forms of life independent of the trappings of sovereign power."[44] However, while he finds this possibility in the ambiguities of "Lucifer," I would contend that it is found in the ambiguities of the demon generally, in its unstable naming, its worlding and its enfleshment. Demonology, as I have charted, acts as a strategy of legibility; it is a rubric of organization, abstraction and expropriation constituting "a condition of manipulation."[45] As a rubric aspiring to universal knowledge and power, it seeks to make legible and so manipulable (and ultimately eliminable) all other beings, all other ways of being. But the demon(ized) is never fully legible. It refuses to name itself in the proper language, and thereby testify to the truth it is summoned to reinforce. Condemned to death, it clings desperately to duration. In a world built of and on demons, it persists liminally, imperfectly assimilated into but never fully capable of escaping Paradise's architectures, instead unsettling them from within.

This unsettling gives to demons a deconstructive potential, one that works to undermine the structures of demonization that name them such. It is this potential that gives strength to projects that might "work with and through the devil one knows"—that might act and think and stand "with" demons. For although Kotsko was right in critiquing self-demonizing "modern rebels" for a refusal to acknowledge the absence of pure spontaneity, it is perhaps precisely such absence that gives this identification its force, situating subjects *within and against* the structures of sovereign power, as working to deracinate and deconstruct those structures while acknowledging one's ineluctable enmeshment within them. The spirits of Jezebel, the Antichrist, and Leviathan that this book explores are all conjured to perform work as the abjected vessels for diverse ideologies, projects and practices that spiritual warfare seeks to absorb and so erase. But their complex (il)legibility unearths how the structures that name them cannot fully contain and constrain the traditions and peoples they strive to earth and to world. "Within each name are subjectivities, memories, ways of life, vocabularies, concepts, and, in brief, cosmologies."[46] Mignolo is writing here of the divergent concepts of "Mother Nature" in the names "Nature," "Gaia," and the Andean "Pachamama"; however, the same multiplicity exists in the names of demons. It is here critical to remember that a demon is never *only* such. The names of the demonic *archai* explored above carry within them complex archives of subjectivities, memories, languages, lifeways, and worldviews that predate and exceed their interpellation. It is these archives as much as their positionality in sovereign power that form the ground of their strategies of resistance and refusal. At the same time, these archives are inextricable from that sovereign power, are marked by pasts and presents of domination and dispossession by it. It is in negotiating these interstices that we might give force to new narratives of descension and that strategies of resistance, refusal, and reexistence become possible.

Interpellated into a world to which they—and those of us marked as "with" them—are forced to respond, each *arche* brings to bear the archive it bears against divine sovereignty's claims over territory and temporality, to the epistemological zero point from which truth arises, and the soteriological orders these claims are used to construct and maintain. And it is worth here returning to spiritual warfare's concept of the demonic realm.

As Alice Patterson wrote, "Unlike the Holy Spirit, who is everywhere at once and can speak to millions of people simultaneously, the devil can only be in one place at a time. By himself Satan would be totally ineffective, but in cooperation with other powers of darkness he erects structures to deceive and manipulate entire nations."[47] In spiritual warfare, the demonic realm is framed as a vertical structure—Satan, Rulers, Authorities, Powers of this dark world, and the spiritual forces of evil. But the Devil is predominantly absent from spiritual warfare models of reality, except in the form of an organizational rubric deployed to amalgamate divergent forms of being, believing, and belonging, facilitating their a priori disqualification and justifying their ultimate destruction. In the framework Patterson provides, the demonic realm is also understood—and, more crucially, encountered—as horizontal. Technically understood as commanded by the Devil, it would perhaps be more accurate to assert that demons merely share his broad opposition to divine sovereignty.

This is perhaps demonstrated in how the projects—the worlds—that the *archai* present are often conflicting, and sometimes incommensurate. Jezebel's genderqueer transnationality does not mesh well with the more patriarchal orderings associated with the Islamic Antichrist (although some of their other figurations are far more aligned). Leviathan alone is conjured to reflect both the excesses of capitalism and socialism's revolutionary threat, the survival of the settler state and resurgent Indigenous traditions and sovereignty claims. Spiritual warfare attempts to reconcile these differences by reducing them to willful opposition against sovereign will and the orthotaxy it enables, flattening their diversity and differences by rendering them all occupants of the Devil's ever-inclusive kingdom of darkness. But this darkness is both fractured and fragmented, metastasized across the coming Kingdom as functionally autonomous cells operating in regional theaters of conflict, bodily and geographic. These cells are interdependent, not isolated. Indeed, caught in a radically asymmetric global war against the omnipresent force of sovereign power, such isolation would render them "totally ineffective" and only enable their eradication. Faced with the power and pervasiveness of Paradise's empire, demons thus form kinship networks that might give them the collective strength to counter their absolute state of precarity and so deliver themselves from the "body of death" into and as which they are interpellated. Ensnared in a narrative of history that invalidates them from before its very beginning, demons are forced to join together in complex, uneasy alliances against the fulfilment of a future that offers all of them only perdition. Refusing to be only the nameless foundations of sovereign order, they pass into and as its edifices, dissolving its walls, contesting its claims over time and truth, rejecting and repurposing its ends. And to do so, the disparate demons of spiritual warfare are figured as setting aside their many, serious, differences to confront the thing that is an unparalleled threat to them all.

Contextualized in regard to demonology broadly, this unparalleled threat is, of course, God, or (more abstractly) sovereign power. Contextualized in regard to contemporary American spiritual warfare, however, this threat is perhaps best described as "America" itself—a normative America: a cisheteropatriarchal, white supremacist, settler colonial imperium that continues to sustain itself on the conjuration of demons. This "America" is never only that, inextricable as it is from discourses of exceptionalism and empire—the paradigmatic pursuit of Paradise, at once elective and all-encompassing—that aim to make "America" a metonym for humanity and US interests those of all humanity: discourses in which "the next big threat to US empire," as Neel Ahuja dryly remarks, "is always taken as a threat to the entire world, humanity itself."[48] Deploying its demonologies as rubrics to conceptualize movements as diverse as feminist and queer liberation, political Islam, Black resistance, Indigenous traditions, and resurgent socialism, the crisis spiritual warfare bears witness to and attempts to manage can be read as epitomizing the crisis of American empire in an increasingly polycentric world—an empire that is the latest and perhaps the last bastion of modernity/coloniality, of the hubris of the onto-epistemological zero point that strives to comprehend and so save the world from being anything otherwise than the selfsame. Binding themselves to a politics of life and light promising the return of and to the zero point—a second advent inseparable from an act of apocalyptic sovereign violence that both obscures the terror of its founding and at last forecloses on any world in which many worlds might coexist—the spiritual warriors whose writings I explored also bind themselves to the architectures of a racial capitalist settler state fueled by new technologies of militarization that, like discourses of spiritual warfare themselves, blur any clear distinction between war and peace.

Spiritual warfare demonology asks its practitioners to understand themselves as always at war with the world—to see that world and its agents as working to deny them access (back) into the garden and therefore to the stability and security, the "idea of permanence," that the garden represents. Yet it is because of this idea of permanence, this drive for stability and security, that their "Paradise is a violent place," as Solnit wrote. It is Paradise only insofar as it is separate from the world—or rather, only insofar as that world can be tamed, cultivated, and demarcated, made into the walled garden that displays the majesty of sovereign power. But for those of us who cohabit outside the walls, the "prohibited and forbidden" who bear witness to the place where damnation grates against salvation and bleeds, spiritual warfare's demonologies hold other, more subversive, messages. They asks us to realize—but differently, errantly—the truth behind its central claim: that Lucifer's war is and has always been our war, that we have been in it always, even and especially when we did not realize it was being waged. They tell us that when confronted by the force of absolute sovereign violence our only chance lies in the creation of networks of collaboration and cooperation, ties of radical kinship that direct our distinct demonizations toward collective strategies of subversion, solidarity, and survival. Finally—but never finally, because nothing in the time of demons is ever final—they tempt us to unearth archives and build architectures with which to imagine futures that might yet be forged. Worlds in which the borders of nations, genders, sexualities are porous. Worlds in which the wretched of the earth might strive for and achieve dignity and justice on that earth. Worlds in which history is never over, and those that sovereign will has deemed over survive until and beyond the death it decrees for them. And like all forgeries, such worlds will always be passing worlds: their archetypes constructed, not natural; their archives transient, not eternal; their architectures replicable, not unique. Worlds of unstable origins and passing orders. Worlds not just without Paradise, but in which Paradise has become impossible.[49]

Acknowledgments

First, I would like to extend thanks to both the UK Arts and Humanities Research Council and the Irish Research Council for funding various stages of this project. This book was completed across three countries and two continents. It began life at SOAS, University of London, United Kingdom, continued over two years at institutions in Tokyo, Japan, and was completed at University College Dublin, Ireland. As such, it is indebted to the various mentors, colleagues, students, and friends made across these spaces and beyond. Among these, I want to particularly thank Sîan Melvill Hawthorne for her careful guidance, critical insight, and continued friendship; Stefan Skrimshire for his detailed critiques and continued support; and Liam Kennedy, for his steady direction and assistance in the closing months. Special appreciation goes to my SOAS cohort—notably Samantha Langsdale, Jennifer Ung Loh, Eleanor Tiplady Higgs, Alexandra Buehler, and Tom Sparrow—for their camaraderie and commiserations, and Anya Benson, without whose friendship, insight, and support I would not be the scholar I am today. I extend gratitude above all to the late Elizabeth Anne Bailey, whose boundless kindness and support is what allowed this book and so much more to exist, as well as to my broader family, including Alison O'Donnell, Michelle O'Donnell, Cole and Alex, and Chris and Sam Bailey. For opportunities to share this work and my long journey with it, professionally and personally, I would like to thank Lilith Acadia, Foxx Cant, Steve Devlin, Rose Devlin, Maryam El-Shall, Sandra Fahy, Iskra Gencheva-Mikami, Jennifer Grubbs, Jamie Hagen, Nina Handjeva-Weller, Sarah Legge, Kodi Maier, Shehzad Raj, Dolores

Resano, Donovan Schaefer, Cheryl Silverman, Valerie M. Thakkar, and Dee Witt. Finally, I would like to thank my editor, Richard Morrison, and the rest of the team at Fordham University Press for believing in this book enough to bring it to fruition.

Fragments of Chapters 1 and 2 have been adapted from my article "The Body Politic(s) of the Jezebel Spirit," *Religion and Gender* 7, no. 2 (2017): 240–255.

Notes

Introduction: Paradise Has Walls

1. Ray Pritchard, *Stealth Attack: Protecting Yourself Against Satan's Plan to Destroy Your Life* (Chicago: Moody Publishers, 2007), 11–12.
2. Ibid., 14.
3. Ibid.
4. For American deployments of demonological imagery in warfare and adjacent social formations, see Robert L. Ivie and Oscar Giner, *Hunt the Devil: A Demonology of US War Culture* (Tuscaloosa: University of Alabama Press, 2015).
5. Pritchard, *Stealth Attack*, 15.
6. Ibid.
7. I take this base/superstructure framing from Sean McCloud's *American Possessions: Fighting Demons in the Contemporary United States* (Oxford: Oxford University Press, 2015).
8. Perhaps the best guide regarding "evil" and the demonological is Jeffrey Burton Russell's valuable and detailed multivolume opus on the Devil: *The Devil: Perceptions of Evil from Antiquity to Primitive Christianity* (Ithaca, NY: Cornell University Press, 1977); *Satan: The Early Christian Tradition* (Ithaca, NY: Cornell University Press, 1981); *Lucifer: The Devil in the Middle Ages* (Ithaca, NY: Cornell University Press, 1984); and *Mephistopheles: The Devil in the Modern World* (Ithaca, NY: Cornell University Press, 1986). For recent works, see, among others, Philip Cole, *The Myth of Evil* (Edinburgh: Edinburgh University Press, 2006); Simona Forti, *New Demons: Rethinking Power and Evil Today*, trans. Zakiya Hanafi (Stanford, CA: Stanford University Press, 2015); Paul W. Kahn, *Out of Eden: Adam and Eve and the Problem of Evil* (Princeton, NJ: Princeton University Press, 2007); Adam Kotsko, *The Prince of This World: The Life and Legacy of the Devil* (Stanford, CA: Stanford University Press, 2016).
9. Michael Foucault, *The Archaeology of Knowledge*, trans. A. M. Sheridan Smith (New York: Routledge, 2002), 49–51. For some discursive approaches to demonology, see David Brakke, *Demons and the Making of the Monk: Spiritual Combat in Early*

Christianity (Cambridge, MA: Harvard University Press, 2006); Stuart Clark, *Thinking with Demons: The Idea of Witchcraft in Early Modern Europe* (Oxford: Oxford University Press, 1997); Margaret Denike, "The Devil's Insatiable Sex: A Genealogy of Evil Incarnate," *Hypatia* 18, no. 1 (2003): 10–43; Neil Forsyth, *The Old Enemy: Satan and the Combat Myth* (Princeton, NJ: Princeton University Press, 1987); Dayna S. Kalleres, *City of Demons: Violence, Ritual, and Christian Power in Late Antiquity* (Berkeley: University of California Press, 2015); Armando Maggi, *Satan's Rhetoric: A Study of Renaissance Demonology* (Chicago: University of Chicago Press, 2001).

10. Stuart Hall, *Representation: Cultural Representations and Signifying Practices* (Milton Keynes: Open University Press, 1997), 6. The discursive turn in witchcraft scholarship is arguably traceable to Clark's *Thinking with Demons*, which rather than reduce witchcraft demonology to economic or psychological causes treated belief in demons as itself generative and productive. See also Virginia Krause, *Witchcraft, Demonology, and Confession in Early Modern France* (Cambridge: Cambridge University Press, 2015); Maggi, *Rhetoric*; and Walter Stephens, *Demon Lovers: Witchcraft, Sex, and the Crisis of Belief* (Chicago: University of Chicago Press, 2002).

11. This mutual imbrication is important. The modern West is assumed to be living in the "afterlife" of demons, in which they persist more as objects of literary or artistic expression than of lived experience. The substance of religious demonologies in the West thus often goes undiscussed in scholarship, perhaps due to what Bruce Lincoln in *Gods and Demons, Priests and Scholars: Critical Explorations in the History of Religions* (Chicago: University of Chicago Press, 2012) calls a "residual anxiety that such foolishness might be contagious" or at least "damage one's reputation" (31). This is true even for the otherwise comprehensive scholarship on conservative American evangelicalism. Jason Bivins's *Religion of Fear: The Politics of Horror in Conservative Evangelicalism* (Oxford: Oxford University Press, 2008) and Sara Moslener's *Virgin Nation: Sexual Purity and American Adolescence* (Oxford: Oxford University Press, 2015) address how demonization demarcates and maintains borders around ideas of self (Bivins) and nation (Moslener), but not the metaphysical or epistemological substance of the demonologies—what demons are, how they work, how we know them—that enable or are enabled by such demarcations. McCloud's *American Possessions* is an exception, constituting the only in-depth study of third-wave spiritual warfare in the United States to date, but does not explore if or how its demonologies work in relation to sociocultural patterns of demonization. By contrast, Adam Kotsko's genealogy of the devil (*Prince*), addresses how Christian demonology operates in secularized form in the United States today, but it does not explore theological demonologies in the country's living religions and if or how they fit into this genealogy.

12. At least since Michael Rogin's *Ronald Reagan: The Movie, and Other Episodes of Political Demonology* (Berkeley: University of California Press, 1987), "demonology" (with or without the modifier "political") has often been used to refer to politicizations of social divides through dehumanization. It is in this sense that the term is used in much current scholarship. To draw on some transdisciplinary examples, see Bonnie Honig, *Emergency Politics: Paradox, Law, Democracy* (Princeton, NJ: Princeton University Press, 2009), 84–85, 164n65; Françoise Vergès, *Monsters and Revolutionaries: Colonial Family Romance and Métissage* (Durham, NC: Duke University Press, 1999), 145ff; Adam Lowenstein, *Shocking Representation: Historical Trauma, National Cinema, and the Modern Horror Film* (New York: Columbia University Press, 2005), 113; and Bivins, *Religion of Fear*, 220–223.

13. Michael Barkun, *Chasing Phantoms: Reality, Imagination, and Homeland Security since 9/11* (Chapel Hill: University of North Carolina Press, 2011), 141.

14. See Andrew Bacevich, *American Empire: The Realities and Consequences of U.S. Diplomacy* (Cambridge, MA: Harvard University Press, 2002).

15. Barkun, *Chasing Phantoms*, 83.

16. Sarah Ahmed, *Strange Encounters: Embodied Others in Post-Coloniality* (New York: Routledge, 2000), 2. Ahmed is here discussing the extraterrestrial alien as an opening into her wider project, and it is worth noting that this alien—particularly in its malevolent iterations—has strong genealogical continuities with Christian demonology. See Christopher Partridge, "Alien Demonology: The Christian Roots of the Malevolent Extraterrestrial in UFO Religions and Abduction Spiritualties," *Religion* 34, no. 3 (2004): 163–189.

17. Jason C. Bivins, "By Demons Driven: Religious Teratologies," in *Speaking of Monsters: A Teratological Anthology*, ed. Caroline Joan S. Picart and John Edgar Browning (New York: Palgrave Macmillan, 2012), 107.

18. Joshua Gunn, "The Rhetoric of Exorcism: George W. Bush and the Return of Political Demonology," *Western Journal of Communication* 68, no. 1 (2004): 12–13.

19. Catherine Keller, *God and Power: Counter-Apocalyptic Journeys* (Minneapolis: Fortress Press, 2005), 37.

20. Stanley Cohen, *Folk Devils and Moral Panics: The Creation of the Mods and Rockers* (New York: Routledge, 2002), 2. For declension narratives, see especially Bivins, *Religion of Fear*, and McCloud, *American Possessions*. For how such narratives intersect with systems of American empire, particularly following the Cold War, see my "Unipolar Dispensations: Exceptionalism, Empire, and the End of One America," *Political Theology* 20, no. 1 (2019): 66–84.

21. See Jan N. Bremmer, *The Rise and Fall of the Afterlife* (New York: Routledge, 2002), 109–127. Thought to stem from Median *paridaeza*, "enclosure," in most variants the Greek *paradeisos* holds a sense of both sovereignty and sacredness. Differentiated from the more practical herb garden (*kêpos*) and uncultivated wilderness, the paradise conveyed the grand design and aesthetic majesty of sovereign power.

22. Bivins, *Religion of Fear*, 219–220.

23. Runions, *Babylon Complex*, 5; Wendy Brown, *Walled States, Waning Sovereignty* (New York: Zone Books, 2010), 58.

24. Nicola A. Menzie, "Does Heaven Have a Wall like the One Trump Wants at the US-Mexico Border?" *Faithfully Magazine*, January 14, 2019. Available online at faithfullymagazine.com/heaven-wall.

25. Among the earliest instances of this phrasing, rendered simply "Heaven has a wall and strict immigration policies. Hell has open borders," seems to be from the Twitter account @TallahForTrump on June 30, 2018, which alone garnered, as of August 2019, more than 8,000 retweets and 20,000 likes.

26. See, respectively, Mark Taylor and Mary Colbert, *The Trump Prophesies: The Astonishing True Story of the Man Who Saw Tomorrow . . . and What He Says Is Coming Next* (Crane, MO: Defender, 2017), 157, and Daily Renegade, "Satan's Witches of Death Aren't Hiding Anymore," *Youtube.com*, 08/28/2019. Available at https://youtu.be/XSBt9rSdo8s.

27. Rebecca Solnit, *Storming the Gates of Paradise: Landscapes for Politics* (Berkeley: University of California Press, 2007), 79–80.

28. For discussion of the serpent/Satan conflation, see Forsyth, *Old Enemy*, 304–305.

29. John S. Tanner, *Anxiety in Eden: A Kierkegaardian Reading of Paradise Lost* (Oxford: Oxford University Press, 1992), 136.

30. Brown, *Walled States*, 24.

31. Jacques Derrida, *Without Alibi*, trans. Peggy Kamuf (Stanford, CA: Stanford University Press, 2002), 51.

32. Jacques Derrida, *Aporias*, trans. Thomas Dutoit (Stanford, CA: Stanford University Press, 1993), 2, 11.

33. Lincoln, *Gods and Demons*, 31

34. See Judith Butler, "Bodies and Power, Revisited," *Radical Philosophy* 114 (2002): 16–17. My framing of the materialization of demonology via demonization here also draws on Margaret Denike's genealogical exploration of witchcraft demonology ("Devil's Insatiable Sex").

35. My reading of demonology is here indebted to discussions of the technology of "race" as a means for managing unruly subject populations through regimes of classification, as outlined by Falguni A. Sheth, *Towards a Political Philosophy of Race* (Albany: State University of New York Press, 2009).

36. Bruce Lincoln, *Religion, Empire, and Torture: The Case of Achaemenian Persia with a Postscript on Abu Ghraib* (Chicago: University of Chicago Press, 2007), 95.

37. Ibid., 79.

38. Ibid., 95.

39. Marcella Althaus-Reid, *The Queer God* (New York: Routledge, 2003), 134.

40. Rebecca Greenwood, *Glory Warfare: How the Presence of God Empowers You to Destroy the Works of Darkness* (Shippensburg, PA: Destiny Image, 2018), 190; Cindy Jacobs, *Possessing the Gates of the Enemy: A Training Manual for Militant Intercession*, 3rd ed. (Grand Rapids, MI: Chosen Books, 2009), 244.

41. Ahmed, *Willful Subjects*, 136. While Ahmed constructs a genealogy of the concept of will(fulness) as rooted in Christian theology, she never discusses demons explicitly, referring only passingly to the "willful affinity" between Eve and the serpent (186).

42. Katherine McKittrick, *Demonic Grounds: Black Women and the Cartographies of Struggle* (Minneapolis: University of Minnesota Press, 2006), xxii–xxv.

43. Philippe Buc, *Holy War, Martyrdom, and Terror: Christianity, Violence, and the West* (Philadelphia: University of Pennsylvania Press, 2015), 15.

44. Paul Boyer, "The Growth of Fundamentalist Apocalyptic in the United States," in *The Encyclopedia of Apocalypticism, Vol. III: Apocalypticism in the Modern Period and the Contemporary Age*, ed. Stephen J. Stein (London: Continuum, 2000), 175.

45. Charles T. Mathewes, *Evil and the Augustinian Tradition* (Cambridge: Cambridge University Press, 2004), 6–7.

46. Jacques Derrida, *Rogues: Two Essays on Reason*, trans. Pascale-Anne Brault and Michael Naas (Stanford, CA: Stanford University Press, 2004), 11–12.

47. Elaine K. Ginsberg, *Passing and the Fictions of Identity* (Durham, NC: Duke University Press, 1996), 2.

48. Eve Kosofsky Sedgwick, *Epistemology of the Closet* (Berkeley: University of California Press, 1990).

49. Laurel C. Schneider, *Beyond Monotheism: A Theology of Multiplicity* (New York: Routledge, 2008), 100.

50. Gayle Wald, *Crossing the Line: Racial Passing in Twentieth-Century U.S. Literature and Culture* (Durham, NC: Duke University Press, 2000), 5–7.

51. Toby Beauchamp, *Going Stealth: Transgender Politics and U.S. Surveillance Practices* (Durham, NC: Duke University Press, 2019), 132.

52. Harryette Mullen, "Optic White: Blackness and the Production of Whiteness," *Diacritics* 24, nos. 2–3 (1994): 82.

53. Frank B. Wilderson III, *Red, White, and Black: Cinema and the Structures of U.S. Antagonisms* (Durham, NC: Duke University Press, 2010), 9–11. See also Saidiya Hartman, *Scenes of Subjection: Terror, Slavery, and Self-Making in Nineteenth-Century America* (Oxford: Oxford University Press, 1997); Jared Sexton, *Amalgamation Schemes: Antiblackness and the Critique of Multiracialism* (Minneapolis: University of Minnesota Press, 2008) and *Black Men, Black Feminism: Lucifer's Nocturne* (New York: Palgrave Macmillan, 2017); Calvin L. Warren, *Ontological Terror: Blackness, Nihilism and Emancipation* (Durham, NC: Duke University Press, 2018); Alexander G. Weheliye, *Habeas Viscus: Racializing Assemblages, Biopolitics, and Black Feminist Theories of the Human* (Durham, NC: Duke University Press, 2014); Sylvia Wynter, "Unsettling the Coloniality of Being/Truth/Power/Freedom: Towards the Human, After Man, Its Overrepresentation—An Argument," *CR: The New Centennial Review* 3, no. 3 (2003): 257–337. Outside antiblackness, similar (albeit not identical) framings operate in antisemitism, as discussed by Forti, *New Demons*.

54. Kotsko, *Prince*, 167.

55. Sara Ahmed, "Bogus," *Feministkilljoys*, October 27, 2016. Available at feministkilljoys.com/2016/10/27/bogus (accessed November 19, 2017).

56. Schneider's analysis of Satan in Dante's *Inferno* is especially helpful for unpacking how the demonic operates as the disavowed foundation of divine order. *Beyond Monotheism*, 91–104.

57. Mary McAleer Balkun, *The American Counterfeit: Authenticity and Identity in American Literature and Culture* (Tuscaloosa: University of Alabama Press, 2006), 17.

58. Mullen, "Optic Whiteness," 80.

59. Hamilton Carroll, *Affirmative Reaction: New Formations of White Masculinity* (Durham, NC: Duke University Press, 2011), 7–9.

60. Linda Schlossberg, "Rites of Passing," in *Passing: Identity and Interpretation in Sexuality, Race, and Religion*, ed. María Carla Sánchez and Linda Schlossberg (New York: New York University Press, 2001), 2.

61. Ibid., 5–6.

62. Sara Ahmed, "Some Striking Feature: Whiteness and Institutional Passing," *Feministkilljoys*, June 14, 2015. Available at feministkilljoys.com/2015/06/14/some-striking-feature-whiteness-and-institutional-passing (accessed January 5, 2018).

63. Derrida, *Without Alibi*, 68.

64. Mary Manjikian, *Apocalypse and Post-Politics: The Romance of the End* (Lanham, MD: Lexington Books, 2012), 43. For more inclusive apocalypticisms, see Keller, *God and Power*, and Schneider, *Beyond Monotheism*.

65. Elizabeth Freeman, *Time Binds: Queer Temporalities, Queer Histories* (Durham, NC: Duke University Press, 2010), 3.

66. Walter Mignolo, *The Darker Side of Western Modernity: Global Futures, Decolonial Options* (Durham, NC: Duke University Press, 2011).

67. This approach is taken by both Bivins in *Religion of Fear* and McCloud in *American Possessions*, as well as by most scholarship on witchcraft demonologies, including Clark's *Thinking with Demons* and Stephens's *Demon Lovers*.

68. Bob Larson is a notable exception, including "radical Islam's beheading of those considered infidels" as a manifestation of Jezebel, alongside Buddhist meditation, belief in universal oneness, Vodou, and Harry Potter. Larson, *Jezebel: Defeating Your #1 Spiritual Enemy* (Shippensburg, PA: Destiny Image Publishers, 2015), 135–136.

1 / Nations unto Light: Spiritual Warfare as Orthotaxic Religiosity

1. Michel de Certeau, *The Possession at Loudun*, trans. Michael B. Smith (Chicago: University of Chicago Press, 2000), 44.

2. Jacques Derrida, *Monolingualism of the Other; Or, The Prosthesis of Origin*, trans. Patrick Mensah (Stanford, CA: Stanford University Press, 1998), 39.

3. Certeau, *Possession*, 44.

4. Bruce Lincoln, *Gods and Demons, Priests and Scholars: Critical Explorations in the History of Religions* (Chicago: University of Chicago Press, 2012), 31.

5. Marcella Althaus-Reid, *The Queer God* (New York: Routledge, 2003), 134.

6. Thomas Horn, *Spiritual Warfare: The Invisible Invasion* (Lafayette, LA: Huntington House, 1998), 13.

7. Ibid., 14–16.

8. Thomas Horn, *Saboteurs: Shadow Government in Quest of the Final World Order* (Crane, MO: Defender, 2017), 289.

9. David Brakke, *Demons and the Making of the Monk: Spiritual Combat in Early Christianity* (Cambridge, MA: Harvard University Press, 2006); Dayna S. Kalleres, *City of Demons: Violence, Ritual, and Christian Power in Late Antiquity* (Berkeley: University of California Press, 2015).

10. Alain Boureau, *Satan the Heretic: The Birth of Demonology in the Medieval West*, trans. Teresa Lavender Fagan (Chicago: University of Chicago Press, 2006); Stuart Clark, *Thinking with Demons: The Idea of Witchcraft in Early Modern Europe* (Oxford: Oxford University Press, 1997); Armando Maggi, *Satan's Rhetoric: A Study of Renaissance Demonology* (Chicago: University of Chicago Press, 2001); Virginia Krause, *Witchcraft, Demonology, and Confession in Early Modern France* (Cambridge: Cambridge University Press, 2015).

11. Charles Taylor, *A Secular Age* (Cambridge, MA: Harvard University Press, 2017).

12. Philip C. Almond, *Satan: A New Biography* (Ithaca, NY: Cornell University Press, 2014).

13. Perhaps the best survey of the limits of Western disenchantment and the influence of its countervailing tendencies is Jason A. Josephson-Storm, *The Myth of Disenchantment: Magic, Modernity, and the Birth of the Human Sciences* (Chicago: University of Chicago Press, 2017).

14. Christopher Partridge, *The Re-Enchantment of the West: Alternative Spiritualities, Sacralization, Popular Culture, and Occulture, Volumes 1 & 2* (London: T&T Clark, 2005).

15. Ideas of the "return" of religion always entail assumptions of location—where is "religion" returning to and from—and frequently contain a disavowal of the reality that, for many, it never really left. For debates on (post)secularism, see Eduardo Mendieta and Jonathan VanAntwerpen, eds., *The Power of Religion in the Public Sphere* (New York: Columbia University Press, 2011); Yolande Jansen, "Postsecularism, Piety and Fanaticism: Reflections on Jürgen Habermas' and Saba Mahmood's Critiques of Secularism," *Philosophy and Social Criticism* 37, no. 9 (2011): 977–998; and Saba Mah-

mood, *Religious Difference in a Secular Age: A Minority Report* (Princeton, NJ: Princeton University Press, 2015). For an overview of political theology, see Hent de Vries and Lawrence E. Sullivan, eds., *Political Theologies: Public Religions in a Post-Secular World*. New York: Fordham University Press, 2006.

16. Cindy Jacobs, *Possessing the Gates of the Enemy: A Training Manual for Militant Intercession*, 3rd ed. (Grand Rapids, MI: Chosen Books, 2009).

17. This is an internal narrative, if one often replicated by outsiders. Several scholars have contested this America-centric narrative in favor of a more diffuse and global origination, for example Donald E. Miller, Kimon H. Sargeant, and Richard W. Flory, *Spirit and Power: The Growth and Global Impact of Pentecostalism* (Oxford: Oxford University Press, 2013).

18. Brad Christerson and Richard W. Flory, *The Rise of Network Christianity: How Independent Leaders Are Changing the Religious Landscape* (Oxford: Oxford University Press, 2017).

19. Sean McCloud, "Mapping the Spatial Limbos of Spiritual Warfare: Haunted Houses, Defiled Land and the Horrors of History," *Material Religion* 9, no. 2 (2013): 171.

20. René Holvast, *Spiritual Mapping in the United States and Argentina, 1989–2005: A Geography of Fear* (Boston: Brill, 2008); Ruth Marshall, "Destroying Arguments and Capitivating Thoughts: Spiritual Warfare Prayer as Global Praxis," *Journal of Religious and Political Practice* 2, no. 1 (2016): 92–113; McCloud, "Mapping the Spatial Limbos."

21. Jacobs, *Possessing*, 228.

22. Steven Conn, *Americans against the City: Antiurbanism in the Twentieth Century* (Oxford: Oxford University Press, 2014), 6.

23. Anna Strhan, *Aliens and Strangers? The Struggle for Coherence in the Everyday Lives of Evangelicals* (Oxford: Oxford University Press, 2015), 191.

24. Larry Richards, *The Full Armor of God: Defending Your Life from Satan's Schemes* (Bloomington, MN: Chosen Books, 2013), 112.

25. Strhan, *Aliens*, 191.

26. Derek Prince, *Secrets of a Prayer Warrior* (Bloomington, MN: Chosen Books, 2009), 112.

27. Medina Isiah, *Defeat. Dethrone. Conquer: Supreme Strategies for Victorious Living* (Bloomington, IN: Westbow Press, 2012), 119.

28. Elizabeth Grosz, *Architecture from the Outside: Essays on Virtual and Real Space* (Cambridge, MA: MIT Press, 2001); Saskia Sassen, *The Global City: New York, London, Tokyo*, 2nd ed. (Princeton, NJ: Princeton University Press, 2001); Xiaojing Zhou, *Cities of Others: Reimagining Urban Spaces in Asian American Literature* (Seattle: University of Washington Press, 2014).

29. Katherine McKittrick, *Demonic Grounds: Black Women and the Cartographies of Struggle* (Minneapolis: University of Minnesota Press, 2006), xv.

30. Ibid., 6.

31. Steve Sampson, *Confronting Jezebel: Discerning and Defeating the Spirit of Control*, rev. ed. (Bloomington, MN: Chosen Books, 2012), 97.

32. Jennifer LeClaire, *Jezebel's Puppets: Exposing the Agenda of False Prophets* (Lake Mary, FL: Charisma House, 2016), 118.

33. Sandy Freed, *Destiny Thieves: Defeating Seducing Spirits and Achieving Your Purpose in God* (Bloomington, MN: Chosen Books, 2007), 227.

34. Alice Patterson, *Bridging the Racial and Political Divide: How Godly Politics Can Transform a Nation* (San Jose, CA: Transformational Publications, 2010), 146.

35. New International Version, as quoted in Jacobs, *Possessing*, 221–222.

36. Thomas White, *The Believer's Guide to Spiritual Warfare* (Ann Arbor, MI: Servant Publications, 1990), 34.

37. Jennifer LeClaire, *Waging Prophetic Warfare: Effective Prayer Strategies to Defeat the Enemy* (Lake Mary, FL: Charisma House, 2016).

38. Charisma House, *Spiritual Warfare Bible: New King James Version* (Lake Mary, FL: Charisma House, 2012), 1858.

39. Jacobs, *Possessing*, 218–219.

40. Bob Larson, *Demon-Proofing Prayers: Bob Larson's Guide to Winning Spiritual Warfare* (Shippensburg, PA: Destiny Image Publishers, 2011), 199–201.

41. Ibid.

42. Jacques Derrida, *Archive Fever: A Freudian Impression*, trans. Eric Prenowitz (Chicago: University of Chicago Press, 1996), 1.

43. Sean McCloud, *American Possessions: Fighting Demons in the Contemporary United States* (Oxford: Oxford University Press, 2015), 115.

44. Ibid., 215.

45. C. Peter Wagner, "The Visible and the Invisible," in *Breaking Spiritual Strongholds in Your City*, ed. C. Peter Wagner (Shippensburg, PA: Destiny Image Publishers, 2015), 67–69.

46. Francis Frangipane, *The Three Battlegrounds: An In-Depth View of the Three Arenas of Spiritual Warfare: The Mind, the Church and the Heavenly Places*, rev. ed. (Cedar Rapids, MI: Arrow Publications, 2006), 109.

47. Yannick Fer, "Pentecostal Prayer as Personal Communication and Invisible Institutional Work," in *A Sociology of Prayer*, ed. Giuseppe Gordon and Linda Woodhead (Farnham: Ashgate, 2015), 62.

48. Cindy Jacobs, *The Supernatural Life* (Grand Rapids, MI: Chosen Books, 2005), 135.

49. Sandie Freed, *Breaking the Threefold Demonic Cord: How to Discern and Defeat the Lies of Jezebel, Athaliah, and Delilah* (Grand Rapids, MI: Chosen Books, 2008), 88.

50. Jacobs, *Possessing*, 244.

51. Armando Maggi, "Christian Demonology in Contemporary American Popular Culture," *Social Research: An International Quarterly* 81, no. 4 (2014): 773.

52. Matthew T. Lee, Margaret M. Poloma, and Stephen G. Post, *The Heart of Religion: Spiritual Empowerment, Benevolence, and the Experience of God's Love* (Oxford: Oxford University Press, 2013), 209.

53. C. Peter Wagner, *Spiritual Warfare Strategy: Confronting Spiritual Powers* (Shippensburg, PA: Destiny Image Publishers, 1996), 219–242; Pierce, "Continue Praying for Japan," *The Elijah List*, April 1, 2011. Available at http://www.elijahlist.com/words/display_word.html?ID=9742 (accessed June 30, 2020).

54. Jacobs, *Possessing*, 220–221.

55. Dag Heward-Mills, *Lay People and the Ministry* (London: Parchment House, 1999), 117.

56. Walter Mignolo, *The Darker Side of Western Modernity: Global Futures, Decolonial Options* (Durham, NC: Duke University Press, 2011), 165–166.

57. Andrea Althoff, *Divided by Faith and Ethnicity: Religious Pluralism and the Problem of Race in Guatemala* (Berlin: De Gruyter, 2014), 330; Melissa Hackman, "A Sinful Landscape: Moral and Sexual Geographies in Cape Town, South Africa," *Social Analysis* 59, no. 3 (2015): 105–125.

58. Marshall, "Destroying Arguments," 102. As Gil Anidjar demonstrates in *Blood: A Critique of Christianity* (New York: Columbia University Press, 2014), blood imagery is not just a core mobilizing image of Christianity but one critical to the evolution of modern racism. This emphasis on blood also influenced on practices of settler colonialism, where notions of blood purity served to override Indigenous kinship structures, as J. Kēhaulani Kauanui demonstrates in *Hawaiian Blood: Colonialism and the Politics of Sovereignty and Indigeneity* (Durham, NC: Duke University Press, 2008).

59. Mignolo, *Darker Side*, 2, xxiv.

60. Kalleres, *City of Demons*, 1–3.

61. Richard Ing, *Spiritual Warfare* (New Kensington, PA: Whitaker House, 1996). 19.

62. Frangipane, *Three Battlegrounds*, 45.

63. Jacobs, *Possessing*, 230–231.

64. LeClaire, *Waging Prophetic Warfare*, 15.

65. Fundamentalist evangelicalisms have a complex relation to the Enlightenment. As Harriet Harris demonstrates in *Fundamentalism and Evangelicals* (Oxford: Oxford University Press, 2008), fundamentalists exhibit a tendency to demonstrate biblical inerrancy through collating empirical evidence. Matthew Avery Sutton notes in *American Apocalypse: A History of Modern Evangelicalism* (Cambridge, MA: Harvard University Press, 2014) that this tendency treats the Bible like a series of propositions that when "properly arranged and classified unveil the plan for the ages" (15–16). For expert coverage of the evangelical indebtedness to paradigms of reason in the US context, see Molly Worthen, *Apostles of Reason: The Crisis of Authority in American Evangelicalism* (Oxford: Oxford University Press, 2013).

66. See Gurminda K. Bhambra, *Rethinking Modernity: Postcolonialism and the Sociological Imagination* (New York: Palgrave Macmillan, 2007), 36.

67. Frangipane, *Three Battlegrounds*, 14.

68. Jacobs, *Possessing*, 218.

69. Frangipane, *Three Battlegrounds*, 112.

70. Jacques Derrida, *Writing and Difference* (New York: Routledge, 2001), 113–114.

71. Jeffrey S. Kahn, *Islands of Sovereignty: Haitian Migration and the Borders of Empire* (Chicago: University of Chicago Press, 2019), 113–114, 103–104.

72. Bob Larson, *Larson's Book of Spiritual Warfare* (Nashville, TN: Thomas Nelson, 1999), 175.

73. Quoted in Elizabeth McAlister, "From Slave Revolt to a Blood Pact with Satan: The Evangelical Rewriting of Haitian History," *Studies in Religion/Sciences Religieuses* 41, no. 2 (2012): 202.

74. Ibid., 193. See also Elizabeth McAlister, "Globalization and the Religious Production of Space," *Journal for the Scientific Study of Religion* 44 (2005): 249–255.

75. The role of Cold War bipolarity in the development of third-wave spiritual warfare's political imaginary is discussed by Holvast in *Spiritual Mapping in the United States and Argentina*.

76. Sarah Miller-Davenport, *Gateway State: Hawai'i and the Cultural Transformation of American Empire* (Princeton, NJ: Princeton University Press, 2019), 2. For critiques of multiculturalism's disavowing tendencies, see Jodi Byrd, *Transit of Empire: Indigenous Critiques of Colonialism* (Minneapolis: University of Minnesota Press, 2011), and Jared Sexton, *Amalgamation Schemes: Antiblackness and the Critique of Multiracialism* (Minneapolis: University of Minnesota Press, 2008). That differences

between Haiti and Hawaii's framings may derive, at least in part, from the specificities of antiblackness among wider regimes of racial ordering should not go unmentioned.

77. Ing, *Spiritual Warfare*, 274, 267, 289, 271.

78. J. Kēhaulani Kauanui, *Paradoxes of Hawaiian Sovereignty: Land, Sex, and the Colonial Politics of State Nationalism* (Durham, NC: Duke University Press, 2019).

79. Audra Simpson, *Mohawk Interruptus: Political Life across the Borders of Settler States* (Durham, NC: Duke University Press, 2014), 11–12. While some Kānaka Maoli reject analogies with Native Americans, as Kauanui details, in the context of spiritual warfare differences between these groups are flattened. Indeed, Ing's stated goal in discussing Hawaiian traditions is to help Christians globally "understand and counteract recent attempts by native peoples to go back to ancient demon religions." *Spiritual Warfare*, 264.

80. Dan Jorgensen, "Third Wave Evangelism and the Politics of the Global in Papua New Guinea: Spiritual Warfare and the Recreation of Place in Telefolmin," *Oceania* 75, no. 4 (2005): 447.

81. Holvast, *Geography of Fear*, 289.

82. Ibid., 286. For spiritual warfare in other national contexts, see Afe Adogame, "Engaging the Rhetoric of Spiritual Warfare: The Public Face of Aladura in Diaspora," *Journal of Religion in Africa* 34, no. 4 (2004): 493–522; Jorgensen, "Third Wave Evangelism"; Marshall, "Destroying Arguments"; McAlister, "Blood Pact"; Amy Stambach, "Spiritual Warfare 101: Preparing the Student for Christian Battle," *Journal of Religion in Africa* 39 (2009): 137–157; Strhan, *Aliens*.

83. Mark Hitchcock, *101 Answers to Questions about Satan, Demons, and Spiritual Warfare* (Eugene, OR: Harvest House, 2014). For analysis of Hitchcock's broader politics and influence, see Tristan Sturm, "Prophetic Eyes: The Theatricality of Mark Hitchcock's Premillennial Geopolitics," *Geopolitics* 11, no. 2 (2011): 231–255.

84. Eddie Smith, *Making Sense of Spiritual Warfare* (Minneapolis, MN: Bethany House, 2008), 115.

85. Linda Rios Brook, *Lucifer's War: Understanding the Ancient Struggle Between God and the Devil* (Lake Mary, FL: Charisma House, 2012), 12.

86. Nicola Perugini and Neve Gordon, *The Human Right to Dominate* (Oxford: Oxford University Press, 2015).

87. Brook, *Lucifer's War*, 12.

88. C. Heike Schotten, *Queer Terror: Life, Death, and Desire in the Settler Colony* (New York: Columbia University Press, 2018), 55–56.

89. Ibid., 60.

90. For *diabolos* in the sense of obstacle or obstruction, see Neil Forsyth, *The Satanic Epic* (Princeton, NJ: Princeton University Press, 2002), 37.

91. McCloud, "Mapping the Spatial Limbos," 169–170.

92. Ibid.

93. Donna Haraway, quoted in Cynthia Weber, *Queer International Relations: Sovereignty, Sexuality, and the Will to Knowledge* (Oxford: Oxford University Press, 2016), 11.

94. See Lucinda Ramberg, *Given to the Goddess: South Indian Devadasis and the Sexuality of Religion* (Durham, NC: Duke University Press, 2014), 31–32.

95. Ranjana Khanna, *Dark Continents: Psychoanalysis and Colonialism* (Durham, NC: Duke University Press, 2003), 4.

96. Gayatri Chakravorty Spivak, "The Rani of Sirmur: An Essay on Reading the Archives," *History and Theory* 24, no. 3 (1985): 264. See also Spivak's *A Critique of Postcolonial Reason: Towards a History of the Vanishing Present* (Cambridge, MA: Harvard University Press, 1999), 211–213.

97. Khanna, *Dark Continents*, 4.

98. Ibid., 5.

99. Scott, *Seeing Like a State*, 183.

100. Spivak, "The Rani of Sirmur," 253.

101. Tala Asad, *Formations of the Secular: Christianity, Islam, Modernity* (Stanford, CA: Stanford University Press, 2003), 147. Asad is discussing the "secular language of redemption" that America often deploys in relation to its foreign pursuit of "democracy" and "human rights"—the "universalizing moral project of the American nation-state" that configures how Americans "see themselves in contrast to their 'evil' opponents" (ibid.).

102. Althaus-Reid, *Queer God*, 135.

103. Nikhil Pal Singh, *Race and America's Long War* (Berkeley: University of California Press, 2017).

104. This interdependency of orthodoxy and orthopraxy is a quality Talal Asad unpacks in his analysis of "discursive traditions." For Asad, traditions are constituted by "discourses that seek to instruct practitioners regarding the correct form and purpose of a given practice" and are bound to constructions of historical temporality. They are formulated in relation to a past (in which they were constituted) and a future (in which they are secured, modified, or abandoned) via the medium of a present (which binds them to institutions and societal conditions). Asad states that focusing on orthopraxy ignores "the centrality of the notion of 'the correct model' to which an instituted practice . . . ought to conform, a model conveyed in authoritative formulas." Asad, "The Idea of an Anthropology of Islam," *Qui Parle* 17, no. 2 (2009): 20. Orthodoxy, he reminds us, "is not a mere body of opinion but a distinctive relationship—a relationship of power to truth" (21). Wherever practitioners, "have the power to regulate, uphold, require, or adjust *correct* practices, and to condemn, exclude, undermine, or replace *incorrect* ones, there is the domain of orthodoxy" (22). My notion of "orthotaxy" here draws on Asad. However, it is not intended as a conceptualization of how tradition discursively functions but of a mode of religiosity that seeks to "properly" order reality in relation to specific discursive and affective pre- and proscriptions.

105. Althaus-Reid, *Queer God*, 134.

106. Khanna, *Dark Continents*, 3–4.

2 / Jezebel Assemblages: Witchcraft, Queerness, Transnationality

1. Mark S. Smith, *The Early History of God: Yahweh and the Other Deities in Ancient Israel* (Cambridge: William B. Eerdmans, 2002), 67.

2. Tina Pippin, *Apocalyptic Bodies: The Biblical End of the World in Text and Image* (New York: Routledge, 1999), 32;

3. Sandie Freed, *Breaking the Threefold Demonic Cord: How to Discern and Defeat the Lies of Jezebel, Athaliah, and Delilah* (Grand Rapids, MI: Chosen Books, 2008), 68; Steve Sampson, *Confronting Jezebel: Discerning and Defeating the Spirit of Control*, rev. ed. (Bloomington, MN: Chosen Books, 2012), 33; Landon Schott, *Jezebel: The Witch*

Is Back (Spokane, WA: Famous Publishing, 2013), 1; John Paul Jackson, *Unmasking the Jezebel Spirit* (Flower Mound, TX: Streams Ministries International, 2002), 10; Diana D. Williams, *The Jezebel Spirit: The Unseen Opponent to Divine Purpose* (Bloomington, IN: Booktango, 2012), 18.

4. For example, Richard Bartholomew in "Publishing, Celebrity, and the Globalisation of Conservative Protestantism," *Journal of Contemporary Religion* 21, no. 1 (2006) sets an author apart solely because he does *not* discuss her (8).

5. Paul Brooks Duff, *Who Rides the Beast? Prophetic Rivalry and the Rhetoric of Crisis in the Churches of the Apocalypse* (Oxford: Oxford University Press, 2001); Janet Howe Gaines, *Music in the Old Bones: Jezebel through the Ages* (Edwardsville: Southern Illinois University Press, 1999); Catherine Keller, *Apocalypse Now and Then: A Feminist Guide to the End of the World* (Boston: Beacon Press, 1996); Jennifer S. Leath, "Revising Jezebel Politics: Towards a New Black Sexual Ethic," in *Black Intersectionalities: A Critique for the 21st Century*, ed. Monica Michlin and Jean-Paul Rocchi (Liverpool: Liverpool University Press, 2013), 195–210; Tamura Lomax, *Jezebel Unhinged: Loosing the Black Female Body in Religion and Culture* (Durham, NC: Duke University Press, 2018); Lee Quinby, *Millennial Seductions: A Skeptic Confronts Apocalyptic Culture* (Ithaca, NY: Cornell University Press, 1999); Pippin, *Apocalyptic Bodies*.

6. Quinby, *Millennial Seductions*, 105. In this vein, it should be noted that the build-up to the 2016 US presidential election saw a proliferation of spiritual warfare manuals about Jezebel, likely owing to long-standing associations with Hillary Clinton. See Charlotte Baker, *The Extreme Jezebel Spirit: False Prophetic Operations* (Paw Creek, NC: It's All About Him Media & Publishing, 2015); Edwin Christiaan, *Divorce Jezebel: Remarry Christ Your Destiny* (Los Angeles: The Original God, Inc., 2015); Douglas Hopson, *Understanding the Traits of Jezebel* (Memphis, TN: PH Publishing, 2015); Bob Larson, *Jezebel: Defeating Your #1 Spiritual Enemy* (Shippensburg, PA: Destiny Image Publishers, 2015); and Jennifer LeClaire, *Jezebel's Puppets: Exposing the Agenda of False Prophets* (Lake Mary, FL: Charisma House, 2016).

7. In contrast to the biblical figure broadly, the Jezebel spirit has received little scholarly attention. She is often only mentioned in passing, as in Leath, "Jezebel Politics," 201; Lomax, *Jezebel Unhinged*, 42; and Sean McCloud, *American Possessions: Fighting Demons in the Contemporary United States* (Oxford: Oxford University Press, 2015), 31–33. Trudie Stark and Hans van Deventer engage with her in detail in "The 'Jezebel Spirit': A Scholarly Inquiry," *Verbum et Ecclesia* 30, no. 2 (2009): 68–76. However, they focus on only two texts and have a theological focus, arguing that notions of a "Jezebel spirit" misread scripture. Here, I am less concerned with whether Jezebel *should* be read as a demonic spirit than that she *has been* read as such, and what discursive and affective relations this reading helps provoke and proscribe.

8. Larson, *Jezebel*, 119. For an inexhaustive sample of spiritual warfare texts that focus chiefly on Jezebel, see Jonas Clark, *Jezebel: Seducing Goddess of War*, rev. ed. (Hallandale Beach, FL: Spirit of Life Publishing, 2004); Francis Frangipane, *The Jezebel Spirit* (Cedar Rapids, IA: Arrow Publications, 1995); Sandie Freed, *The Jezebel Yoke: Breaking Free from Bondage and Deception* (Bloomington, MN: Chosen Books, 2012); Jackson, *Unmasking*; Jennifer LeClaire, *The Spiritual Warrior's Guide to Defeating Jezebel* (Bloomington, MN: Chosen Books, 2013); LeClaire, *Jezebel's Puppets*; Don Richter, *Overcoming the Attack of the Jezebel Spirit: The Church Under Siege* (Maitland, FL: Xulon Press, 2005); Sampson, *Confronting Jezebel*; Landon Schott, *Jezebel*; Williams, *Jezebel Spirit*.

9. Cynthia Weber, *Queer International Relations: Sovereignty, Sexuality, and the Will to Knowledge* (Oxford: Oxford University Press, 2016).

10. Lomax, *Jezebel Unhinged*, 23–24.

11. Jackson, *Unmasking*, 2–3.

12. Jason C. Bivins, *Religion of Fear: The Politics of Horror in Conservative Evangelicalism* (Oxford: Oxford University Press, 2008), 219–220.

13. Schott, *Jezebel*, 4.

14. Ibid., 1, 13, 22.

15. Sara Ahmed, *Willful Subjects* (Durham, NC: Duke University Press, 2014), 175.

16. Leath, "Jezebel Politics," 201–202.

17. Sara Moslener, *Virgin Nation: Sexual Purity and American Adolescence* (Oxford: Oxford University Press, 2015), 15.

18. Alice Patterson, *Bridging the Racial and Political Divide: How Godly Politics Can Transform a Nation* (San Jose, CA: Transformational Publications, 2010), 194, 198.

19. Schott, *Jezebel*, 90.

20. Patterson, *Bridging*, 191; Schott, *Jezebel*, 90. Jezebel's threat to gender is also focal in her associations with media, including Hollywood, which has "spread her perversions and sexuality across the world" (Schott, *Jezebel*, 101–111) via sitcoms "that undermine the family and male authority . . . [and are] largely written by homosexuals" (Sampson, *Confronting Jezebel*, 52), and "semi-pornographic broadcasts that air on prime-time television" (LeClaire, *Defeating Jezebel*, 101), which—like pornography proper—are presumably intended to "prepare individuals to destroy their marriages" (Schott, *Jezebel*, xv).

21. Francis Frangipane, *The Three Battlegrounds: An In-Depth View of the Three Arenas of Spiritual Warfare: The Mind, the Church and the Heavenly Places*, rev. ed. (Cedar Rapids, MI: Arrow Publications, 2006), 123; Sandie Freed, *Destiny Thieves: Defeating Seducing Spirits and Achieving Your Purpose in God* (Bloomington, MN: Chosen Books, 2007), 191; Sampson, *Confronting Jezebel*, 27; Schott, *Jezebel*, 9. Spirits habitually gendered male rarely elicit defenses of or explanations for their assigned gender. Authors nonetheless fluctuate between and within texts on whether they refer to Jezebel as "it" or "she," as well as on the genderedness of her operations: for example, Freed uses "her," Schott fluctuates between the two, and LeClaire refers to the spirit mostly as "it." However, she also glosses "it" as a "goddess" (*Defeating Jezebel*, 24). Due to her persistent gendering and associations with classical images of (deviant) femininity, I have opted to use "her" throughout this work.

22. Frangipane, *Three Battlegrounds*, 123.

23. Michael Kleu and Madelene Eayrs, *Who Are You? A Practical Deliverance Guide* (Maitland, FL: Xulon Press 2010), 285.

24. Frangipane, *Three Battlegrounds*, 123.

25. Sampson, *Confronting Jezebel*, 42.

26. Schott, *Jezebel*, xi, xv; LeClaire, *Defeating Jezebel*, 37–40.

27. Lee Edelman, *No Future: Queer Theory and the Death Drive* (Durham, NC: Duke University Press, 2004), 60.

28. Lee Edelman, "Ever After: History, Negativity, and the Social," *South Atlantic Quarterly* 106, no. 3 (2007): 471.

29. C. Heike Schotten, *Queer Terror: Life, Death, and Desire in the Settler Colony* (New York: Columbia University Press, 2018), 35.

30. Michael L. Brown, *Jezebel's War with America: The Plot to Destroy Our Country and What we Can do to Turn the Tide* (Lake Mary, FL: Charisma House, 2019), 115.

31. Schott, *Jezebel*, 106–108.

32. LeClaire, *Defeating Jezebel*, 37; Schott, *Jezebel*, 93.

33. Sampson, *Confronting Jezebel*, 50. See also LeClaire, *Defeating Jezebel*, 37–38, and Schott, *Jezebel*, 93.

34. Schott, *Jezebel*, 93.

35. LeClaire, *Defeating Jezebel*, 30, 133. For analysis of pathologizing language vis-à-vis homosexuality, see Thomas L. Long, *AIDS and American Apocalypse: The Cultural Semiotics of an Epidemic* (Albany: State University of New York Press, 2005). For the history of Christian associations between the sins of Sodom and (male) homosexuality, see Mark D. Jordan, *The Invention of Sodomy in Christian Theology* (Chicago: University of Chicago Press, 2007).

36. Athaliah's status as Jezebel's biological daughter is disputed. Spiritual warriors generally ignore this disputation (LeClaire, *Jezebel's Puppets*, 37) or evade it by casting her as Jezebel's "spiritual daughter" (Freed, *Threefold Cord*, 102).

37. Freed, *Threefold Cord*, 102, 107.

38. Jasbir K. Puar, *Terrorist Assemblages: Homonationalism in Queer Times* (Durham, NC: Duke University Press, 2007), 211.

39. José Esteban Muñoz, *Cruising Utopia: The Then and There of Queer Futurity* (New York: New York University Press, 2009), 94.

40. Schotten, *Queer Terror*.

41. Sandie Freed, *Destiny Thieves*, 195.

42. I here draw on Patrick Wolfe's framing of settler colonialism as "a structure not an event" in "Settler Colonialism and the Elimination of the Native," *Journal of Genocide Research* 8, no. 4 (2006): 387–409, 388.

43. Freed, *Threefold Cord*, 104–105, 110.

44. Althaus-Reid, *Queer God*, 134.

45. Quoted in Lomax, *Jezebel Unhinged*, 41.

46. Ibid.

47. Lomax, *Jezebel Unhinged*, 42–43.

48. Ibid., 32, xvii, 2.

49. Ibid., 23–24.

50. Ibid., 42.

51. Leath, "Jezebel Politics," 201–202.

52. Patterson, *Bridging*, 159, 163. Emphasis in original. Patterson here draws on the genetic fallacy, citing Margaret Sanger's eugenicist views to code the organization is inherently and eternally antiblack. For links between slavery and abortion in evangelical discourse, see Carol Mason, "Cracked Babies." For a nuanced analysis of the strange consequences this analogy has for black reproductive justice if taken to its logical conclusion, see Sexton, *Lucifer's Nocturne*, 86–89

53. Patterson, *Bridging*, 160.

54. Brown, *Jezebel's War*, 107–110.

55. Ibid., 109. Emphasis in original.

56. This assumed present takes places within a history that constructs black life as always already queered and trans, as Christina Sharpe outlines in *In the Wake: On Blackness and Being* (Durham: Duke University Press, 2016), 30–32.

57. Lomax, *Jezebel Unhinged*, 119.

58. Frangipane, *Three Battlegrounds*, 29.
59. Schott, *Jezebel*, xvi.
60. Schott, *Gay Awareness*, 112, 212.
61. Sampson, *Confronting Jezebel*, 107.
62. Freed, *Destiny Thieves*, 185–187.
63. Ahmed, *Willful Subjects*, 128.
64. Ibid., 2.
65. See, for example, Timothy J. McMillan, "Black Magic: Witchcraft, Race, and Resistance in Colonial New England," *Journal of Black Studies* 25, no. 1 (1994): 99–117.
66. Gil Anidjar, *Blood: A Critique of Christianity* (New York: Columbia University Press, 2014).
67. Janet R. Jakobsen and Ann Pellegrini, *Love the Sin: Sexual Regulation and the Limits of Religious Tolerance* (New York: New York University Press, 2003), 45.
68. Lomax, *Jezebel Unhinged*, 42.
69. Leath, "Jezebel Politics," 207. Emphasis in original.
70. Puar, *Terrorist Assemblages*, 215.
71. Ibid., 207–208.
72. Biblical ideas of "witchcraft" derive primarily from the Hebrew *keshep*, which appears in 2 Kings 9:22, Isaiah 47:9 and 12, Micah 5:12, and twice in Nahum 3:4, all in condemnatory fashion. The term in 1 Samuel, however, is not *keshep* but *qesem* (divination).
73. LeClaire, *Satan's Deadly Trio*, 23.
74. Freed, *Destiny Thieves*, 99.
75. Sampson, *Confronting Jezebel*, 25. While narratives of psychological and emotional abuse are often used by spiritual warriors to categorize "witchcraft," the incidents relayed are rarely figured as terrible *in themselves*: their apparent demonic nature—their being "witchcraft"—is not due to the damaging effects of abuse or addiction but the impact these have on the integrated unity and functioning of the Church and normative family. Happy resolutions come only through the rededication of self to God and so to the integrated personal and communal unity divine will is seen to enable. Sampson, *Confronting Jezebel*, 157–159; Schott, *Jezebel*, 11–12; LeClaire, *Defeating Jezebel*, 28, 118–119.
76. Freed, *Destiny Thieves*, 166.
77. Ibid.
78. LeClaire, *Satan's Deadly Trio*, 19.
79. LeClaire, *Jezebel's Puppets*, 132.
80. Alain Boureau, *Satan the Heretic: The Birth of Demonology in the Medieval West*, trans. Teresa Lavender Fagan (Chicago: University of Chicago Press, 2006), 201.
81. Armando Maggi, *Satan's Rhetoric: A Study of Renaissance Demonology* (Chicago: University of Chicago Press, 2001), 25, 233.
82. Ibid., 26, 233.
83. Jacobs, *Possessing*, 130.
84. Freed, *Jezebel Yoke*, 65.
85. Ibid.
86. Freed, *Destiny Thieves*, 216–217.
87. See Elias Kifon Bongma, *African Witchcraft and Otherness: A Philosophical and Theological Critique of Intersubjective Relations* (Albany: State University of New York Press, 2001); Karen Fields, *Revival and Rebellion in Colonial Central Africa* (Princeton,

NJ: Princeton University Press, 1985); James W. Perkinson, "Reversing the Gaze: European Race Discourses as Modern Witchcraft Practice," *Journal of the American Academy of Religion* 72, no. 3 (2004): 603–629.

88. Perkinson, "Reversing the Gaze," 620; McMillan, "Black Magic."

89. LeClaire, *Defeating Jezebel*, 164.

90. Freed, *Destiny Thieves*, 103.

91. Victor Lorenzo, "Evangelizing a City Dedicated to Darkness," in *Breaking Spiritual Strongholds in Your City*, ed. C. Peter Wagner (Shippensburg, PA: Destiny Images Publisher, 2015), 180.

92. LeClaire, *Deadly Trio*, 78.

93. Jennifer Eivaz, *The Intercessors Handbook: How to Pray with Boldness, Authority, and Supernatural Power* (Bloomington, MN: Chosen Books, 2016), 153.

94. Roberto Strongman, *Queering Black Atlantic Religion: Transcorporeality in Candomblé, Santería, and Vodou* (Durham, NC: Duke University Press, 2019), 21.

95. For the welfare queen as demonological figure, see Adam Kotsko, *Neoliberalism's Demons: On the Political Theology of Late Capital* (Stanford, CA: Stanford University Press, 2018), 72.

96. William C. Connolly, *Christianity and Capitalism, American Style* (Durham, NC: Duke University Press, 2008), 29.

97. Ibid.

98. Ibid., 166.

99. For the relation between race and the urban imaginary, see Liam Kennedy, *Race and Urban Space in Contemporary American Culture* (Chicago: Fitzroy Dearborn, 2000).

100. LeClaire, *Deadly Trio*, 78.

101. It is worth noting that the *arche* to which Haiti pledged allegiance in the revolution is sometimes named as Jezebel, under the guise of the *lwa* Ezili, as explored by Elizabeth McAlister in "Race, Gender, and Christian Diaspora: New Pentecostal Intersectionalities and Haiti," in *Spirit on the Move: Black Women and Pentecostalism in Africa and the Diaspora*, ed. Judith Casselberry and Elizabeth A. Pritchard (Durham, NC: Duke University Press, 2019), 59–61.

102. Steven Conn, *Americans against the City: Anti-Urbanism in the Twentieth Century* (Oxford: Oxford University Press, 2014), 6, 299.

103. Erin Runions, *The Babylon Complex: Theopolitical Fantasies of War, Sex, and Sovereignty* (New York: Fordham University Press, 2014), 2–3.

104. Ibid., 2. For scriptural parallels, see Revelation 2:23 and 17:5, 2:20 and 18:23, 2:20–22 and 17:1–5, 2:20 and 17:6, and 2:22 and 17:16. For discussion of such parallels, see Duff, *Who Rides the Beast?* 91.

105. LeClaire, *Defeating Jezebel*, 59; Schott, *Jezebel*, 101.

106. Frangipane, *Three Battlegrounds*, 155, 131.

107. Richard Ing, *Spiritual Warfare*, (New Kensington, PA: Whitaker House, 1996), 47, 45.

108. Jackson, *Unmasking*, 2–3.

109. James Gardner, *The War with Babylon* (Maitland, FL: Xulon Press, 2004), 271, 142.

110. LeClaire, *Defeating Jezebel*, 66, 68.

111. Kath Weston, *Families We Choose: Lesbians, Gays, Kinship* (New York: Columbia University Press, 1997), 153.

112. LeClaire, *Defeating Jezebel*, 59–64.
113. Ibid., 70.
114. Elizabeth Derry, *Lucifer Is Not Satan, Part II* (Maitland, FL: Xulon Press, 2007), 205.
115. John Goldingay and David Payne, *Isaiah 40–55, Volume 1: A Critical and Exegetical Commentary* (London: Continuum, 2006), 99–100.
116. Runions, *Babylon Complex*, 83.
117. The claim that Nimrod built Babel stems chiefly from Jewish historian Josephus. For Nimrod in Babylon narratives broadly, see ibid.
118. Ibid., 83–85.
119. Weber, *Queer International Relations*, 3–4.
120. Ibid., 37.
121. Ibid., 39–41.
122. Ibid., 196.
123. Ibid., 196–197.
124. Arjun Appadurai, *Fear of Small Numbers: An Essay on the Geography of Anger* (Durham, NC: Duke University Press, 2006), 11, 52, 117.
125. Eric Stanley, "Near Life, Queer Death: Overkill and Ontological Capture," *Social Text* 107 (2011): 9–10, 15.
126. Appadurai, *Small Numbers*, 70, 100–107.
127. Stanley, "Near Life," 12.
128. Frangipane, *Three Battlegrounds*, 110.
129. See, for example, Natasha V. Chang, *The Crisis-Woman: Body Politics and the Modern Woman in Fascist Italy* (Toronto: University of Toronto Press, 2015).
130. Sampson, *Confronting Jezebel*, 39.

3 / The Islamic Antichrist: An Eschatology of Blowback

1. "A Spirit of Rage—John Guandolo & Joel Richardson on The Jim Bakker Show," April 27, 2017. Available at www.youtube.com/watch?v=yPhetBv3kxQ (accessed March 16, 2018).
2. For the complex relation between blackness and Islam in America and broadly, see Edward E. Curtis IV, *The Call of Bilal: Islam in the African Diaspora* (Princeton, NJ: Princeton University Press, 2016); Sherman A. Jackson, *Islam and the Blackamerican: Looking toward the Third Resurrection* (Oxford: Oxford University Press, 2005); Su'ad Abdul Khabeer, *Muslim Cool: Race, Religion, and Hip Hop in the United States* (New York: New York University Press, 2016); Ricardo René Laremont, "Race, Islam, and Politics: Differing Visions among Black American Muslims," *Journal of Islamic Studies* 10, no. 1 (1999): 33–49; Judith Weisenfeld, *New World A-Coming: Black Religion and Racial Identity during the Great Migration* (New York: New York University Press, 2016).
3. Darryl Li, "A Jihadism Anti-Primer," *MERP* 276. 2015, available at https://merip.org/2015/12/a-jihadism-anti-primer (accessed June 17, 2020).
4. Whereas demonologies of Jezebel reflected ideas of abjected femininity, those of the Islamic Antichrist draw heavily on dehumanizing discourses of Muslim and Black masculinity as inherently patriarchal, violent, dogmatic, illiberal, thuggish, and criminal (see Khabeer, *Muslim Cool*, 173). Women are mostly absent from these demonologies—except as victims—while (Black, Muslim) men are enfleshed as its hypervisible avatars, forerunners of the (male) Antichrist to come, and the texts discussed often

fluctuate between referring to the figure as "he" or "it." To capture this gendered dimension, I refer to the Antichrist spirit as "he."

5. Emmanouela Grypeou, "'A People Will Emerge from the Desert': Apocalyptic Perceptions of the Early Muslim Conquests in Contemporary Eastern Christian Literature," in *Apocalypticism and Eschatology in Late Antiquity: Encounters in the Abrahamic Religions, 6th–8th Centuries*, ed. Hagil Amirav, Emmanouela Grypeou, and Guy Stroumsa (Leuven: Peeters, 2017), 291–310.

6. Frederick Quinn, *The Sum of All Heresies* (Oxford: Oxford University Press, 2008), 30.

7. John L. Esposito, *The Islamic Threat: Myth or Reality?* (Oxford: Oxford University Press, 1999); Thomas S. Kidd, *American Christians and Islam: Evangelical Culture and Muslims from the Colonial Period to the Age of Terrorism* (Princeton, NJ: Princeton University Press, 2009), 1–18.

8. Reza F. Safa, *The Coming Fall of Islam in Iran: Thousands of Muslims Find Christ in the Midst of Persecution* (Lake Mary, FL: Charisma House, 2006), 5.

9. Don Richardson, *Secrets of the Koran: Revealing Insights into Islam's Holy Book* (Minneapolis, MN: Bethany House, 2003), 38.

10. Walid Shoebat and Joel Richardson, *God's War on Terror: Islam, Prophecy and the Bible* (N.P.: Top Executive Media, 2008), 63.

11. Reza F. Safa, in Richardson, *Secrets*, 9. The centrality of 9/11 is highlighted by Safa in regard to the sales figures of his works, reporting that while three thousand copies of his 1996 book *Inside Islam* sold in its first few months, after 9/11 "some thirty thousand copies were sold in a matter of weeks" (*Coming Fall*, 1).

12. Safa, *Coming Fall*, 100.

13. Arshin Adib-Moghaddam, *A Metahistory of the Clash of Civilizations: Us and Them beyond Orientalism* (New York: Columbia University Press, 2009).

14. See also Richardson, *Secrets*, 169; Shoebat and Richardson, *God's War*; T. W. Tramm, *From Abraham to Armageddon: The Convergence of Current Events, Biblical Prophecy, and Islam* (N.P.: TW Press, 2008), 217–221; Michael Youssef, *Jesus, Jihad and Peace: What Bible Prophecy Says About World Events* (Brentwood, TN: Worthy Books, 2015), 169–170.

15. Ralph W. Stice, *Arab Spring, Christian Winter: Islam Unleashed on the Church and the World* (Abbotsford, WI: ANEKO Press, 2014), xxiii–xxiv.

16. C. Heike Schotten, *Queer Terror: Life, Death, and Desire in the Settler Colony* (New York: Columbia University Press, 2018), 128.

17. Safa, *Coming Fall*, 100, 1.

18. Ralph W. Stice, *From 9/11 to 666: The Convergence of Current Events, Biblical Prophecy and the Vision of Islam* (Nashville, TN: ACW Press, 2005), 34.

19. Richardson, *Secrets*, 224; Safa, *Inside Islam*, 8, 10, 15.

20. This genealogy is given added force by the common attempt in Islamic Antichrist texts to position "Allah" as "secretly" the Baal of the Hebrew Bible (Safa, *Inside Islam*, 22; Youssef, *Peace*, 68; Shoebat and Richardson, *God's War*, 383), although this is not shared by all (Richardson, *Secrets*, 232).

21. Erin Runions, *The Babylon Complex: Theopolitical Fantasies of War, Sex, and Sovereignty* (New York: Fordham University Press, 2014), 227–234.

22. Safa, *Inside Islam*, 17. Faisal Malick differs in situating the spirit behind Islam as "the political spirit" in his *The Political Spirit* (Shippensburg, PA: Destiny Image Publishing, 2008). However, his description of it as one that "opposes the work of Christ in

the earth" (117) is functionally indistinguishable from the Antichrist spirit as outlined by other authors.

23. Richardson, *Secrets*, 18.

24. Shoebat and Richardson, *God's War*, 54.

25. Ibid., 22.

26. Safa, *Coming Fall*, 36; emphasis added. Joel Richardson also engages with ideas of "Islamic Supersessionism" in *When a Jew Rules the World: What the Bible Really Says about Israel in the Plan of God* (Washington, DC: WND Books, 2015).

27. Kathleen Biddick, *The Typological Imaginary: Circumcision, Technology, History* (Philadelphia: University of Pennsylvania Press, 2003), 4, 6.

28. Ibid., 6.

29. Such cross-tradition apocalyptic fusions are more common in Islam. See David Cook, *Contemporary Muslim Apocalyptic Literature* (Syracuse, NY: Syracuse University Press, 2005), and Jean-Pierre Filiu, *Apocalypse in Islam*, trans. M. B. DeBevoise (Berkeley: University of California Press, 2011).

30. Youssef, *Peace*, 90.

31. While Richardson's work popularized the idea after 9/11, it was forwarded earlier by both Stice's *9/11 to 666* and Robert Livingston's *Christianity and Islam: The Final Clash* (Enumclaw, WA: Wine Press Publishing, 2004), and is traceable at least to George Otis's *The Last of the Giants: Lifting the Veil on Islam and the End Times* (Grand Rapids: Baker Books, 1991).

32. Joel Richardson, *The Islamic Antichrist* (Washington, DC: WND Books, 2009), 33–50, 61–70, 77–80.

33. Ibid., 33–39, 28, 62–64.

34. Drew Griffin and Kathleen Johnson, "'Ex-Terrorist' Rakes in Homeland Security Bucks," *CNN*, July 14, 2010, available at http://www.edition.cnn.com/2011/US/07/11/terrorism.expert (accessed August 28, 2018).

35. Shoebat and Richardson, *God's War*, 57–183.

36. Steve Magill, *Revelation and the Age of Antichrist: A 21st Century Guide Through the Book of Revelation* (Enumclaw, WA: Redemption Press, 2015).

37. The most detailed counter is Chris White, *The Islamic Antichrist Debunked: A Comprehensive Critique of the Muslim Antichrist Theory* (Ducktown, TN: CWM Publishing, 2015). See also Ron Rhodes, *Unmasking the Antichrist: Dispelling the Myths, Discovering the Truth* (Eugene, OR: Harvest House, 2012); Thomas R. Horn and Cris Putnam, *On the Path of the Immortals: Exo-Vaticana, Project LUCIFER, and the Strategic Sites Where Entities Await the Appointed Time* (Crane, MO: Defender, 2015), and *The Final Roman Emperor, the Islamic Antichrist, and the Vatican's Last Crusade* (Crane, MO: Defender, 2016); and S. Douglas Woodward, *Mistaken Identity: The Case against the Islamic Antichrist* (Oklahoma City: Faith Happens Publishing, 2016).

38. For example, the Mahdi's seven-year treaty is listed as three, nine, ten, forty, or even seventy years depending on the Islamic source (Filiu, *Apocalypse in Islam*, 43), and comparisons of Mahdi and Antichrist as riding on white horses draw on framings of the white rider of Revelation 6: 2 as the Antichrist, a specific reading that stems from Billy Graham's *Approaching Hoofbeats* and omits many other interpretations of the figure—including as Christ himself. See Andrew Cunningham and Ole Peter Grell, *The Four Horsemen of the Apocalypse: Religion, War, Famine, and Death in Reformation Europe* (Cambridge: Cambridge University Press, 2000).

39. Richardson, *Islamic Antichrist*, 3–4.

40. The prominence of *taqiyya* in spiritual warfare texts seemingly emerges with Richardson's *Islamic Antichrist*. It is also found in other Islamophobic works, as discussed by Maryam El-Shall in "From Risk to Terror: Islamist Conspiracies and the Paradoxes of Post-9/11 Government," *Open Cultural Studies* 2, no. 1 (2018): 39–49.

41. Jack Smith, *Islam: The Cloak of Antichrist* (Sisters, OR: Trusted Books, 2012), 160.

42. J. Richardson, *Islamic Antichrist*, 153;

43. Shoebat and Richardson, *God's War on Terror*, 75.

44. Youssef, *Peace* 132. This claim about "concealed means" references wider Islamophobic narratives of "civilization jihad," which I cover extensively in "Islamophobic Conspiracism and Neoliberal Subjectivity: The Inassimilable Society," *Patterns of Prejudice* 52, no. 1 (2018): 1–23. This is a recurrent motif in spiritual warfare texts that discuss *taqiyya*, which often also cite the allegedly deleterious effect of "political correctness" and multiculturalism on "Western civilization" (Smith, *Islam*, 165; Tramm, *Abraham to Armageddon*, 33).

45. Richardson, *Islamic Antichrist*, 154–156.

46. Shoebat and Richardson, *God's War*. 83.

47. Youssef, *Peace*, 23; Walid Shoebat and Ben Barrack, *The Case for Islamophobia: Jihad by the Sword—America's Final Warning* (N.P.: Walid Shoebat Foundation, 2013), 70.

48. Youssef, *Peace*, 137.

49. Richardson, *Islamic Antichrist*; 156. Shoebat and Richardson, *God's War*, 75. As El-Shall notes, reading this clause "as a lie, produc[es] an odd configuration of lying that is permitted as a generalized strategy of deceit (without regard for ends or reasons) that is itself licensed by a lie" ("Risk to Terror," 44–45). While she is correct that this reading might "logically seem to undo itself" (ibid.), in spiritual warfare discourse this construction is given coherence by a demonological framework that deprives the demon(ized) of ontological and epistemological validity a priori.

50. Richardson, *Islamic Antichrist*, 162.

51. Shoebat and Barrack, *Islamophobia*, 385.

52. Analyses of the coding of the "Muslim" as inassimilable to Euro-American or Judeo-Christian selfhood are vast. For some explorations, see Khaled A. Beydoun, "'Muslim Bans' and the (Re)Making of Political Islamophobia," *University of Illinois Law Review* (2017): 1733–1774; Saba Mahmood, *Religious Difference in a Secular Age: A Minority Report* (Princeton, NJ: Princeton University Press, 2015); O'Donnell, "Islamophobic Conspiracism"; Samina Yasmeen and Nina Marković, eds. , *Muslim Citizens in the West: Spaces and Agents of Inclusion and Exclusion* (Farnham: Ashgate, 2014).

53. The symbiotic relation between domestic policing and overseas intervention is by now well-testified. See Christopher J. Coyne and Abigail R. Hall, *Tyranny Comes Home: The Domestic Fate of U.S. Militarism* (Stanford, CA: Stanford University Press, 2018); Stuart Schrader, *Badges without Borders: How Global Counterinsurgency Transformed American Policing* (Berkeley: University of California Press, 2019); Micol Seigel, *Violence Work: State Power and the Limits of Police* (Durham, NC: Duke University Press, 2018).

54. Safa, *Coming Fall*, 128. See also Malick, *Political Spirit*, 128.

55. Safa, *Coming Fall*, 101.

56. Quoted in Thomas Cincotta, *Manufacturing the Muslim Menace* (Somerville, MA: Political Research Associates, 2011), 1.

57. Shoebat and Barrack, *Islamophobia*, 365; see also Shoebat and Richardson, *God's War*, 27, 470–475.

58. Faisal Malick, *The Destiny of Islam in the End Times: Understanding God's Heart for the Muslim People* (Shippensburg, PA: Destiny Image Publishing, 2007), 223.

59. Ibid., 109.

60. Ibid., 221.

61. See Andrew Bacevich, *American Empire: The Realities and Consequences of U.S. Diplomacy* (Cambridge, MA: Harvard University Press, 2002).

62. Gil Anidjar, *Blood: A Critique of Christianity* (New York: Columbia University Press, 2014), 70.

63. Ibid., 85.

64. See also J. Kēhaulani Kauanui, *Hawaiian Blood: Colonialism and the Politics of Sovereignty and Indigeneity* (Durham, NC: Duke University Press, 2008); Saidiya Hartman, *Scenes of Subjection: Terror, Slavery, and Self-Making in Nineteenth-Century America* (Oxford: Oxford University Press, 1997).

65. Safa, *Coming Fall*, 145, 157.

66. Ibid., 157. See also Richardson, *Secrets*, 112–113; Smith, *Islam*, 25–28; Tramm, *Abraham to Armageddon*, 5–14; and Youssef, *Peace*, 51–55. Malick deviates by blaming Arab hostility to Israel on a "spirit of Esau," but the fraternal and fratricidal focus is the same (*Political Spirit*, 119–144). Such works attempt to make Muslim antisemitism a problem with "Islam," obscuring the influence of European antisemitism imported in the nineteenth and twentieth centuries. The broad use of notorious antisemitic forgery *The Protocols of the Elders of Zion* in the modern Middle East, for example, is passed over in favor of a narrow discussion of Islamic sources. For the complex roots of modern Muslim antisemitism, see Esther Webman, "Adoption of the *Protocols* in the Arab Discourse on the Arab-Israeli Conflict, Zionism, and the Jews," in *The Global Impact of the Protocols of the Elders of Zion: A Century-Old Myth*, ed. Esther Webman (New York: Routledge, 2012), 196–219, and "The Challenge of Assessing Arab/Muslim Antisemitism," *Middle Eastern Studies* 46, no. 5 (2010): 677–697.

67. For the history of "Judeo-Christianity" in Europe, see Paul Hanebrink, *A Specter Haunting Europe: The Myth of Judeo-Bolshevism* (Cambridge, MA: Harvard University Press, 2018); in America, see Amy Kaplan, *Our American Israel: The Story of an Entangled Alliance* (Cambridge, MA: Harvard University Press, 2018). For spiritual warrior's conflation between Jews and Christians, see Richardson, *Islamic Antichrist*, 6; Richardson, *Secrets*, 239; Shoebat and Richardson, *God's War*, 88.

68. Gil Anidjar, *The Jew, the Arab: A History of the Enemy* (Stanford, CA: Stanford University Press, 2003), xxi–xxii, 3–40.

69. Li, "Exception to Empire," 470–471.

70. Youssef, *Peace*, 38.

71. Safa, *Coming Fall*, 73–91, 129–150.

72. Ibid., 51.

73. Stice, *From 9/11 to 666*, and *Arab Spring, Christian Winter*.

74. Homi K. Bhabha, *The Location of Culture* (New York: Routledge, 1994), 86, 90.

75. Ibid., 91.

76. This is noteworthy given that concepts of the nation-state and the "Muslim world" itself are themselves colonial constructions. Roxanne Euben's *Enemy in the Mirror: Islamic Fundamentalism and the Limits of Modern Rationalism—A Work of Comparative Political Theory* (Princeton, NJ: Princeton University Press, 1999) and Cemil

Aydin's *The Idea of the Muslim World: A Global Intellectual History* (Cambridge, MA: Harvard University Press, 2017) both show how ideas about an essentially or originally unified *ummah* or "Muslim world" used by Islamists are rooted in a colonial fantasy of Islamic homogeneity. The Islamic menace that spiritual warriors envision is thus one produced by Western colonialism, not just in its material exigencies but also in its core ideological premises.

77. Philippe Buc, *Holy War, Martyrdom, and Terror: Christianity, Violence, and the West* (Philadelphia: University of Pennsylvania Press, 2015), 15.

78. Teresa Brennan, *Exhausting Modernity: Grounds for a New Economy* (New York: Routledge, 2000), 160.

79. Tramm, *Abraham to Armageddon*, 11.

80. Youssef, *End Times*, 195, 144.

81. Mark Hitchcock, *ISIS, Iran, Israel and the End of Days* (Eugene, OR: Harvest House, 2013), 132.

82. Youssef, *End Times*, 196; Frantz Fanon, *The Wretched of the Earth*, trans. Richard Philcox (New York: Grove Press, 2004), 16.

83. Fanon, *Wretched*, 5.

84. I take this phrase from Frantz Fanon, *Black Skin, White Masks*, trans. Charles Lam Markmann (London: Pluto, 2008), 147.

85. Safa, *Coming Fall*, 117.

86. Ibid., 111.

87. Ibid., 112.

88. Youssef, *Peace*, 210.

89. Ibid.

90. Ibid., 213.

91. Safa, *Coming Fall*, 107.

92. Stice, *From 9/11 to 666*, 30–31.

93. Safa, *Coming Fall*, 115. It is worth noting that the acts of "radical Muslim" violence Safa and others fixate on, like suicide bombings, are notoriously indiscriminate, and antiblack racism is found in many Muslim communities. For one discussion of how antiblackness and Islamophobia structure Black Muslims through distinct, even opposing regimes of identity, see Muna Mire, "Towards a Black Muslim Ontology of Resistance," *The New Inquiry*, April 29, 2015, available at https://thenewinquiry.com/towards-a-black-muslim-ontology-of-resistance (accessed June 17, 2020).

94. For the systemic exclusion of nonwhite Americans from the social contract, see Charles W. Mills, *The Racial Contract* (Ithaca, NY: Cornell University Press, 1997). For the "Black Muslim" as separatist threat, see Khabeer, *Muslim Cool*; Weisenfeld, *New World*.

95. Brittany Friedman and Zachary Sommers, "Solitary Confinement and the Nation of Islam," May 30, 2018, available at http://tif.ssrc.org/2018/05/30/solitary-confinement-and-the-nation-of-islam (accessed June 17, 2020).

96. Tramm, *Abraham to Armageddon*, 228.

97. Shoebat and Richardson, *God's War*, 464.

98. Richardson, *Secrets*, 201. Saudi "oil money" broadly is also key to the narratives of Smith (*Islam*, 218) and Youssef (*Peace*, 169). Despite its focal point in Joel Richardson's interchange with Guandolo, it is a recent addition to his eschatology, emerging with his 2016 *Mystery Babylon*.

99. Richardson, *Secrets*, 199–201. This argument is also deployed by Perry Stone in *Unleashing the Beast: The Coming Fanatical Dictator and his Ten-Nation Coalition* (Lake Mary, FL: Charisma House, 2011), 213–216. For a historical overview of Black slavery in the Muslim world, see David M. Goldenberg, *The Curse of Ham: Race and Slavery in Early Judaism, Christianity, and Islam* (Princeton, NJ: Princeton University Press, 2003).

100. Safa, *Inside Islam*, 55.

101. Laremont, "Race, Islam, and Politics," 33.

102. Ibid., 56.

103. Youssef, *Peace*, 173.

104. Jessilyn Justice, "Revival-Minded Black Pastors Denounce 'Demonic' Black Lives Matter Movement," *Charisma News*, December 5, 2015, available at www.charismanews.com/us/53756-revival-minded-black-pastors-denounce-demonic-black-lives-matter-movement (accessed November 13, 2018).

105. Gerald Flurry, "The Real Agenda Behind Black Lives Matter," *The Philadelphia Trumpet* 27, no. 5 (2016): 25.

106. Stephen E. Strang, *God and Donald Trump* (Lake Mary, FL: Charisma House, 2017), 8–9.

107. Robert L. Maginnis, *The Deeper State: Inside the War on Trump by Corrupt Elites, Secret Societies, and the Builders of an Imminent Final Empire* (Crane, MO: Defender, 2017).

108. The demonological elements of Brown's framing by his killer have been explored by Adam Kotsko in *The Prince of This World: The Life and Legacy of the Devil* (Stanford, CA: Stanford University Press, 2016), 1–4, 201, and Jared Sexton, *Black Men, Black Feminism: Lucifer's Nocturne* (New York: Palgrave Macmillan, 2017), 13–16.

109. John Burton, "Satan's Grand Strategy and God's Answer to the Black Lives Matter Crisis," *Charisma Magazine*, September 30, 2016, available online at www.charismamag.com/life/culture/27684-satan-s-strategy-and-god-s-answer-to-the-black-lives-matter-crisis (accessed November 13, 2018).

110. I adapt this term from Miriyam Aouragh, "'White Privilege' and Shortcuts to Anti-Racism," *Race and Class* 61, no. 2 (2019): 3–26. For Aouragh, "radical kinship" refers to the foundation of a new universalist alliance that both overcomes divisive tendencies and pushes towards collective emancipation, "claiming equality and justice in collective coalitions, with strong comrades not submissive allies" (21).

111. Jasbir K. Puar, *The Right to Maim: Debility, Capacity, Disability* (Durham, NC: Duke University Press, 2017), ix–xiii.

112. For the claim that support for/rejection of Israel leads directly to national flourishing/destruction, see Sean Durbin, *Righteous Gentiles: Religion, Identity, and Myth in John Hagee's Christians United for Israel* (Boston: Brill, 2019), 202–242.

113. Joel Richardson, *Mideast Beast: The Scriptural Case for an Islamic Antichrist* (Washington, DC: WND Books, 2012), 19, 52. This framing of ancient antagonism joins contemporary constructions of Israel as a "muscular nation, uncorrupted by European decadence" and thus "the epicentre of the fight to defend western civilization" from the "Islamic onslaught," a well-documented element of far-right discourse. See Liz Fekete, "The Muslim Conspiracy Theory and the Oslo Massacre," *Race and Class* 53, no. 3 (2012): 30–57.

114. Kaplan, *American Israel*, 239–241.

115. Patrisse Khan-Cullors and Asha Bendele, *When They Call You a Terrorist: A Black Lives Matter Memoir* (Edinburgh: Canongate Books, 2018); Schotten, *Queer Terror*, 129–130.

116. Schotten, *Queer Terror*, 130.

117. Katie Walker Grimes, "'Birtherism' and Anti-Blackness: The Anti-Islamic Ante-Life of Africanized Slavery," *Political Theology* 18, no. 8 (2017): 709–729. For a history of Islam in the Americas, see Sylviane Diouf, *Servants of Allah: African Muslims Enslaved in the Americas* (New York: New York University Press, 2013).

118. Grimes, "Birtherism," 717.

119. Ibid., 723.

120. Calvin L. Warren, *Ontological Terror: Blackness, Nihilism and Emancipation* (Durham, NC: Duke University Press, 2018), 9.

121. Fanon, *Black Skin*, 82–83.

122. Warren, *Ontological Terror*, 5.

123. Ibid., 6.

124. See Chapter 2. See also David Brakke, *Demons and the Making of the Monk: Spiritual Combat in Early Christianity* (Cambridge, MA: Harvard University Press, 2006), 157–181; Fanon, *Black Skin*, 146; Goldenberg, *Curse of Ham*, 50; Sexton, *Lucifer's Nocturne*. Frank B. Wilderson III also points to the Christian root of metaphysics and how "Settler power" channeled via Christianity "asserts supreme dominance over the elements of the universe" and thus shapes the "ontological modality of sovereignty." Wilderson, *Red, White, and Black: Cinema and the Structures of U.S. Antagonisms* (Durham, NC: Duke University Press, 2010), 165. However, neither he nor Warren discuss the relation to demonology directly.

125. Grimes, "Birtherism," 723.

126. Ibid. It should be clarified that this framing runs counter to certain principles of afro-pessimism, which presumes a globalization of ontological absence on the basis of antiblackness. This globalization has been criticized, for example by Annie Olaloku-Teriba in "Afro-Pessimism and the (Un)Logic of Anti-Blackness," *Historical Materialism* 26, no. 2 (2018): 96–122. My focus here is specifically on how constructions of blackness qua absence intersect with those of Islam within spiritual warfare discourse. However, a framing of Grimes's format more coherent with afro-pessimism might be effected via Calvin Warren's concept of "onticide" as a procedure for conceptualizing "(un)differentiating violence" within the fungible commodity of blackness, a "conceptual crisis" beyond humanist grammar in which the term of the human is written under erasure, both necessary and impossible. Calvin L. Warren, "Onticide: Afro-Pessimism, Gay Nigger #1, and Surplus Violence," *GLQ* 23(3) (2017): 407–408. For Warren, this is the Black queer. Here, it would be the Black Muslim. This process of (un)differentiating violence would then account for the intensified carceral logics applied to Black Muslims.

127. Weisenfeld, *New World*.

128. bell hooks, *Killing Rage: Ending Racism* (New York: Henry Holt, 1995), 12.

129. Ibid., 13.

130. Ibid., 19.

131. Safa, *Coming Fall*, 111–112.

132. Smith, *Islam*, 175. See also Tramm, *Abraham to Armageddon*, 136–137.

133. Patrick Wolfe, "Settler Colonialism and the Elimination of the Native," *Journal of Genocide Research* 8, no. 4 (2006): 388–389.

134. Saidiya Hartman, "The Belly of the World: A Note on Black Women's Labors," in *Afro-Pessimism: An Introduction*, ed. Frank B. Wilderson III (Minneapolis: Racked and Dispatched, 2017), 83.
135. Fanon, *Black Skin*, 71.
136. Safa, *Coming Fall*, 27.
137. Fanon, *Black Skin*, 146.
138. Ibid., 147, 2.

4 / Leviathan's Wake: Demonology and the Passing of Order

1. Jonas Clark, *Saboteurs in the Republic: Battling Spiritual Wickedness in High Places* (Hallandale, FL: Spirit of Life Publishing, 2010), 5–7.
2. Jonas Clark, *Destined for Dominion* (Hallandale Beach, FL: Spirit of Life Ministries, 2012), 202–206.
3. Angela Powers Flippen, *Diary of an Unlikely Warrior: A Practical Guide for Spiritual Warfare* (Bloomington, IN: WestBow Press, 2013), 44; Shawn Beaton, *Defeating the Leviathan Spirit* (Seattle: CreateSpace Independent, 2017), 4–5. In *The Leviathan Factor* (Eugene, OR: Wipf & Stock, 2017), Lawrence E. Burkholder uses the name as a direct synonym. Leviathan's gender assignment fluctuates in the texts discussed, with Beaton coding Leviathan as male, for example, while Derek P. Gilbert and Josh Peck gender the serpent female in *The Day the Earth Stands Still: Unmasking the Old Gods behind ETs, UFOs, and the Official Disclosure Movement* (Crane, MO: Defender, 2017), 162. Due to both this ambiguity and Leviathan's inherent multiplicity, I use "they" throughout this chapter.
4. Clark, *Destined*, 202.
5. Linda Rios Brook, *Lucifer's War: Understanding the Ancient Struggle between God and the Devil* (Lake Mary, FL: Charisma House, 2012), 13.
6. See Jacques Derrida, *The Death Penalty, Volume I*, trans. Peggy Kamuf (Chicago: University of Chicago Press, 2014), 24.
7. Richard Ing, *Spiritual Warfare* (New Kensington, PA: Whitaker House, 1996), 203.
8. John Robertson, *Winning the Battles in Spiritual Warfare* (Bloomington, IN: WestBow Press, 2013), 314; Clark, *Destined*, 202–206.
9. Ing, *Spiritual Warfare*, 203.
10. Ron Phillips, *Everyone's Guide to Demons and Spiritual Warfare: Simple, Powerful Tools for Outmaneuvering Satan in your Daily Life* (Lake Mary, FL: Charisma House, 2010), 147.
11. Jennifer LeClaire, *The Spiritual Warfare Battle Plan: Unmasking 15 Harassing Demons That Want to Destroy Your Life* (Lake Mary, FL: Charisma House, 2017), 28; Brook, *Lucifer's War*, 36.
12. John Eckhardt, *Deliverance and Spiritual Warfare Manual: A Comprehensive Guide to Living Free* (Lake Mary, FL: Charisma House, 2014), 150.
13. Donald C. Polaski, *Authoring the End: The Isaiah Apocalypse and Intertextuality* (Boston: Brill, 2001), 284.
14. Neil Forsyth, *The Old Enemy: Satan and the Combat Myth* (Princeton, NJ: Princeton University Press, 1987), 62. Forsyth's text remains perhaps the best overview of pre-Christian precedents of the "combat myth."
15. LeClaire, *Battle Plan*, 26.
16. Robertson, *Winning the Battles*, 314.

17. Eckhardt, *Deliverance Manual*, 145.

18. Michael S. Heiser, *The Unseen Realm: Recovering the Supernatural Worldview of the Bible* (Bellingham, WA: Lexham, 2015), 153.

19. For connections between Psalms 74:12–17, Genesis 1, and earlier *chaoskampf* narratives, see John Day, *God's Conflict with the Dragon of the Sea: Echoes of a Canaanite Myth in the Old Testament* (Cambridge: Cambridge University Press, 1985).

20. Gilbert and Peck, *Earth Stands Still*, 157.

21. Ibid., 159.

22. Ibid., 162.

23. Heiser, *Unseen Realm*, 382–3.

24. Catherine Keller, *Face of the Deep: A Theology of Becoming* (New York: Routledge, 2003), 26, 62. See Burkholder (*Leviathan Factor*) for a direct mapping of Leviathan onto nature's unstable elements.

25. Michael Kleu and Madelene Eayrs, *Who Are You? A Practical Deliverance Guide* (Maitland, FL: Xulon Press 2010), 154–155.

26. Ibid.

27. Bill Vincent, *Spiritual Warfare: The Complete Collection* (Litchfield, IL: Revival Waves of Glory Books & Publishing, 2015), 510.

28. LeClaire, *Battle Plan*, 28.

29. Flippen, *Diary*, 49.

30. Robertson, *Winning the Battles*, 315.

31. LeClaire, *Battle Plan*, 26.

32. Richard Hotchkin, *Leviathan Exposed: Overcoming the Hidden Schemes of a Demonic King* (Maricopa, AZ: XP Publications, 2015), 23.

33. Phillips, *Everyone's Guide*, 149.

34. For the role of "political correctness" in the political right, see John K. Wilson, *The Myth of Political Correctness: The Conservative Attack on Higher Education* (Durham, NC: Duke University Press, 1995).

35. LeClaire, *Battle Plan*, 25.

36. Right Wing Watch, "Jacobs: OWS Protests Driven By 'A Power of Darkness,'" www.youtube.com/watch?v=niQaw8Kq2qw.

37. Lance Wallnau, "Three Secrets of American Politics," *7m Underground*, March 17, 2016.

38. Lance Wallnau, "Breaking Controlling Spirits," *Mishpochah* 1706 (November 2017), n.p.

39. Dave Williams, *The Miracle Results of Fasting: Discover the Amazing Benefits in Your Spirit, Soul and Body* (Tulsa, OK: Harrison House, 2004), 65–67.

40. Sara Ahmed, *On Being Included: Racism and Diversity in Institutional Life* (Durham, NC: Duke University Press, 2012), 153.

41. W. Scott Poole, *Never Surrender: Confederate Memory and Conservatism in the South Carolina Upcountry* (Athens: University of Georgia Press, 2004), 80.

42. David M. Goldenberg, *The Curse of Ham: Race and Slavery in Early Judaism, Christianity, and Islam* (Princeton, NJ: Princeton University Press, 2003), 160–161.

43. Clark, *Destined*, 123.

44. See Paul Hanebrink, *A Specter Haunting Europe: The Myth of Judeo-Bolshevism* (Cambridge, MA: Harvard University Press, 2018).

45. Gil Anidjar, *Blood: A Critique of Christianity* (New York: Columbia University Press, 2014), 143.

46. Adam Kotsko, *Neoliberalism's Demons: On the Political Theology of Late Capital* (Stanford, CA: Stanford University Press, 2018), 73, 85.

47. Ibid., 85–95.

48. Phillips, *Everyone's Guide*, 147; Ing, *Spiritual Warfare*, 203.

49. Eckhardt, *Deliverance Manual*, 154–155.

50. Pier Giuseppe Monateri, *Dominus Mundi: Political Sublime and World Order* (London: Bloomsbury, 2018).

51. Clark is not alone here. See Eckhardt, *Deliverance Manual*, 150; Robertson, *Winning the Battles*, 313; Cindy Trimm, *The Rules of Engagement: The Art of Strategic Prayer and Spiritual Warfare* (Lake Mary, FL: Charisma House, 2008), 169, 180.

52. Jean Bodin, *On the Demon-Mania of Witches*, trans. Randy A. Scott (Toronto: Centre for Reformation and Renaissance Studies, 1995), 48. For an in-depth analysis of Bodin's political demonology, see my article "Witchcraft, Statecraft, Mancraft: On the Demonological Foundations of Sovereignty," *Political Theology* 21, no. 6 (2020): 530–549.

53. Monateri, *Dominus Mundi*.

54. C. Heike Schotten, *Queer Terror: Life, Death, and Desire in the Settler Colony* (New York: Columbia University Press, 2018), 41.

55. Ibid., 44–45.

56. A. P. Martinich, *The Two Gods of Leviathan: Thomas Hobbes on Religion and Politics* (Cambridge: Cambridge University Press, 1992), 336.

57. Thomas Hobbes, *Leviathan* (Cambridge: Cambridge University Press, 1996), 418.

58. Ibid., 416–417; italics in original.

59. Ibid., 316.

60. Ibid., 306–320.

61. James Martel, *Subverting the Leviathan: Reading Thomas Hobbes as a Radical Democrat* (New York: Columbia University Press, 2007), 112.

62. Ibid., 120–122.

63. Geoffrey Bennington, "Sovereign Stupidity and Autoimmunity," in *Derrida and the Time of the Political*, ed. Pheng Cheah and Suzanne Guerlac (Durham, NC: Duke University Press, 2009), 97–113.

64. Tess Maltese, *Instruction Handbook for Deliverance, AKA Exorcism* (Maitland, FL: Xulon Press, 2007), 49.

65. Ing, *Spiritual Warfare*, 204.

66. LeClaire, *Battle Plan*, 32.

67. Ing, *Spiritual Warfare*, 205.

68. Christopher Pye, "The Sovereign, the Theater, and the Kingdome of Darkness: Hobbes and the Spectacle of Power," *Representations* 8 (1984): 96.

69. Peter J. Steinberger, "Hobbes, Rousseau and the Modern Conception of the State," *Journal of Politics* 70, no. 3 (2008): 596.

70. Hobbes, *Leviathan*, 111.

71. Teresa Brennan, *Exhausting Modernity Exhausting Modernity: Grounds for a New Economy* (New York: Routledge, 2000), 160.

72. Flippen, *Diary*, 44.

73. Hobbes, *Leviathan*, 269. Hobbes held that when entering into the collective authoring of the sovereign by/as the general will, an individual divests "himselfe of the liberty of hindering another of the benefit of his own right to the same thing" (190).

74. Hobbes, *Leviathan*, 18.
75. Michael P. Krom, *The Limits of Reason in Hobbes's Commonwealth* (New York: Continuum, 2011), 159.
76. Sara Melzer, *Colonizer or Colonized? The Hidden Stories of Early Modern French Culture* (Philadelphia: University of Pennsylvania Press, 2012), 181.
77. Ing, *Spiritual Warfare*, 203.
78. Robertson, *Winning the Battles*, 314.
79. Hobbes, *Leviathan*, 89.
80. Srinivas Aravamudan, "Hobbes and America," in *The Postcolonial Enlightenment: Eighteenth-Century Colonialism and Postcolonial Theory*, ed. Daniel Carey and Lynn Festa (Oxford: Oxford University Press, 2009), 42–43.
81. Ibid., 53–55.
82. Horn and Putnam, *Immortals*, 120–129.
83. Bob Larson and Laura Larson, *Set Your Family Free: Breaking Satan's Assignments Against Your Household* (Shippensburg, PA: Destiny Image, 2017), 45–46.
84. "Cindy Jacobs, Television Prophet, Says Native Americans Must Repent For Ancestor's Pagan Beliefs," *Huffington Post*, August 28, 2013, available at https://www.huffingtonpost.com/2013/06/05/cindy-jacobs-native-americans-repent_n_3390601.html (accessed June 25, 2018).
85. Horn and Putnam, *Immortals*, 125.
86. See, for example, Olivia A. Bloechl, *Native American Song at the Frontier of Early Modern Music* (Cambridge: Cambridge University Press, 2008), 58–79; David Tavárez, *The Invisible War: Indigenous Devotions, Discipline, and Dissent in Colonial Mexico* (Stanford, CA: Stanford University Press, 2011), 279.
87. Andrea Smith, *Native Americans and the Christian Right: The Gendered Politics of Unlikely Alliances* (Durham, NC: Duke University Press, 2008).
88. For the complex history of Quetzalcoatl, see David Carrasco, *Quetzalcoatl and the Irony of Empire: Myth and Prophecies in the Aztec Tradition* (Chicago: University of Chicago Press, 1982).
89. Ing, *Spiritual Warfare*, 266–267. For one discussion of the politics of blood quantum, see J. Kēhaulani Kauanui, *Hawaiian Blood: Colonialism and the Politics of Sovereignty and Indigeneity* (Durham, NC: Duke University Press, 2008).
90. Ing, *Spiritual Warfare*, 275, 289.
91. Lorenzo Veracini, "Introducing *Settler Colonial Studies*," *Settler Colonial Studies* 1, no. 1 (2011): 3.
92. Audra Simpson, *Mohawk Interruptus: Political Life across the Borders of Settler States* (Durham, NC: Duke University Press, 2014), 11–12.
93. Mark Rifkin, *Beyond Settler Time: Temporal Sovereignty and Indigenous Self-Determination* (Durham, NC: Duke University Press, 2017), vii.
94. Nicole Anderson, *Derrida: Ethics under Erasure* (New York: Continuum, 2012), 91, 99.
95. Jacques Derrida, *Specters of Marx: The State of the Debt, the Work of Mourning, and the New International*, trans. Peggy Kamuf (New York: Routledge, 1993), 64–65.
96. Kotsko, *Neoliberalism's Demons*, 97–99.
97. Stefano Harney and Fred Moten, *The Undercommons: Fugitive Planning and Black Study* (New York: Minor Compositions, 2013), 11.
98. Ibid., 96.
99. Sara Ahmed, *Willful Subjects* (Durham, NC: Duke University Press, 2014), 207.

100. Stephen Dillon, *Fugitive Life: The Queer Politics of the Prison State* (Durham, NC: Duke University Press, 2018), 145.

101. Yountae An, *The Decolonial Abyss: Mysticism and Cosmopolitics from the Ruins* (New York: Fordham University Press, 2016), 119.

102. Ibid., 94, 92.

103. Ibid., 114.

104. Christina Sharpe, *In the Wake: On Blackness and Being* (Durham, NC: Duke University Press, 2016), 14.

105. Ibid., 9, 11.

106. Vincent, *Spiritual Warfare*, 486.

107. I use "flesh" here in two intertwined senses. The first is as the site of the high crime committed on African women and men that precedes and exceeds discursive obfuscation, and the capture of which strips it as a site of ethics, outlined by Hortense J. Spillers in "Mama's Baby, Papa's Maybe: An American Grammar Book," in *Afro-Pessimism: An Introduction*, edited by Frank B. Wilderson III (Minneapolis: Racked and Dispatched, 2017), 95–97. The second is the theological sense in which "Flesh is defined as a kind of law of sin," a "counterfeit" of "vital corporeality" whose invocation is "used to control the malleability of bodies," as discussed by Mayra Rivera, *Poetics of the Flesh* (Durham, NC: Duke University Press, 2015), 92, 154.

108. Neil Forsyth has discussed the origin of demonic subjectivity through the experience of subjection to divine power, here via *Paradise Lost*. Neil Forsyth, *The Satanic Epic* (Princeton, NJ: Princeton University Press, 2002), 150.

109. Polaski, *Authoring the End*, 285.

110. Giorgio Agamben, *The Time That Remains: A Commentary on the Letter to the Romans*, trans. Patricia Daily (Stanford, CA: Stanford University Press, 2005), 77.

111. Martel, *Subverting the Leviathan*, 3.

112. Ibid., 239.

113. Ibid., 247.

114. Quoted in ibid., 10.

115. Hamilton Carroll, *Affirmative Reaction: New Formations of White Masculinity* (Durham, NC: Duke University Press, 2011), 8.

116. Polaski, *Authoring the End*, 285.

117. Elizabeth Freeman, *Time Binds: Queer Temporalities, Queer Histories* (Durham, NC: Duke University Press, 2010), 3.

118. Monateri, *Dominus Mundi*.

119. Michael Hardt and Antonio Negri, *Assembly* (Oxford: Oxford University Press, 2017), xx–xxi.

120. Jared Sexton, *Black Men, Black Feminism: Lucifer's Nocturne* (New York: Palgrave Macmillan, 2017), 19.

121. Ibid.

122. Jacques Derrida, *Rogues: Two Essays on Reason*, trans. Pascale-Anne Brault and Michael Naas (Stanford, CA: Stanford University Press, 2004), 114.

123. Ibid., 124.

124. Hotchkin, *Leviathan Exposed*, 47–48.

125. An, *Abyss*, 115–116; emphasis in original.

126. Freeman, *Time Binds*, 109.

127. Dillon, *Fugitive Life*, 154.

Conclusion: Paradise Refused

1. Mark Taylor and Mary Colbert, *The Trump Prophesies: The Astonishing True Story of the Man Who Saw Tomorrow . . . and What He Says Is Coming Next* (Crane, MO: Defender, 2017), 146–147.
2. Ibid., 157.
3. Ibid.,154.
4. Ibid., 133–134, 206–207.
5. Steve Strang, "Prophesies of Trump Revealed with Mark Taylor," podcast, *Strang Report by Steve Strang*, Charisma Podcast Network, January 15, 2018.
6. Walter Mignolo, *The Darker Side of Western Modernity: Global Futures, Decolonial Options* (Durham, NC: Duke University Press, 2011).
7. Taylor and Colbert, *Trump Prophecies*, 94.
8. Jennifer LeClaire, "Prophecy: After Wicked Kingdom Toppled—Jezebel Curse Broken off America," *Awakening*, November 9, 2016, available at www.jenniferleclaire.org/articles/prophecy-after-wicked-kingdom-toppled-jezebel-curse-broken-off-america.
9. Gil Anidjar, *Blood: A Critique of Christianity* (New York: Columbia University Press, 2014), 32.
10. Gloria Anzaldúa, *Borderland/La Frontera: The New Mestiza* (San Francisco: Aunt Lute Books, 1987), 3, 85.
11. Linda Rios Brook, *Lucifer's War: Understanding the Ancient Struggle Between God and the Devil* (Lake Mary, FL: Charisma House, 2012), 13.
12. Jacques Derrida, *Given Time: I. Counterfeit Money*, trans. Peggy Kamuf (Chicago: Chicago University Press, 1992), 160.
13. Ibid., 161.
14. Achille Mbembe, "Necropolitics," trans. Libby Meintjes, *Public Culture* 15, no. 1 (2003): 27.
15. Ray Pritchard, *Stealth Attack: Protecting Yourself Against Satan's Plan to Destroy Your Life* (Chicago: Moody Publishers, 2007), 18.
16. Ibid., 12, 19.
17. Ibid., 18, 20.
18. C. Heike Schotten, *Queer Terror: Life, Death, and Desire in the Settler Colony* (New York: Columbia University Press, 2018), 147.
19. Ibid., 21.
20. Judith Halberstam, *The Queer Art of Failure* (Durham, NC: Duke University Press, 2011), 88.
21. Marcella Althaus-Reid, *The Queer God* (New York: Routledge, 2003), 134.
22. Pritchard, *Stealth Attack*, 20–21.
23. Cindy Jacobs, *Possessing the Gates of the Enemy: A Training Manual for Militant Intercession*, 3rd ed. (Grand Rapids, MI: Chosen Books, 2009), 74; Bill Johnson and Lance Wallnau, *Invading Babylon: The 7 Mountain Mandate* (Shippensburg, PA: Destiny Image Publishing, 2013), 22; Jennifer Eivaz, *The Intercessors Handbook: How to Pray with Boldness, Authority, and Supernatural Power* (Bloomington, MN: Chosen Books, 2016), 168.
24. Derek Prince, *Pulling Down Strongholds* (Charlotte, NC: Whitaker House, 2013), 6.
25. Brook, *Lucifer's War*, 24.

26. Jacques Derrida, *The Death Penalty, Volume I*, trans. Peggy Kamuf (Chicago: University of Chicago Press, 2014), 24. For a longer discussion of this use of demons, see my essay "Literature, Theology, Survival," in *The Hermeneutics of Hell: Visions and Representations of the Devil in World Literature*, ed. Gregor Thuswaldner and Daniel Russ (New York: Palgrave Macmillan, 2017), 143–164.

27. Adam Kotsko, *The Prince of This World: The Life and Legacy of the Devil* (Stanford, CA: Stanford University Press, 2016), 187.

28. Ibid., 192–3.

29. Sara Ahmed, *Willful Subjects* (Durham, NC: Duke University Press, 2014), 136.

30. Kotsko, *Prince*, 192.

31. Jared Sexton, *Black Men, Black Feminism: Lucifer's Nocturne* (New York: Palgrave Macmillan, 2017), 15

32. Kotsko, *Prince*, 204.

33. Ibid., 206.

34. Ahmed, *Willful Subjects*, 177.

35. Ibid., 184.

36. Adam Kotsko, *Neoliberalism's Demons: On the Political Theology of Late Capital* (Stanford, CA: Stanford University Press, 2018), 143–144.

37. Ibid., 144.

38. I take the term "martial politics" here from Alison Howell, "Forget 'Militarization': Race, Disability and the 'Martial Politics' of the Police and of the University," *International Feminist Journal of Politics* 20, no. 2 (2018): 117–136.

39. Schotten, *Queer Terror*, 45.

40. Lauren Berlant, *Cruel Optimism* (Durham, NC: Duke University Press, 2011).

41. I take this phrase from Ruben van Luijk, *Children of Lucifer: The Origins of Modern Religious Satanism* (Oxford: Oxford University Press, 2016), 392.

42. Walter Mignolo, *The Darker Side of Western Modernity: Global Futures, Decolonial Options* (Durham, NC: Duke University Press, 2011), xxv.

43. Quoted in Jared Sexton, "The *Vel* of Slavery: Tracking the Figure of the Unsovereign," in *Afro-Pessimism: An Introduction*, ed. Frank B. Wilderson III (Minneapolis: Racked & Dispatched, 2017), 148–169.

44. Sexton, *Lucifer's Nocturne*, 19.

45. James C. Scott, *Seeing Like a State: How Certain Schemes to Improve the Human Condition Have Failed* (New Haven, CT: Yale University Press, 1999), 183.

46. Mignolo, *Darker Side*, 310.

47. Alice Patterson, *Bridging the Racial and Political Divide: How Godly Politics Can Transform a Nation* (San Jose, CA: Transformational Publications, 2010), 146.

48. Neel Ahuja, *Biosecurities: Disease Intervention, Empire, and the Government of Species* (Durham, NC: Duke University Press, 2016), 166.

49. I adapt this closing adage from Stefano Harney and Fred Moten's framing of the goal of abolition in *The Undercommons: Fugitive Planning and Black Study* (New York: Minor Compositions, 2013).

Bibliography

Adib-Moghaddam, Arshin. *A Metahistory of the Clash of Civilizations: Us and Them beyond Orientalism*. New York: Columbia University Press, 2009.

Adogame, Afe. "Engaging the Rhetoric of Spiritual Warfare: The Public Face of Aladura in Diaspora." *Journal of Religion in Africa* 34, no. 4 (2004): 493–522.

Agamben, Giorgio. *The Time That Remains: A Commentary on the Letter to the Romans*. Translated by Patricia Daily. Stanford, CA: Stanford University Press, 2005.

Ahmed, Sara. "Bogus." *Feministkilljoys*. October 27, 2016. Available at feministkilljoys.com/2016/10/27/bogus (accessed November 19, 2017).

———. *On Being Included: Racism and Diversity in Institutional Life*. Durham, NC: Duke University Press, 2012.

———. "Some Striking Feature: Whiteness and Institutional Passing." *Feministkilljoys*. June 14, 2015. Available at feministkilljoys.com/2015/06/14/some-striking-feature-whiteness-and-institutional-passing (accessed January 5, 2018).

———. *Strange Encounters: Embodied Others in Post-Coloniality*. New York: Routledge, 2000.

———. *Willful Subjects*. Durham, NC: Duke University Press, 2014.

Ahuja, Neel. *Bioinsecurities: Disease Intervention, Empire, and the Government of Species*. Durham, NC: Duke University Press, 2016.

Almond, Philip C. *Satan: A New Biography*. Ithaca, NY: Cornell University Press, 2014.

Althaus-Reid, Marcella. *The Queer God*. New York: Routledge, 2003.

Althoff, Andrea. *Divided by Faith and Ethnicity: Religious Pluralism and the Problem of Race in Guatemala*. Berlin: De Gruyter, 2014.

An, Yountae. *The Decolonial Abyss: Mysticism and Cosmopolitics from the Ruins*. New York: Fordham University Press, 2016.
Anderson, Ben. "Affective Atmospheres." *Emotion, Space and Society* 2 (2009): 77–81.
Anderson, Nicole. *Derrida: Ethics under Erasure*. New York: Continuum, 2012.
Anidjar, Gil. *Blood: A Critique of Christianity*. New York: Columbia University Press, 2014.
———. *The Jew, the Arab: A History of the Enemy*. Stanford, CA: Stanford University Press, 2003.
Anzaldúa, Gloria. *Borderland/La Frontera: The New Mestiza*. San Francisco: Aunt Lute Books, 1987.
Aouragh, Miriyam. "'White Privilege' and Shortcuts to Anti-Racism." *Race and Class* 61, no. 2 (2019): 3–26.
Appadurai, Arjun. *Fear of Small Numbers: An Essay on the Geography of Anger*. Durham, NC: Duke University Press, 2006.
Aravamudan, Srinivas. "Hobbes and America." In *The Postcolonial Enlightenment: Eighteenth-Century Colonialism and Postcolonial Theory*, edited by Daniel Carey and Lynn Festa, 37–70. Oxford: Oxford University Press, 2009.
Asad, Talal. *Formations of the Secular: Christianity, Islam, Modernity*. Stanford, CA: Stanford University Press, 2003.
———. "The Idea of an Anthropology of Islam." *Qui Parle* 17, no. 2 (2009): 1–30.
Aydin, Cemil. *The Idea of the Muslim World: A Global Intellectual History*. Cambridge, MA: Harvard University Press, 2017.
Bacevich, Andrew. *American Empire: The Realities and Consequences of U.S. Diplomacy*. Cambridge, MA: Harvard University Press, 2002.
Baker, Charlotte. *The Extreme Jezebel Spirit: False Prophetic Operations*. Paw Creek, NC: It's All About Him Media & Publishing, 2015.
Balkun, Mary McAleer. *The American Counterfeit: Authenticity and Identity in American Literature and Culture*. Tuscaloosa: University of Alabama Press, 2006.
Barkun, Michael. *Chasing Phantoms: Reality, Imagination, and Homeland Security since 9/11*. Chapel Hill: University of North Carolina Press, 2011.
Bartholomew, Richard. "Publishing, Celebrity, and the Globalisation of Conservative Protestantism." *Journal of Contemporary Religion* 21, no. 1 (2006): 1–13.
Beaton, Shawn. *Defeating the Leviathan Spirit*. Seattle: CreateSpace Independent, 2017.
Beauchamp, Toby. *Going Stealth: Transgender Politics and U.S. Surveillance Practices*. Durham, NC: Duke University Press, 2019.
Bennington, Geoffrey. "Sovereign Stupidity and Autoimmunity." In *Derrida and the Time of the Political*, edited by Pheng Cheah and Suzanne Guerlac, 97–113. Durham, NC: Duke University Press, 2009.
Berlant, Lauren. *Cruel Optimism*. Durham, NC: Duke University Press, 2011.
Beydoun, Khaled A. "'Muslim Bans' and the (Re)Making of Political Islamophobia." *University of Illinois Law Review* (2017): 1733–1774.

Bhabha, Homi K. *The Location of Culture*. New York: Routledge, 1994.
Bhambra, Gurminda K. *Rethinking Modernity: Postcolonialism and the Sociological Imagination*. New York: Palgrave Macmillan, 2007.
Biddick, Kathleen. *The Typological Imaginary: Circumcision, Technology, History*. Philadelphia: University of Pennsylvania Press, 2003.
Bivins, Jason C. "By Demons Driven: Religious Teratologies." In *Speaking of Monsters: A Teratological Anthology*, edited by Caroline Joan S. Picart and John Edgar Browning, 105–116. New York: Palgrave Macmillan, 2012.
———. *Religion of Fear: The Politics of Horror in Conservative Evangelicalism*. Oxford: Oxford University Press, 2008.
Bloechl, Olivia A. *Native American Song at the Frontier of Early Modern Music*. Cambridge: Cambridge University Press, 2008.
Bodin, Jean. *On the Demon-Mania of Witches*. Translated by Randy A. Scott. Toronto: Centre for Reformation and Renaissance Studies, 1995.
Bongma, Elias Kifon. *African Witchcraft and Otherness: A Philosophical and Theological Critique of Intersubjective Relations*. Albany: State University of New York Press, 2001.
Boureau, Alain. *Satan the Heretic: The Birth of Demonology in the Medieval West*. Translated by Teresa Lavender Fagan. Chicago: University of Chicago Press, 2006.
Boyer, Paul. "The Growth of Fundamentalist Apocalyptic in the United States." In *The Encyclopedia of Apocalypticism, Vol. III: Apocalypticism in the Modern Period and the Contemporary Age*, edited by Stephen J. Stein, 140–178. London: Continuum, 2000.
Brakke, David. *Demons and the Making of the Monk: Spiritual Combat in Early Christianity*. Cambridge, MA: Harvard University Press, 2006.
Bremmer, Jan N. *The Rise and Fall of the Afterlife*. New York: Routledge, 2002.
Brennan, Teresa. *Exhausting Modernity: Grounds for a New Economy*. New York: Routledge, 2000.
Brook, Linda Rios. *Lucifer's War: Understanding the Ancient Struggle Between God and the Devil*. Lake Mary, FL: Charisma House, 2012.
Brown, Michael L. *Jezebel's War with America: The Plot to Destroy Our Country and What We Can Do to Turn the Tide*. Lake Mary, FL: Charisma House, 2019.
Brown, Wendy. *Walled States, Waning Sovereignty*. New York: Zone Books, 2010.
Buc, Philippe. *Holy War, Martyrdom, and Terror: Christianity, Violence, and the West*. Philadelphia: University of Pennsylvania Press, 2015.
Burkholder, Lawrence E. *The Leviathan Factor*. Eugene, OR: Wipf & Stock, 2017.
Butler, Judith. "Bodies and Power, Revisited." *Radical Philosophy* 114 (2002): 13–19.
Byrd, Jodi. *Transit of Empire: Indigenous Critiques of Colonialism*. Minneapolis: University of Minnesota Press, 2011.

Carrasco, David. *Quetzalcoatl and the Irony of Empire: Myth and Prophecies in the Aztec Tradition*. Chicago: University of Chicago Press, 1982.
Carroll, Hamilton. *Affirmative Reaction: New Formations of White Masculinity*. Durham, NC: Duke University Press, 2011.
Certeau, Michel de. *The Possession at Loudun*. Translated by Michael B. Smith. Chicago: University of Chicago Press, 2000.
Chang, Natasha V. *The Crisis-Woman: Body Politics and the Modern Woman in Fascist Italy*. Toronto: University of Toronto Press, 2015.
Charisma House. *Spiritual Warfare Bible: New King James Version*. Lake Mary, FL: Charisma House, 2012.
Christerson, Brad, and Richard W. Flory, *The Rise of Network Christianity: How Independent Leaders Are Changing the Religious Landscape*. Oxford: Oxford University Press, 2017.
Christiaan, Edwin. *Divorce Jezebel: Remarry Christ Your Destiny*. Los Angeles: The Original God, Inc., 2015.
Cincotta, Thomas. *Manufacturing the Muslim Menace*. Somerville, MA: Political Research Associates, 2011.
Clark, Jonas. *Destined for Dominion*. Hallandale Beach, FL: Spirit of Life Ministries, 2012.
———. *Jezebel: Seducing Goddess of War*. Revised edition. Hallandale Beach, FL: Spirit of Life Publishing, 2004.
———. *Saboteurs in the Republic: Battling Spiritual Wickedness in High Places*. Hallandale, FL: Spirit of Life Publishing, 2010.
Clark, Stuart. *Thinking with Demons: The Idea of Witchcraft in Early Modern Europe*. Oxford: Oxford University Press, 1997.
Cohen, Stanley. *Folk Devils and Moral Panics: The Creation of the Mods and Rockers*. New York: Routledge, 2002.
Cole, Philip. *The Myth of Evil*. Edinburgh: Edinburgh University Press, 2006.
Conn, Steven. *Americans against the City: Anti-Urbanism in the Twentieth Century*. Oxford: Oxford University Press, 2014.
Connolly, William C. *Christianity and Capitalism, American Style*. Durham, NC: Duke University Press, 2008.
Cook, David. *Contemporary Muslim Apocalyptic Literature*. Syracuse, NY: Syracuse University Press, 2005.
Coyne, Christopher J., and Abigail R. Hall. *Tyranny Comes Home: The Domestic Fate of U.S. Militarism*. Stanford, CA: Stanford University Press, 2018.
Cunningham, Andrew, and Ole Peter Grell. *The Four Horsemen of the Apocalypse: Religion, War, Famine, and Death in Reformation Europe*. Cambridge: Cambridge University Press, 2000.
Curtis, Edward E., IV. *The Call of Bilal: Islam in the African Diaspora*. Princeton, NJ: Princeton University Press, 2016.
Day, John. *God's Conflict with the Dragon of the Sea: Echoes of a Canaanite Myth in the Old Testament*. Cambridge: Cambridge University Press, 1985.

Denike, Margaret. "The Devil's Insatiable Sex: A Genealogy of Evil Incarnate." *Hypatia* 18, no. 1 (2003): 10–43.
Derrida, Jacques. *Aporias*. Translated by Thomas Dutoit. Stanford, CA: Stanford University Press, 1993.
———. *Archive Fever: A Freudian Impression*. Translated by Eric Prenowitz. Chicago: University of Chicago Press, 1996.
———. *The Death Penalty, Volume I*. Translated by Peggy Kamuf. Chicago: University of Chicago Press, 2014.
———. *Given Time: I. Counterfeit Money*. Translated by Peggy Kamuf. Chicago: University of Chicago Press, 1992.
———. *Monolingualism of the Other; Or, The Prosthesis of Origin*. Translated by Patrick Mensah. Stanford, CA: Stanford University Press, 1998.
———. *Rogues: Two Essays on Reason*. Translated by Pascale-Anne Brault and Michael Naas. Stanford, CA: Stanford University Press, 2004.
———. *Specters of Marx: The State of the Debt, the Work of Mourning, and the New International*. Translated by Peggy Kamuf. New York: Routledge, 1993.
———. *Without Alibi*. Translated by Peggy Kamuf. Stanford, CA: Stanford University Press, 2002.
———. *Writing and Difference*. New York: Routledge, 2001.
Derry, Elizabeth. *Lucifer Is Not Satan, Part II*. Maitland, FL: Xulon Press, 2007.
de Vries, Hent, and Lawrence E. Sullivan, eds. *Political Theologies: Public Religions in a Post-Secular World*. New York: Fordham University Press, 2006.
Dillon, Stephen. *Fugitive Life: The Queer Politics of the Prison State*. Durham, NC: Duke University Press, 2018.
Diouf, Sylviane A. *Servants of Allah: African Muslims Enslaved in the Americas*. New York: New York University Press, 2013.
Duff, Paul Brooks. *Who Rides the Beast? Prophetic Rivalry and the Rhetoric of Crisis in the Churches of the Apocalypse*. Oxford: Oxford University Press, 2001.
Durbin, Sean. *Righteous Gentiles: Religion, Identity, and Myth in John Hagee's Christians United for Israel*. Boston: Brill, 2019.
Eckhardt, John. *Deliverance and Spiritual Warfare Manual: A Comprehensive Guide to Living Free*. Lake Mary, FL: Charisma House, 2014.
Edelman, Lee. "Ever After: History, Negativity, and the Social." *South Atlantic Quarterly* 106, no. 3 (2007): 469–476.
———. *No Future: Queer Theory and the Death Drive*. Durham, NC: Duke University Press, 2004.
Eivaz, Jennifer. *The Intercessors Handbook: How to Pray with Boldness, Authority, and Supernatural Power*. Bloomington, MN: Chosen Books, 2016.
El-Shall, Maryam. "From Risk to Terror: Islamist Conspiracies and the Paradoxes of Post-9/11 Government." *Open Cultural Studies* 2, no. 1 (2018): 39–49.
Esposito, John L. *The Islamic Threat: Myth or Reality?* Oxford: Oxford University Press, 1999.

Euben, Roxanne. *Enemy in the Mirror: Islamic Fundamentalism and the Limits of Modern Rationalism—A Work of Comparative Political Theory*. Princeton, NJ: Princeton University Press, 1999.

Fanon, Frantz. *Black Skin, White Masks*. Translated by Charles Lam Markmann. London: Pluto, 2008.

———. *The Wretched of the Earth*. Translated by Richard Philcox. New York: Grove Press, 2004.

Fekete, Liz. "The Muslim Conspiracy Theory and the Oslo Massacre." *Race and Class* 53, no. 3 (2012): 30–57.

Fer, Yannick. "Pentecostal Prayer as Personal Communication and Invisible Institutional Work." In *A Sociology of Prayer*, edited by Giuseppe Gordon and Linda Woodhead, 49–66. Farnham: Ashgate, 2015.

Fields, Karen. *Revival and Rebellion in Colonial Central Africa*. Princeton, NJ: Princeton University Press, 1985.

Filiu, Jean-Pierre. *Apocalypse in Islam*. Translated by M. B. DeBevoise. Berkeley: University of California Press, 2011.

Flippen, Angela Powers. *Diary of an Unlikely Warrior: A Practical Guide for Spiritual Warfare* Bloomington, IN: WestBow Press, 2013.

Flurry, Gerald. "The Real Agenda Behind Black Lives Matter." *The Philadelphia Trumpet* 27, no. 5 (2016): 15–17, 23–25.

Forsyth, Neil. *The Old Enemy: Satan and the Combat Myth*. Princeton, NJ: Princeton University Press, 1987.

———. *The Satanic Epic*. Princeton, NJ: Princeton University Press, 2002.

Forti, Simona. *New Demons: Rethinking Power and Evil Today*. Translated by Zakiya Hanafi. Stanford, CA: Stanford University Press, 2015.

Foucault, Michel. *The Archaeology of Knowledge*. Translated by A. M. Sheridan Smith. New York: Routledge, 2002.

Frangipane, Francis. *The Jezebel Spirit*. Cedar Rapids, IA: Arrow Publications, 1995.

———. *The Three Battlegrounds: An In-Depth View of the Three Arenas of Spiritual Warfare: The Mind, the Church and the Heavenly Places*. Revised edition. Cedar Rapids, MI: Arrow Publications, 2006.

Freed, Sandie. *Breaking the Threefold Demonic Cord: How to Discern and Defeat the Lies of Jezebel, Athaliah, and Delilah* Grand Rapids, MI: Chosen Books, 2008.

———. *Destiny Thieves: Defeating Seducing Spirits and Achieving Your Purpose in God*. Bloomington, MN: Chosen Books, 2007.

———. *The Jezebel Yoke: Breaking Free from Bondage and Deception*. Bloomington, MN: Chosen Books, 2012.

Freeman, Elizabeth. *Time Binds: Queer Temporalities, Queer Histories*. Durham, NC: Duke University Press, 2010.

Gaines, Janet Howe. *Music in the Old Bones: Jezebel through the Ages*. Edwardsville: Southern Illinois University Press, 1999.

Gardner, James. *The War with Babylon*. Maitland, FL: Xulon Press, 2004.

Gilbert, Derek P. *The Great Inception: Satan's PSYOPS from Eden to Armageddon*. Crane, MO: Defender, 2016.

Gilbert, Derek P., and Josh Peck, *The Day the Earth Stands Still: Unmasking the Old Gods behind ETs, UFOs, and the Official Disclosure Movement*. Crane, MO: Defender, 2017.

Ginsberg, Elaine K. *Passing and the Fictions of Identity*. Durham, NC: Duke University Press, 1996.

Goldenberg, David M. *The Curse of Ham: Race and Slavery in Early Judaism, Christianity, and Islam*. Princeton, NJ: Princeton University Press, 2003.

Goldingay, John, and David Payne. *Isaiah 40–55, Volume 1: A Critical and Exegetical Commentary*. London: Continuum, 2006.

Graham, Billy. *Approaching Hoofbeats: The Four Horsemen of the Apocalypse*. New York: Avon, 1985.

Greenwood, Rebecca. *Glory Warfare: How the Presence of God Empowers You to Destroy the Works of Darkness*. Shippensburg, PA: Destiny Image, 2018.

Grimes, Katie Walker. "'Birtherism' and Anti-Blackness: The Anti-Islamic Ante-Life of Africanized Slavery." *Political Theology* 18, no. 8 (2017): 709–729.

Grosz, Elizabeth. *Architecture from the Outside: Essays on Virtual and Real Space*. Cambridge, MA: MIT Press, 2001.

Grypeou, Emmanouela. "'A People Will Emerge from the Desert': Apocalyptic Perceptions of the Early Muslim Conquests in Contemporary Eastern Christian Literature." In *Apocalypticism and Eschatology in Late Antiquity: Encounters in the Abrahamic Religions, 6th–8th Centuries*, edited by Hagil Amirav, Emmanouela Grypeou, and Guy Stroumsa, 291–310. Leuven: Peeters, 2017.

Gunn, Joshua. "The Rhetoric of Exorcism: George W. Bush and the Return of Political Demonology." *Western Journal of Communication* 68, no. 1 (2004): 1–23.

Hackman, Melissa. "A Sinful Landscape: Moral and Sexual Geographies in Cape Town, South Africa." *Social Analysis* 59, no. 3 (2015): 105–125.

Halberstam, Judith. *The Queer Art of Failure*. Durham, NC: Duke University Press, 2011.

Hall, Stuart. *Representation: Cultural Representations and Signifying Practices*. Milton Keynes: Open University Press, 1997.

Hanebrink, Paul. *A Specter Haunting Europe: The Myth of Judeo-Bolshevism*. Cambridge, MA: Harvard University Press, 2018.

Harney, Stefano, and Fred Moten. *The Undercommons: Fugitive Planning and Black Study*. New York: Minor Compositions, 2013.

Hardt, Michael, and Antonio Negri. *Assembly*. Oxford: Oxford University Press, 2017.

Harris, Harriet. *Fundamentalism and Evangelicals*. Oxford: Oxford University Press, 2008.

Hartman, Saidiya V. "The Belly of the World: A Note on Black Women's Labors." In *Afro-Pessimism: An Introduction*, edited by Frank B. Wilderson III, 80–90. Minneapolis: Racked and Dispatched, 2017.

———. *Scenes of Subjection: Terror, Slavery, and Self-Making in Nineteenth-Century America.* Oxford: Oxford University Press, 1997.
Heiser, Michael S. *The Unseen Realm: Recovering the Supernatural Worldview of the Bible.* Bellingham, WA: Lexham, 2015.
Heward-Mills, Dag. *Lay People and the Ministry.* London: Parchment House, 1999.
Hitchcock, Mark. *ISIS, Iran, Israel and the End of Days.* Eugene, OR: Harvest House, 2013.
———. *101 Answers to Questions about Satan, Demons, and Spiritual Warfare.* Eugene, OR: Harvest House, 2014.
Hobbes, Thomas. *Leviathan.* Cambridge: Cambridge University Press, 1996.
Holvast, René. *Spiritual Mapping in the United States and Argentina, 1989–2005: A Geography of Fear.* Boston: Brill, 2008.
Honig, Bonnie. *Emergency Politics: Paradox, Law, Democracy.* Princeton, NJ: Princeton University Press, 2009.
hooks, bell. *Killing Rage: Ending Racism.* New York: Henry Holt, 1995.
Hopson, Douglas. *Understanding the Traits of Jezebel.* Memphis, TN: PH Publishing, 2015.
Horn, Thomas R. *Saboteurs: Shadow Government in Quest of the Final World Order.* Crane, MO: Defender, 2017.
———. *Spiritual Warfare: The Invisible Invasion.* Lafayette, LA: Huntington House, 1998.
Horn, Thomas R., and Cris Putnam. *The Final Roman Emperor, the Islamic Antichrist, and the Vatican's Last Crusade* Crane, MO: Defender, 2016.
———. *On the Path of the Immortals: Exo-Vaticana, Project LUCIFER, and the Strategic Sites Where Entities Await the Appointed Time.* Crane, MO: Defender, 2015.
Hotchkin, Richard. *Leviathan Exposed: Overcoming the Hidden Schemes of a Demonic King.* Maricopa, AZ: XP Publications, 2015.
Howell, Alison. "Forget 'Militarization': Race, Disability and the 'Martial Politics' of the Police and of the University." *International Feminist Journal of Politics* 20, no. 2 (2018): 117–136.
Ing, Richard. *Spiritual Warfare.* New Kensington, PA: Whitaker House, 1996.
Isiah, Medina. *Defeat. Dethrone. Conquer: Supreme Strategies for Victorious Living.* Bloomington, IN: WestBow Press, 2012.
Ivie, Robert L., and Oscar Giner. *Hunt the Devil: A Demonology of US War Culture.* Tuscaloosa: University of Alabama Press, 2015.
Jackson, John Paul. *Unmasking the Jezebel Spirit.* Flower Mound, TX: Streams Ministries International, 2002.
Jackson, Sherman A. *Islam and the Blackamerican: Looking toward the Third Resurrection.* Oxford: Oxford University Press, 2005.
Jacobs, Cindy. *Possessing the Gates of the Enemy: A Training Manual for Militant Intercession.* 3rd edition. Grand Rapids, MI: Chosen Books, 2009.
———. *The Supernatural Life.* Grand Rapids, MI: Chosen Books, 2005.

Jakobsen, Janet R., and Ann Pellegrini. *Love the Sin: Sexual Regulation and the Limits of Religious Tolerance*. New York: New York University Press, 2003.

Jansen, Yolande. "Postsecularism, Piety and Fanaticism: Reflections on Jürgen Habermas' and Saba Mahmood's Critiques of Secularism." *Philosophy and Social Criticism* 37, no. 9 (2011): 977–998.

Johnson, Bill, and Lance Wallnau. *Invading Babylon: The 7 Mountain Mandate*. Shippensburg, PA: Destiny Image Publishing, 2013.

Jordan, Mark D. *The Invention of Sodomy in Christian Theology*. Chicago: University of Chicago Press, 2007.

Jorgensen, Dan. "Third Wave Evangelism and the Politics of the Global in Papua New Guinea: Spiritual Warfare and the Recreation of Place in Telefolmin." *Oceania* 75, no. 4 (2005): 444–461.

Josephson-Storm, Jason A. *The Myth of Disenchantment: Magic, Modernity, and the Birth of the Human Sciences*. Chicago: University of Chicago Press, 2017.

Kahn, Jeffrey S. *Islands of Sovereignty: Haitian Migration and the Borders of Empire*. Chicago: University of Chicago Press, 2019.

Kahn, Paul W. *Out of Eden: Adam and Eve and the Problem of Evil*. Princeton, NJ: Princeton University Press, 2007.

Kalleres, Dayna S. *City of Demons: Violence, Ritual, and Christian Power in Late Antiquity*. Berkeley: University of California Press, 2015.

Kaplan, Amy. *Our American Israel: The Story of an Entangled Alliance*. Cambridge, MA: Harvard University Press, 2018.

Kauanui, J. Kēhaulani. *Hawaiian Blood: Colonialism and the Politics of Sovereignty and Indigeneity*. Durham, NC: Duke University Press, 2008.

———. *Paradoxes of Hawaiian Sovereignty: Land, Sex, and the Colonial Politics of State Nationalism*. Durham, NC: Duke University Press, 2019.

Keller, Catherine. *Apocalypse Now and Then: A Feminist Guide to the End of the World*. Boston: Beacon Press, 1996.

———. *Face of the Deep: A Theology of Becoming*. New York: Routledge, 2003.

———. *God and Power: Counter-Apocalyptic Journeys*. Minneapolis: Fortress Press, 2005.

Kennedy, Liam. *Race and Urban Space in Contemporary American Culture*. Chicago: Fitzroy Dearborn, 2000.

Khabeer, Su'ad Abdul. *Muslim Cool: Race, Religion, and Hip Hop in the United States*. New York: New York University Press, 2016.

Khan-Cullors, Patrisse, and Asha Bendele. *When They Call You a Terrorist: A Black Lives Matter Memoir*. Edinburgh: Canongate Books, 2018.

Khanna, Ranjana. *Dark Continents: Psychoanalysis and Colonialism*. Durham, NC: Duke University Press, 2003.

Kidd, Thomas S. *American Christians and Islam: Evangelical Culture and Muslims from the Colonial Period to the Age of Terrorism*. Princeton, NJ: Princeton University Press, 2009.

Kleu, Michael, and Madelene Eayrs. *Who Are You? A Practical Deliverance Guide* Maitland, FL: Xulon Press 2010.

Kotsko, Adam. *Neoliberalism's Demons: On the Political Theology of Late Capital*. Stanford, CA: Stanford University Press, 2018.

———. *The Prince of This World: The Life and Legacy of the Devil*. Stanford, CA: Stanford University Press, 2016.

Krause, Virginia. *Witchcraft, Demonology, and Confession in Early Modern France*. Cambridge: Cambridge University Press, 2015.

Krom, Michael P. *The Limits of Reason in Hobbes's Commonwealth*. New York: Continuum, 2011.

Laremont, Ricardo René. "Race, Islam, and Politics: Differing Visions among Black American Muslims." *Journal of Islamic Studies* 10, no. 1 (1999): 33–49.

Larson, Bob. *Demon-Proofing Prayers: Bob Larson's Guide to Winning Spiritual Warfare*. Shippensburg, PA: Destiny Image Publishers, 2011.

———. *Jezebel: Defeating Your #1 Spiritual Enemy*. Shippensburg, PA: Destiny Image Publishers, 2015.

———. *Larson's Book of Spiritual Warfare*. Nashville, TN: Thomas Nelson, 1999.

Larson, Bob, and Laura Larson, *Set Your Family Free: Breaking Satan's Assignments against Your Household*. Shippensburg, PA: Destiny Image, 2017.

Leath, Jennifer S. "Revising Jezebel Politics: Towards a New Black Sexual Ethic." In *Black Intersectionalities: A Critique for the 21st Century*, edited by Monica Michlin and Jean-Paul Rocchi. 195–210. Liverpool: Liverpool University Press, 2013.

LeClaire, Jennifer. *Jezebel's Puppets: Exposing the Agenda of False Prophets*. Lake Mary, FL: Charisma House, 2016.

———. *Satan's Deadly Trio: Defeating the Deceptions of Jezebel, Religion and Witchcraft*. Bloomington, MN: Chosen Books, 2014.

———. *The Spiritual Warfare Battle Plan: Unmasking 15 Harassing Demons That Want to Destroy Your Life*. Lake Mary, FL: Charisma House, 2017.

———. *The Spiritual Warrior's Guide to Defeating Jezebel*. Bloomington, MN: Chosen Books, 2013.

———. *Waging Prophetic Warfare: Effective Prayer Strategies to Defeat the Enemy*. Lake Mary, FL: Charisma House, 2016.

Lee, Matthew T., Margaret M. Poloma, and Stephen G. Post. *The Heart of Religion: Spiritual Empowerment, Benevolence, and the Experience of God's Love*. Oxford: Oxford University Press, 2013.

Li, Darryl. "From Exception to Empire: Sovereignty, Carceral Circulation, and the 'Global War on Terror.'" In *Ethnographies of U.S. Empire*, edited by Carole McGranahan and John F. Collins, 456–475. Durham, NC: Duke University Press, 2018.

———. "A Jihadism Anti-Primer." *MERP* 276. 2015. Available at https://merip.org/2015/12/a-jihadism-anti-primer.

Lincoln, Bruce. *Gods and Demons, Priests and Scholars: Critical Explorations in the History of Religions*. Chicago: University of Chicago Press, 2012.

———. *Religion, Empire, and Torture: The Case of Achaemenian Persia with a Postscript on Abu Ghraib*. Chicago: University of Chicago Press, 2007.

Livingston, Robert. *Christianity and Islam: The Final Clash.* Enumclaw, WA: WinePress Publishing, 2004.
Lomax, Tamura. *Jezebel Unhinged: Loosing the Black Female Body in Religion and Culture.* Durham, NC: Duke University Press, 2018.
Long, Thomas L. *AIDS and American Apocalypse: The Cultural Semiotics of an Epidemic.* Albany: State University of New York Press, 2005.
Lorenzo, Victor. "Evangelizing a City Dedicated to Darkness." In *Breaking Spiritual Strongholds in Your City,* edited by C. Peter Wagner, 163–182. Shippensburg, PA: Destiny Images Publisher, 2015.
Lowenstein, Adam. *Shocking Representation: Historical Trauma, National Cinema, and the Modern Horror Film.* New York: Columbia University Press, 2005.
Maggi, Armando. "Christian Demonology in Contemporary American Popular Culture." *Social Research: An International Quarterly* 81, no. 4 (2014): 769–793.
———. *Satan's Rhetoric: A Study of Renaissance Demonology.* Chicago: University of Chicago Press, 2001.
Magill, Steve. *Revelation and the Age of Antichrist: A 21st Century Guide through the Book of Revelation.* Enumclaw, WA: Redemption Press, 2015.
Maginnis, Robert L. *The Deeper State: Inside the War on Trump by Corrupt Elites, Secret Societies, and the Builders of an Imminent Final Empire.* Crane, MO: Defender, 2017.
Mahmood, Saba. *Religious Difference in a Secular Age: A Minority Report.* Princeton, NJ: Princeton University Press, 2015.
Malick, Faisal. *The Destiny of Islam in the End Times: Understanding God's Heart for the Muslim People.* Shippensburg, PA: Destiny Image Publishing, 2007.
———. *The Political Spirit.* Shippensburg, PA: Destiny Image Publishing, 2008.
Maltese, Tess. *Instruction Handbook for Deliverance, AKA Exorcism.* Maitland, FL: Xulon Press, 2007.
Manjikian, Mary. *Apocalypse and Post-Politics: The Romance of the End.* Lanham, MD: Lexington Books, 2012.
Marshall, Ruth. "Destroying Arguments and Capitivating Thoughts: Spiritual Warfare Prayer as Global Praxis." *Journal of Religious and Political Practice* 2, no. 1 (2016): 92–113.
Martel, James. *Subverting the Leviathan: Reading Thomas Hobbes as a Radical Democrat.* New York: Columbia University Press, 2007.
Martinich, A. P. *The Two Gods of Leviathan: Thomas Hobbes on Religion and Politics.* Cambridge: Cambridge University Press, 1992.
Mason, Carol. "Cracked Babies and the Partial Birth of a Nation: Millennialism and Fetal Citizenship." *Cultural Studies* 14, no. 1 (2000): 35–60.
Mathewes, Charles T. *Evil and the Augustinian Tradition.* Cambridge: Cambridge University Press, 2004.
Mbembe, Achille. "Necropolitics." Translated by Libby Meintjes. *Public Culture* 15, no. 1 (2003): 11–40.

McAlister, Elizabeth. "From Slave Revolt to a Blood Pact with Satan: The Evangelical Rewriting of Haitian History." *Studies in Religion/Sciences Religieuses* 41, no. 2 (2012): 187–215.

———. "Globalization and the Religious Production of Space." *Journal for the Scientific Study of Religion* 44 (2005): 249–255.

———. "Race, Gender, and Christian Diaspora: New Pentecostal Intersectionalities and Haiti." In *Spirit on the Move: Black Women and Pentecostalism in Africa and the Diaspora*, edited by Judith Casselberry and Elizabeth A. Pritchard, 44–64. Durham, NC: Duke University Press, 2019.

McCloud, Sean. *American Possessions: Fighting Demons in the Contemporary United States*. Oxford: Oxford University Press, 2015.

———. "Mapping the Spatial Limbos of Spiritual Warfare: Haunted Houses, Defiled Land and the Horrors of History." *Material Religion* 9, no. 2 (2013): 166–185.

McKittrick, Katherine. *Demonic Grounds: Black Women and the Cartographies of Struggle*. Minneapolis: University of Minnesota Press, 2006.

McMillan, Timothy J. "Black Magic: Witchcraft, Race, and Resistance in Colonial New England." *Journal of Black Studies* 25, no. 1 (1994): 99–117.

Melzer, Sara. *Colonizer or Colonized? The Hidden Stories of Early Modern French Culture*. Philadelphia: University of Pennsylvania Press, 2012.

Mendieta, Eduardo, and Jonathan VanAntwerpen, eds. *The Power of Religion in the Public Sphere*. New York: Columbia University Press, 2011.

Menzie, Nicola A. "Does Heaven Have a Wall like the One Trump Wants at the US-Mexico Border?" *Faithfully Magazine*, January 14, 2019.

Mignolo, Walter. *The Darker Side of Western Modernity: Global Futures, Decolonial Options*. Durham, NC: Duke University Press, 2011.

Miller, Donald E., Kimon H. Sargeant, and Richard W. Flory. *Spirit and Power: The Growth and Global Impact of Pentecostalism*. Oxford: Oxford University Press, 2013.

Miller-Davenport, Sarah. *Gateway State: Hawai'i and the Cultural Transformation of American Empire*. Princeton, NJ: Princeton University Press, 2019.

Mills, Charles W. *The Racial Contract*. Ithaca, NY: Cornell University Press, 1997.

Milton, John. *Paradise Lost*. Oxford: Oxford University Press, 2008.

Monateri, Pier Giuseppe. *Dominus Mundi: Political Sublime and World Order*. London: Bloomsbury, 2018.

Moslener, Sara. *Virgin Nation: Sexual Purity and American Adolescence*. Oxford: Oxford University Press, 2015.

Mullen, Harryette. "Optic White: Blackness and the Production of Whiteness." *Diacritics* 24, nos. 2–3 (1994): 71–89.

Muñoz, José Esteban. *Cruising Utopia: The Then and There of Queer Futurity*. New York: New York University Press, 2009.

O'Donnell, S. Jonathon. "Islamophobic Conspiracism and Neoliberal Subjectivity: The Inassimilable Society." *Patterns of Prejudice* 52, no. 1 (2018): 1–23.

———. "Literature, Theology, Survival." In *The Hermeneutics of Hell: Visions and Representations of the Devil in World Literature*, edited by Gregor Thuswaldner and Daniel Russ, 143–164. New York: Palgrave Macmillan, 2017.
———. "Unipolar Dispensations: Exceptionalism, Empire, and the End of One America." *Political Theology* 20, no. 1 (2019): 66–84.
———. "Witchcraft, Statecraft, Mancraft: On the Demonological Foundations of Sovereignty." *Political Theology* 21, no. 6 (2020): 530–549.
Olaloku-Teriba, Annie. "Afro-Pessimism and the (Un)Logic of Anti-Blackness." *Historical Materialism* 26, no. 2 (2018): 96–122.
Otis, George. *The Last of the Giants: Lifting the Veil on Islam and the End Times*. Minneapolis: Chosen Books, 1991.
Partridge, Christopher. "Alien Demonology: The Christian Roots of the Malevolent Extraterrestrial in UFO Religions and Abduction Spiritualties." *Religion* 34, no. 3 (2004): 163–189.
———. *The Re-Enchantment of the West: Alternative Spiritualities, Sacralization, Popular Culture, and Occulture, Volumes 1 & 2*. London: T&T Clark, 2005.
Patterson, Alice. *Bridging the Racial and Political Divide: How Godly Politics Can Transform a Nation*. San Jose, CA: Transformational Publications, 2010.
Perkinson, James W. "Reversing the Gaze: European Race Discourses as Modern Witchcraft Practice." *Journal of the American Academy of Religion* 72, no. 3 (2004): 603–629.
Perugini, Nicola, and Neve Gordon. *The Human Right to Dominate*. Oxford: Oxford University Press, 2015.
Phillips, Ron. *Everyone's Guide to Demons and Spiritual Warfare: Simple, Powerful Tools for Outmaneuvering Satan in your Daily Life*. Lake Mary, FL: Charisma House, 2010.
Pippin, Tina. *Apocalyptic Bodies: The Biblical End of the World in Text and Image*. New York: Routledge, 1999.
Polaski, Donald C. *Authoring the End: The Isaiah Apocalypse and Intertextuality*. Boston: Brill, 2001.
Poole, W. Scott. *Never Surrender: Confederate Memory and Conservatism in the South Carolina Upcountry*. Athens: University of Georgia Press, 2004.
Prince, Derek. *Pulling Down Strongholds* Charlotte, NC: Whitaker House, 2013.
———. *Secrets of a Prayer Warrior*. Bloomington, MN: Chosen Books, 2009.
Pritchard, Ray. *Stealth Attack: Protecting Yourself Against Satan's Plan to Destroy Your Life*. Chicago: Moody Publishers, 2007.
Puar, Jasbir K. *The Right to Maim: Debility, Capacity, Disability*. Durham, NC: Duke University Press, 2017.
———. *Terrorist Assemblages: Homonationalism in Queer Times*. Durham, NC: Duke University Press, 2007.
Pye, Christopher. "The Sovereign, the Theater, and the Kingdome of Darkness: Hobbes and the Spectacle of Power." *Representations* 8 (1984): 84–106.
Quinby, Lee. *Millennial Seductions: A Skeptic Confronts Apocalyptic Culture*. Ithaca, NY: Cornell University Press, 1999.

Quinn, Frederick. *The Sum of All Heresies*. Oxford: Oxford University Press, 2008.
Ramberg, Lucinda. *Given to the Goddess: South Indian Devadasis and the Sexuality of Religion*. Durham, NC: Duke University Press, 2014.
Rhodes, Ron. *Unmasking the Antichrist: Dispelling the Myths, Discovering the Truth*. Eugene, OR: Harvest House, 2012.
Richards, Larry. *The Full Armor of God: Defending Your Life from Satan's Schemes*. Bloomington, MN: Chosen Books, 2013.
Richardson, Don. *Secrets of the Koran: Revealing Insights into Islam's Holy Book*. Minneapolis, MN: Bethany House, 2003.
Richardson, Joel. *The Islamic Antichrist*. Washington, DC: WND Books, 2009.
———. *Mideast Beast: The Scriptural Case for an Islamic Antichrist*. Washington, DC: WND Books, 2012.
———. *Mystery Babylon: Unlocking the Bible's Greatest Prophetic Mystery*. Washington, DC: WND Books, 2016.
———. *When a Jew Rules the World: What the Bible Really says about Israel in the Plan of God*. Washington, DC: WND Books, 2015.
Richter, Don. *Overcoming the Attack of the Jezebel Spirit: The Church under Siege*. Maitland, FL: Xulon Press, 2005.
Rifkin, Mark. *Beyond Settler Time: Temporal Sovereignty and Indigenous Self-Determination*. Durham, NC: Duke University Press, 2017.
Rivera, Mayra. *Poetics of the Flesh*. Durham, NC: Duke University Press, 2015.
Robertson, John. *Winning the Battles in Spiritual Warfare*. Bloomington, IN: WestBow Press, 2013.
Rogin, Michael Paul. *Ronald Reagan: The Movie, and Other Episodes of Political Demonology*. Berkeley: University of California Press, 1987.
Runions, Erin. *The Babylon Complex: Theopolitical Fantasies of War, Sex, and Sovereignty*. New York: Fordham University Press, 2014.
Russell, Jeffrey Burton. *The Devil: Perceptions of Evil from Antiquity to Primitive Christianity*. Ithaca, NY: Cornell University Press, 1977.
———. *Lucifer: The Devil in the Middle Ages*. Ithaca, NY: Cornell University Press, 1984.
———. *Mephistopheles: The Devil in the Modern World*. Ithaca, NY: Cornell University Press, 1986.
———. *Satan: The Early Christian Tradition*. Ithaca, NY: Cornell University Press, 1981.
Safa, Reza F. *The Coming Fall of Islam in Iran: Thousands of Muslims Find Christ in the Midst of Persecution*. Lake Mary, FL: Charisma House, 2006.
———. *Inside Islam: Exposing and Reaching the World of Islam*. Lake Mary, FL: Charisma House, 1996.
———. *The Rise and Fall of Islam: How America Can Win the War Against Radical Islam and Terrorism*. Sevierville, TN: Insight, 2004.
Sampson, Steve. *Confronting Jezebel: Discerning and Defeating the Spirit of Control*. Revised edition. Bloomington, MN: Chosen Books, 2012.

Sassen, Saskia. *The Global City: New York, London, Tokyo.* 2nd ed. Princeton, NJ: Princeton University Press, 2001.
Schlossberg, Linda. "Rites of Passing." In *Passing: Identity and Interpretation in Sexuality, Race, and Religion,* edited by María Carla Sánchez and Linda Schlossberg, 1–12. New York: New York University Press, 2001.
Schneider, Laurel C. *Beyond Monotheism: A Theology of Multiplicity.* New York: Routledge, 2008.
Schott, Landon. *Gay Awareness: Discovering the Heart of the Father & the Mind of Christ on Sexuality.* Austin, TX: Famous Publishing, 2016.
———. *Jezebel: The Witch Is Back.* Spokane, WA: Famous Publishing, 2013.
Schotten, C. Heike. *Queer Terror: Life, Death, and Desire in the Settler Colony.* New York: Columbia University Press, 2018.
Schrader, Stuart. *Badges without Borders: How Global Counterinsurgency Transformed American Policing.* Berkeley: University of California Press, 2019.
Scott, James C. *Seeing Like a State: How Certain Schemes to Improve the Human Condition Have Failed.* New Haven, CT: Yale University Press, 1999.
Sedgwick, Eve Kosofsky. *Epistemology of the Closet.* Berkeley: University of California Press, 1990.
Seigel, Micol. *Violence Work: State Power and the Limits of Police.* Durham, NC: Duke University Press, 2018.
Sexton, Jared. *Amalgamation Schemes: Antiblackness and the Critique of Multiracialism.* Minneapolis: University of Minnesota Press, 2008.
———. *Black Men, Black Feminism: Lucifer's Nocturne.* New York: Palgrave Macmillan, 2017.
———. "The *Vel* of Slavery: Tracking the Figure of the Unsovereign." In *Afro-Pessimism: An Introduction,* edited by Frank B. Wilderson III, 148–169. Minneapolis: Racked & Dispatched, 2017.
Sharpe, Christina. *In the Wake: On Blackness and Being.* Durham, NC: Duke University Press, 2016.
Sheth, Falguni A. *Towards a Political Philosophy of Race.* Albany: State University of New York Press, 2009.
Shoebat, Walid, and Joel Richardson. *God's War on Terror: Islam, Prophecy and the Bible.* N.P.: Top Executive Media, 2008.
Shoebat, Walid, and Ben Barrack. *The Case for Islamophobia: Jihad by the SWord—America's Final Warning.* N.P.: Walid Shoebat Foundation, 2013.
Simpson, Audra. *Mohawk Interruptus: Political Life across the Borders of Settler States.* Durham, NC: Duke University Press, 2014.
Singh, Nikhil Pal. *Race and America's Long War.* Berkeley: University of California Press, 2017.
Smith, Andrea. *Native Americans and the Christian Right: The Gendered Politics of Unlikely Alliances.* Durham, NC: Duke University Press, 2008.
Smith, Eddie. *Making Sense of Spiritual Warfare.* Minneapolis: Bethany House, 2008.
Smith, Jack. *Islam: The Cloak of Antichrist.* Sisters, OR: Trusted Books, 2012.

Smith, Mark S. *The Early History of God: Yahweh and the Other Deities in Ancient Israel*. Cambridge: William B. Eerdmans, 2002.
Solnit, Rebecca. *Storming the Gates of Paradise: Landscapes for Politics*. Berkeley: University of California Press, 2007.
Spillers, Hortense J. "Mama's Baby, Papa's Maybe: An American Grammar Book." In *Afro-Pessimism: An Introduction*, edited by Frank B. Wilderson III, 91–122. Minneapolis: Racked and Dispatched, 2017.
Spivak, Gayatri Chakravorty. *A Critique of Postcolonial Reason: Towards a History of the Vanishing Present*. Cambridge, MA: Harvard University Press, 1999.
———. "The Rani of Sirmur: An Essay on Reading the Archives." *History and Theory* 24, no. 3 (1985): 247–272.
Stambach, Amy. "Spiritual Warfare 101: Preparing the Student for Christian Battle." *Journal of Religion in Africa* 39 (2009): 137–157.
Stanley, Eric. "Near Life, Queer Death: Overkill and Ontological Capture." *Social Text* 107 (2011): 1–19.
Stark, Trudie, and Hans van Deventer. "The 'Jezebel Spirit': A Scholarly Inquiry." *Verbum et Ecclesia* 30, no. 2 (2009): 68–76.
Steinberger, Peter J. "Hobbes, Rousseau and the Modern Conception of the State." *Journal of Politics* 70, no. 3 (2008): 595–611.
Stephens, Walter. *Demon Lovers: Witchcraft, Sex, and the Crisis of Belief*. Chicago: University of Chicago Press, 2002.
Stice, Ralph W. *Arab Spring, Christian Winter: Islam Unleashed on the Church and the World*. Abbotsford, WI: ANEKO Press, 2014.
———. *From 9/11 to 666: The Convergence of Current Events, Biblical Prophecy and the Vision of Islam*. Nashville, TN: ACW Press, 2005.
Stone, Perry. *Unleashing the Beast: The Coming Fanatical Dictator and his Ten-Nation Coalition*. Lake Mary, FL: Charisma House, 2011.
Strang, Stephen E. *God and Donald Trump*. Lake Mary, FL: Charisma House, 2017.
Strhan, Anna. *Aliens and Strangers? The Struggle for Coherence in the Everyday Lives of Evangelicals*. Oxford: Oxford University Press, 2015.
Strongman, Roberto. *Queering Black Atlantic Religion: Transcorporeality in Candomblé, Santería, and Vodou*. Durham, NC: Duke University Press, 2019.
Sturm, Tristan. "Prophetic Eyes: The Theatricality of Mark Hitchcock's Premillennial Geopolitics." *Geopolitics* 11, no. 2 (2011): 231–255.
Sutton, Matthew Avery. *American Apocalypse: A History of Modern Evangelicalism*. Cambridge, MA: Harvard University Press, 2014.
Tanner, John S. *Anxiety in Eden: A Kierkegaardian Reading of Paradise Lost*. Oxford: Oxford University Press, 1992.
Tavárez, David. *The Invisible War: Indigenous Devotions, Discipline, and Dissent in Colonial Mexico*. Stanford, CA: Stanford University Press, 2011.
Taylor, Charles. *A Secular Age*. Cambridge, MA: Harvard University Press, 2017.

Taylor, Mark, and Mary Colbert. *The Trump Prophesies: The Astonishing True Story of the Man Who Saw Tomorrow . . . and What He Says Is Coming Next.* Crane, MO: Defender, 2017.
Tramm, T. W. *From Abraham to Armageddon: The Convergence of Current Events, Biblical Prophecy, and Islam.* N.P.: TW Press, 2008.
Trimm, Cindy. *The Rules of Engagement: The Art of Strategic Prayer and Spiritual Warfare.* Lake Mary, FL: Charisma House, 2008.
van Luijk, Ruben. *Children of Lucifer: The Origins of Modern Religious Satanism.* Oxford: Oxford University Press, 2016.
Veracini, Lorenzo. "Introducing *Settler Colonial Studies*." *Settler Colonial Studies* 1, no. 1 (2011): 1–12.
Vergès, Françoise. *Monsters and Revolutionaries: Colonial Family Romance and Métissage.* Durham, NC: Duke University Press, 1999.
Vincent, Bill. *Spiritual Warfare: The Complete Collection.* Litchfield, IL: Revival Waves of Glory Books & Publishing, 2015.
Wagner, C. Peter. *Spiritual Warfare Strategy: Confronting Spiritual Powers.* Shippensburg, PA: Destiny Image Publishers, 1996.
——. "The Visible and the Invisible." In *Breaking Spiritual Strongholds in Your City,* edited by C. Peter Wagner, 51–72. Shippensburg, PA: Destiny Image Publishers, 2015.
Wald, Gayle. *Crossing the Line: Racial Passing in Twentieth-Century U.S. Literature and Culture.* Durham, NC: Duke University Press, 2000.
Wallnau, Lance. "Breaking Controlling Spirits." *Mishpochah* 1706 (November 2017).
——. "Three Secrets of American Politics." *7m Underground,* March 17, 2016.
Warren, Calvin L. "Onticide: Afro-Pessimism, Gay Nigger #1, and Surplus Violence." *GLQ* 23, no. 3 (2017): 391–418.
——. *Ontological Terror: Blackness, Nihilism and Emancipation.* Durham, NC: Duke University Press, 2018.
Weber, Cynthia. *Queer International Relations: Sovereignty, Sexuality, and the Will to Knowledge.* Oxford: Oxford University Press, 2016.
Webman, Esther. "Adoption of the *Protocols* in the Arab Discourse on the Arab-Israeli Conflict, Zionism, and the Jews." In *The Global Impact of the Protocols of the Elders of Zion: A Century-Old Myth,* edited by Esther Webman, 196–219. New York: Routledge, 2012.
——. "The Challenge of Assessing Arab/Muslim Antisemitism." *Middle Eastern Studies* 46, no. 5 (2010): 677–697.
Weheliye, Alexander G. *Habeas Viscus: Racializing Assemblages, Biopolitics, and Black Feminist Theories of the Human.* Durham, NC: Duke University Press, 2014.
Weisenfeld, Judith. *New World A-Coming: Black Religion and Racial Identity during the Great Migration.* New York: New York University Press, 2016.
Weston, Kath. *Families We Choose: Lesbians, Gays, Kinship.* New York: Columbia University Press, 1997.

White, Chris. *The Islamic Antichrist Debunked: A Comprehensive Critique of the Muslim Antichrist Theory.* Ducktown, TN: CWM Publishing, 2015.

White, Thomas. *The Believer's Guide to Spiritual Warfare.* Ann Arbor, MI: Servant Publications, 1990.

Wilderson, Frank B, III. *Red, White, and Black: Cinema and the Structures of U.S. Antagonisms.* Durham, NC: Duke University Press, 2010.

Williams, Dave. *The Miracle Results of Fasting: Discover the Amazing Benefits in Your Spirit, Soul and Body.* Tulsa, OK: Harrison House, 2004.

Williams, Diana D. *The Jezebel Spirit: The Unseen Opponent to Divine Purpose.* Bloomington, IN: Booktango, 2012.

Wilson, John K. *The Myth of Political Correctness: The Conservative Attack on Higher Education.* Durham, NC: Duke University Press, 1995.

Wolfe, Patrick. "Settler Colonialism and the Elimination of the Native." *Journal of Genocide Research* 8, no. 4 (2006): 387–409.

Woodward, S. Douglas. *Mistaken Identity: The Case Against the Islamic Antichrist.* Oklahoma City: Faith Happens Publishing, 2016.

Worthen, Molly. *Apostles of Reason: The Crisis of Authority in American Evangelicalism.* Oxford: Oxford University Press, 2013.

Wynter, Sylvia. "Unsettling the Coloniality of Being/Truth/Power/Freedom: Towards the Human, After Man, Its Overrepresentation—An Argument." *CR: The New Centennial Review* 3, no. 3 (2003): 257–337.

Yasmeen, Samina, and Nina Marković, eds. *Muslim Citizens in the West: Spaces and Agents of Inclusion and Exclusion.* Farnham: Ashgate, 2014.

Youssef, Michael. *The Barbarians Are Here: Preventing the Collapse of Western Civilization in Times of Terrorism.* Franklin, TN: Worthy Books, 2017.

———. *End Times and the Secret of the Mahdi: Unlocking the Mystery of Revelation and the Antichrist.* Brentwood, TN: Worthy Books, 2016.

———. *Jesus, Jihad and Peace: What Bible Prophecy Says About World Events.* Brentwood, TN: Worthy Books, 2015.

Zhou, Xiaojing. *Cities of Others: Reimagining Urban Spaces in Asian American Literature.* Seattle: University of Washington Press, 2014.

S. JONATHON O'DONNELL is a postdoctoral fellow in American Studies at University College Dublin.

Index

Ahmed, Sara, 9–10, 15–16, 55, 63, 116, 131, 149, 151
Althaus-Reid, Marcella, 9, 24, 47, 59, 147
An, Yountae, 131–132, 140
antiblackness, 13–15, 42, 63–64, 68–71, 103–104, 131–132, 169–170, 182, 184; and being, 103–106, 131–32; and demonology, 13–15, 68, 104; and the Human, 13–14, 106–108
Antichrist, 11, 20–21, 119, 124, 135–136, 145–146; as anticolonial, 96–98, 105–108, 145–146; as antiracist, 20, 82, 97, 100–101, 105–108; and blackness, 81–83, 98–108; and empire, 89–91, 93–94, 97, 101–103, 106–108; Islamic, 20–21, 82, 83–89, 90, 96–98, 101–102, 106–108, 155, 177–178; and rage, 81–83, 95–97, 105–106, 115, 119, 124, 146, 177, 178; and resemblance, 85–86, 95–96, 124, 135
antisemitism, 14, 66–67, 78, 117–118, 130, 165, 181
antiurbanism, 25, 27–30, 37–38, 69–71
Anidjar, Gil, 91–93, 118, 169
Anzaldúa, Gloria, 143
apocalypse, 6, 16–18, 33–34, 53, 72, 82–84, 87–89, 102, 106–108, 111, 132–137, 152–156; and chrononormativity, 16–18, 135–137; as decision, 16–18, 85–86, 106–108, 136–137; and Islam, 83–89; and sovereignty, 16–18, 121–125, 135–137

Appadurai, Arjun, 77–78
arche (demon), 18–19, 31–35, 36–42, 46–47, 48–51, 53, 72–73, 78 84, 96, 100–101, 110, 136, 140, 154–155; as object of knowledge, 36–38; as origin and order, 31–32; as orthotaxy's other, 31–35, 46–47, 48–51, 78, 136; as structural, 33–34, 49–50
asymmetry, 2–3, 9–10, 17–18, 76, 82–83, 135–136, 146–147, 155–157; and sovereignty, 9–10, 17–18, 42–44, 76, 90–94, 152; war, 2–3, 20, 42–44, 90–93, 110, 139–140, 146–147

Baal, 52, 54, 57, 85–86, 112, 178; and abortion, 54, 57; and Islam, 85–86, 178
Babylon, 19, 71–76
Bhabha, Homi, 94–95
Black Lives Matter, 81, 100–103, 116
blood, 30, 35–36, 54, 60, 63–64, 84, 86, 91–3, 101–102, 118, 127–128, 143–144, 152, 169; and capital, 117–119; as extractive, 91–93; and flesh, 30, 63–64, 84; and generational iniquity, 35, 58–59, 92, 126–128; and othering, 35–36, 58–59, 91–93, 101–102, 118–119, 127–128; and settler colonialism, 35, 126–128, 169; and soteriology, 86, 91–92, 143, 153
biopolitics, 17–18, 39–42, 58–65, 117–119, 121, 133–136, 144–145, 149–153; of hell, 149–153; and sovereignty, 121, 144–145,

212 / INDEX

biopolitics (*continued*)
151–153; and temporality, 17–18, 39–42, 58–60, 121, 133–136. *See also* blood; necropolitics
Birtherism, 104–105

capitalism, 18, 29, 35–36, 47, 69–70, 91–93, 107, 117–119, 130, 137, 152, 155–156; and blood, 91–93, 117–119, 152; neoliberal, 118–119, 130; as nomadic, 69–93, 93
Certeau, Michel de, 23–24, 38
chaos, 7, 21, 47, 85, 110, 111–114, 115–116, 125–126, 132–133, 139, 186; and colonialism, 125–126; conquest of, 111–114, 186; and *creatio ex nihilo*, 113–114, 129; as illegitimate order, 114–120. *See also* Leviathan
Christian Zionism, 101–102
civilization, 25, 36–37, 42–43, 54, 56–57, 70, 82–83, 84, 88, 92, 99–100, 102, 106, 125, 137, 146, 180, 183; clash of, 84, 99–100, 106, 146, 180, 183. *See* death; empire
colonialism, 3, 11, 17–19, 21, 24, 35–37, 39–42, 43–46, 47–48, 58–60, 62, 68, 82–83, 94–95, 97–100, 106–107, 110, 126–130, 131–132, 140, 143–146, 152–153, 156, 181–182; epistemic violence of, 43–47, 156; heliopolitics of, 47–48, 51, 62; mimicry, 20, 94–95; settler, 41–47, 58–60, 62, 92, 101–102, 106–107, 126–130 152–153, 156, 169, 174; and sexuality, 59, 68; spiritual warfare as, 43–45, 110, 126–130, 143–146; as worlding, 21, 24, 45–46, 145–146
coloniality, 9, 19, 36–37, 39, 47–49, 131; as abyssal wound, 131, 140; as modernity/coloniality, 19, 35–37, 47, 145–146, 156
counterfeit, 11, 13–17, 19, 21–22, 34–35, 67–69, 73, 120, 123–125, 127–129, 130–135, 139, 141–142, 144, 152; as guarantor of authenticity, 15–16, 21, 34–35, 67–69, 73, 123–125, 127, 130–135, 144–145; and racialization, 13–15, 67–70, 127–129, 152; and sovereignty, 127–129, 130–133, 135, 139, 141–142; witchcraft as, 67–69

darkness, 2, 25–26, 30, 32, 34–39, 47–48, 63–65, 70–71, 75, 78, 80, 84, 91, 97, 109, 122, 130, 138, 141, 150, 155; and blackness, 63–65, 70–71, 103–106, 138, 150; forces of, 5, 25–26, 30, 75, 109, 122, 155; as site of illegitimacy, 34–39, 63, 78, 80, 91, 97, 122, 141, 155. *See also* heliopolitics; light

death, 7, 33–34, 37, 39–40, 44–45, 52, 57–59, 60, 66–67, 83, 91, 100, 111, 119, 121, 131–132, 133–134, 138–139, 140, 143–145, 146–149, 151–153; of normativity, 44–45, 57–59, 66–67, 83, 100, 121, 151–153, 155–157; penalty, 91, 111, 133–134, 143, 146–149, 151–152, 157; and queerness, 44–45, 57–58, 59–60; and the settler state, 39, 42, 44–45; social, 104–106; structures, 33–34, 39–40, 42, 45. *See* necropolitics
decoloniality, 82, 94–100, 129–137; decolonial violence, 82, 94–100; and temporality, 129–137
demon, 1–10, 11–14, 19, 25–36, 42–45, 48–51, 54, 62, 70–71, 78–80, 104, 131, 136–137, 144–145; and American empire, 2, 4–11, 39–45, 82–3, 89–94, 97–106, 131–136, 141–143, 145–146, 153–157; counter-appeal of, 9–10, 50–51, 99–100, 106–108, 137–140, 142–143 153–157; gender of, 56, 173, 177–178, 185; human collaboration, 25–26, 65–67, 70–71, 83–85; as object of knowledge, 1–10, 36–39, 45–48, 49, 76, 87–89; and passing, 11–15, 66–67, 90, 122–124; possession, 23–24, 25–30, 62; and racialization, 13–14, 39–42, 60–65, 84–85, 100–106; reproductive capacity, 57–59; speech of, 66–67; in spiritual warfare, 25–29, 30–36, 145–147; as structural, 30–36; variations of, 19, 21, 30–32; witchcraft as product of, 65–67, 70–71. *See also arche* (demon)
demonology, 3, 7–9, 12–14, 19, 23–24, 30–35, 36–42, 45–46, 82, 93–94, 96, 104, 118–119, 133–134, 145–147, 153–157, 161, 162; afterlife of, 26–27; of blackness, 81–83, 98–106; as colonial, 36–42, 45, 125–131; as counter-narrative, 9–11, 106–108, 153–157; as crisis, 23–24, 120–123, 133–137; of gender, 56–60, 78–79, 173, 177, 185; and ontotheology, 14, 100–108; as strategy of legibility, 8, 46, 85, 139–140, 153–154; third wave, 30–36, 48–49, 145–147
Derrida, Jacques, 7–8, 12, 17, 23, 31–32, 38–39, 85, 130, 138–139, 144, 148–149
devil, 1–2, 6–7, 30, 43–44, 68–71, 80, 95, 101, 118, 124–125, 132, 144, 149–153, 154–155; as contingent, 30; fall of, 118–119; folk devil, 5, 16; as passing, 6–7, 11; salvation of, 149–153; as structuring rubric, 31, 101, 155

economy, 15, 29, 34–36, 69–70, 92, 110–111, 115–120, 131–134, 151, 162; soteriological, 115–120, 130, 132–134, 137, 144
Edelman, Lee, 44, 57–59
empire, 3–5, 8–9, 17–19, 20, 34, 42–47, 67, 71, 82–83, 88–90, 91–94, 95, 97, 105–108, 110, 126–128, 142, 144-145, 155–156; American, 3–5, 34, 42–45, 47–49, 91–94, 103, 145, 156; as retention, 9, 59–60; spirits of, 34, 97. *See also* paradise
envy, 95–96, 114, 124–125; colonial, 95–96; and sovereignty, 124–125, 133, 135

Fanon, Frantz, 95–96, 103–104, 108, 124, 131
Ferguson uprising, 81–82, 100–102
Freeman, Elizabeth, 17–18, 135–136
futurity, 10, 17–18, 20–22, 67–68, 73, 78–80, 88–90, 91, 102–106, 110, 121–122, 129, 131–136, 137–138, 140, 148–149, 155–157; Black, 102–106, 138; claim over, 25–26, 44–47, 54, 56–60, 67–68, 91, 106–108, 123, 125, 129–130, 152–153; denial of, 3, 18, 44–45, 56–60, 78–80, 88–90, 103–107, 129–130, 136, 142, 152–153; queer, 18, 44–45, 56, 131; reproductive, 9, 17–18, 20, 56–60, 73. *See also* temporality; time

gender, 9, 11–13, 16–17, 20, 29, 41–42, 53–57, 60–64, 72, 73–76, 79, 106–107, 130, 134–135, 151–152, 155, 157, 173, 177–178, 185; cis and trans, 13; of demons, 56, 173, 177–178, 185; and colonialism, 41–42; and passing, 11–13; and race, 53–54, 60–64, 106–107, 134–135; and sovereignty, 53–54,73–76, 151–152, 157. *See* Jezebel
geography, 27–30, 37–38, 39–41, 75, 77–78; as pathologized, 39–41, 68–71; urban, 27–30, 37–38. *See also* antiurbanism; territory

Haiti, 39–42, 68–70, 128, 169–170; and antiblackness, 68–70, 169–170; as pathologized geography, 39–41; as diabolic rupture; 40, 128; and witchcraft, 68–70
Halberstam, J. Jack, 130–131, 147
Hawaii, 37, 41–42, 128, 169, 170; and blood, 41–42, 128, 169, 170
heaven, 2, 5–7, 13, 146, 152; new, 113, 131; and securitization, 5–7, 13; at war for reality, 2, 33, 43–46, 139–140, 146. *See also* empire; paradise

heliopolitics, 38–39, 42, 46–48, 58–59, 62–64, 65, 68–69, 76–78, 79–80, 84, 108, 121–122, 126, 130, 145–146, 152–153. *See also* light; possession; sovereignty
hell, 12–13, 27–28, 30, 33, 46, 50, 91, 108, 122, 147–153; as carceral, 147–153; at war for reality, 33, 46, 139–140; worlding of, 46, 50–51, 91
Hobbes, Thomas, 21, 120–125, 126, 133–134, 144, 187
hooks, bell, 105–106
homophobia, 25, 34, 41, 54, 57–58, 60–62, 66, 68–70, 74–80, 101, 115; and antiblackness, 60–62, 68–70; and antiurbanism, 25–26, 68–70; and sexualsovereign order, 74–77. *See also* Jezebel

idolatry, 25, 35–36, 53, 55, 58, 62–65, 73, 92, 121–123, 126–129; accusation as epistemic violence, 35–36, 92, 126–129; self-determination as, 62–65, 127–128; sovereignty and, 121–123
illegality, 6, 9–10, 14–15, 27, 31–36, 46–47, 63, 66, 69–70, 110, 129, 141–142, 144; demonic, 9–10, 27, 31–36, 46–47, 63, 66, 110, 129, 141–142, 144; migrant, 6, 14–15, 69–70, 141–142
immigration, 4–6, 14–15, 39–41, 63, 68–71, 76, 89–90, 93, 143–144, 163
Indigenous, 21, 32–33, 35–36, 41–42, 44, 68, 102, 104, 110, 169; kinship, 41–42, 169; sovereignties, 41–42, 126–130, 137, 155; survival, 42, 59, 126–130, 132; traditions, 21, 41–42, 68, 126–130
Islam, 3, 20–21, 34–35, 69, 78, 96–97, 156, 166; as anti-imperial, 82, 93–94, 97–100, 107; as antiracist, 97–98; as apocalyptic, 82–85, 86–89; and blackness, 82, 98–100, 104–106, 107; deceptiveness of, 89–90, and generational iniquity, 92, 95; as imperial, 34, 87–90, 93; justification for violence against, 90–91, 96, 104–106; as mirror image, 20, 82–83, 86–88, 96; Shi'a, 88; and supersession, 86–88
Islamophobia, 3, 20, 78, 81–82, 90–91, 92–93, 96, 142
Israel, 52–53, 55, 78, 86, 93–94, 101–102, 145, 181, 183; ancient, 52–53, 55, 78, 102; state of 93–94, 101–102, 145, 181, 183. *See also* Christian Zionism

214 / INDEX

Japan, 32–34
Jezebel, 19–20, 21, 37, 53–54, 57–60, 60–65, 71–73, 75, 77–80; and abortion, 57–58; and Babylon, 71–76; as biblical queen, 53, 55, 60, 64–65, 70–71; and blackness, 53, 55, 60–65; name of, 52–53; as transterritorial spirit, 54; and queerness, 54–60, 71–73, 75, 77–80; and reproductive futurity, 57–60; as willful subject, 54–56; and witchcraft, 56–58, 75–76, 135
Judeo-Christian, 82, 88, 92–93, 130, 181. See Christian Zionism

Kauanui, J. Kēhaulani, 41–42, 169, 170
Kotsko, Adam, 14, 118–119, 130, 149–152, 154, 162
kosmos, 28–29, 46, 132. See also world

Leviathan, 21, 109–111, 113, 114–117, 119–120, 126–131, 132, 137–140; as chaos, 111–114, 125–126, 136; as colonial, 126–131, 132, 136–137, 140; as counterfeit, 123–125, 135; as divisive, 114–117; Hobbesian, 120–125, 133–134; and Indigenous traditions, 126–129; as the multitude, 110, 119–120, 137–140; and the state, 109–111, 117–120, 130; and temporality, 118, 127–129, 133–136; and whiteness, 116–117, 124–135
light, 2, 11, 32, 37–39, 46–49, 51, 89, 121–122, 124–125, 141, 147, 156; as colonial, 37–39, 46–49, 96, 156; and counterfeiture, 11, 123; as order, 32, 38–39, 46–49, 84, 121–122; as violence, 37–39, 46–49, 141, 156; and whiteness, 96, 108, 124–125, 156. See heliopolitics
Lomax, Tamura, 60–62, 64
Lucifer, 83, 138, 150, 153–154. See also Satan

Malcolm X, 99, 105–106
Manifest Destiny, 42–43. See also empire; paradise
Martel, James, 122, 133–134, 137–138
McKittrick, Katherine, 10, 28–29, 39
Middle Passage, 106–107, 131–132
Mignolo, Walter, 35–36, 39, 75, 142, 153–154
mimicry, 10, 20–22, 28, 67, 123–124; colonial, 94–95; demonic, 20–22, 67, 94–95, 123–124
modernity, 26–27, 35–36, 47–49, 66–67, 142; logic of salvation, 35–36, 75, 143–145; race and, 91, 103–105; spiritual warfare as product of, 38. See also coloniality

naming, 3, 12–15, 48, 55, 57, 72, 77–78, 82–83, 90–91, 92–93, 120–121, 149, 153–154; of demons, 8–11, 23–24, 52–53, 64–65, 100–101, 106–108, 109–110, 112, 116, 138, 144–145; as technique of order, 12–15, 34–35, 50–51, 106–108, 131–132
Nation of Islam, 98–99, 105
necropolitics, 17–18, 34–35, 39–42, 56–57, 58–59, 73, 77–78, 118–120, 133–134, 144–145, 149–153

ontology, 14, 31–32, 40, 100–106; and hauntology, 130–131; negation of, 14, 63–64, 90, 100–106, 108, 131–132; in spiritual warfare, 14–16, 33–35, 49–50
ontotheology, 13–16, 149–153; blackness and, 100–106; demons as absence of, 18, 20–21, 55, 63–64, 79–80, 84–85, 90, 140
orthotaxy, 9–10, 18–19, 21–22, 24, 49–51, 136; as apocalyptic, 21–22, 128–131, 133–136; as mode of religiosity, 49–51; traits of, 18–19, 29, 34–35, 38–39; and whiteness, 134–135

paradise, 5–9, 16, 24, 41, 47–48, 82–83, 85, 108, 142, 143–146, 149–152, 153–154, 156–157; demon as deconstructive of, 5–9, 153–154; as imperial, 8–9, 35–36, 82–83, 140, 145–146, 155–156; and securitization, 5–8, 16–18, 47–48, 96, 143–144, 156–157. See also empire
passing, 6–7, 9–10, 11–18, 46–47, 76, 78–79, 88–89, 93–94, 110, 120–125, 137, 142, 143–147, 148–149, 157; demonic, 6–7, 9, 11–12, 21–22, 38, 46–47, 67, 110, 133–135, 143–145; racial, 12–14; registers of, 11
possession, 4–5, 12–13, 23–24, 25, 29–32, 38–39, 62–64, 78, 90, 129, 144–145; of selfhood, 62–64, 69; of territory, 25, 29–32, 38, 59–60
pride, 99, 114, 123, 128
Puar, Jasbir, 58–59, 76, 101–102

queerness, 9, 56–60, 62, 64–65, 69, 72–76, 77–80, 108, 113, 140, 143, 151, 155–156; antinormative, 44–45, 57–59, 146, 151; sovereignty and, 75–76, 121; violence against, 64, 77–80; witchcraft and, 65–68

race, 12–15, 39–42, 60–64, 68–71, 79, 91–93, 116–117, 128–129, 134–135, 151

racialization, 9, 13–15, 35–36, 39–42, 55–60, 63–65, 68–71, 82–83, 84, 88–89, 91–93, 94–96, 117–119, 120–121; as demonization, 14, 85, 117–119, 127–128, 149–151
rage, 20, 78–79, 82, 95–96, 108, 115; anticolonial, 97–98; Black, 81, 100–101, 105–106, 135; generative, 105–106, 108; Islam and 95–96, 105–106
Rifkin, Mark, 129–130
Runions, Erin, 5, 19, 71–72, 74, 85–87

Satan, 6–7, 9–10, 11–13, 26–28, 30–33, 37–38, 61–62, 67–68, 81, 95–96, 101, 129, 146–148, 155–157; as anti-slavery, 40–41; and blackness, 63–64, 81–82, 100–101; in hell, 147–148; and homosexuality, 62; and Leviathan, 110, 113, 120–121; as organizing rubric, 31, 48; as passing figure, 6–7, 11–12, 95; salvation of, 149–153; as terrorist, 2, 34, 43–44, 84–85, 146–147
Schotten, C. Heike, 44–45, 57–59, 84–85, 102, 121–122, 146, 152–153
secular, 5, 8, 17, 26–27, 38, 47, 83, 150–151, 162, 166, 171
security, 4–8, 12–13, 18, 39–40, 55–56, 138–139, 156–157; blackness and, 98, 102–104; national, 4–8, 82–85, 90–94, 95–96; soteriology and, 122, 137
Sexton, Jared, 138, 150, 153, 174
Sharpe, Christina, 131–132, 174
Simpson, Audra, 42, 129
Solnit, Rebecca, 6, 143–144, 156
soteriology, 35–36, 39–42, 92–94, 95, 117–119, 128, 135–136, 138–139, 143–145, 149–153, 157; and demonization, 59, 67–68, 92–94, 95–96, 128, 130, 143–145; and development, 35–36, 40–41, 117–119, 128, 145; as economy, 117–119, 130, 132; and Satan, 95–96, 149–153
sovereignty, 4–11, 29–30, 42, 53–55, 59–60, 73–76, 77–80, 93, 102–103, 133–137, 143–147, 153–157; as absolute, 34–35, 118–119, 120–125; as biopolitical, 44–45, 93, 121–122, 133–134; and democracy, 138–139; and demons, 3, 4–11, 107–108, 118–119, 124–125, 129–130, 137–138, 153–157; Hobbesian, 120–125, 133; Indigenous, 41–42, 126–130, 137, 155; as indivisible, 29–30, 77, 121–123; and ipseity, 12; and orthotaxy, 21–22, 48–51; settler, 44–45, 48–49, 59, 102–103, 127–130; sexual, 53–54, 55, 59–60, 73–76, 78–80, 151; temporal, 18, 21, 33–37, 49, 92, 108, 121–122, 125–130, 140, 152, 154–157; and willful will, 9–10, 30, 65, 75, 105, 113, 144–145, 149
space, 8–9, 11, 18–19, 27–30, 33–34, 36–42, 45–46, 101, 144, 152; uneven geographies of, 28–29, 39–42, 110, 129, 152; time and, 19, 33–34, 67–68, 130, 144, 146–147
spiritual warfare, 1–3, 9–10, 18–19, 21, 25–30, 33, 45–48, 55, 63–64, 69–70, 76, 86, 92–94, 101, 126–131, 134–135, 137, 139–140, 145–147, 152, 153–157; and American empire, 42–45; as assemblage, 69–70, 76; as conflict over hegemony, 31–33, 45–48; demonic hierarchy in, 30–32, 72–73; as epistemic violence, 35, 39–42, 45–48; manuals, 2, 36–37, 87–88; as modern, 37–39; and normative order, 9–10, 28–29, 39–42, 57–59, 60–64, 79–80, 101, 124–125, 126–131; as orthotaxic religiosity, 24, 29, 34, 38–39, 48–51; third wave, 25–28; and whiteness, 134–135; witchcraft and 65–66, 67–71. See also demonology
Spivak, Gayatri Chakravorty, 45–46

taqiyya, 90–94, 180
temporality, 11–12, 16–19, 33–34, 36–37, 39–42, 45–46, 56–57, 74–75, 92, 118, 121–130, 133–137, 140, 141–143, 144–147; of exorcism, 33–34, 80–81; and rupture, 39–42; as temporal sovereignty, 18, 21, 33–37, 49, 92, 108, 121–122, 126–130, 152, 154–157; and typology, 86–87. See also territory; time
territorialization, 9, 13
territorial spirit, 18–19, 27–28, 30–35, 37–38, 39–42, 46–47, 66, 70, 126–131, 154–155; as trans-territorial, 34, 54, 72–76, 93. See also *arche* (demon)
territory, 2, 9, 19, 27–28, 33, 36–37, 39–42, 48–50, 66, 72–76, 91, 126–131, 140, 141–145, 152; dominion over, 6, 29, 33–35, 38, 55, 93, 126–131; household as, 55–58; and temporality, 21, 39, 47–49, 108, 110–111, 126–131, 134, 136–137, 142
terror, 2, 13–14, 20–21, 70, 79, 82, 98, 100–108; and antiblackness, 13–14, 82–83, 103–106; at nothing, 100–106; at porosity, 70; and queerness, 13, 44–45, 70, 78–79; at resemblance, 13–14, 82–83, 95; as world-making, 82–83, 103–106, 108, 156

terrorism, 1–2, 4, 13, 26, 34, 43–45, 84–85, 88, 102; demonic as, 1–2, 34, 42, 84, 146; Islamic, 34, 84–85, 97–98; resistance to orthotaxy as, 44–45, 56–57, 102–103

teleology, 17–19, 36, 39–42, 59–60, 79–80, 83, 86–89, 130–137, 152–157; and colonialism, 39–42, 126–127, 130–134

time, 7, 11, 16–18, 33–34, 39–42, 45–46, 77–80, 96–97, 121–122, 128–129, 135–136, 141–143, 146, 152–153; for demons, 33–34, 80, 146, 148–149; as duration, 140, 146; end times, 2, 11, 16–18, 20, 27, 73, 81–82, 83–84, 86–88, 113, 141–143, 146–147; and reproduction, 16–18, 56–58; as settler colonial, 21, 39–42, 128–131, 152–153; vs temporality, 121–122

typology, 86–87, 112, 132, 135

Voudou, 39–41, 68–69

War on Terror, 1–2, 4–11, 39–40, 43–45, 83–85, 88, 93–94, 102, 146–147. *See also* asymmetry

Warren, Calvin, 103–105

whiteness, 13–16, 28–29, 35–36, 41, 55, 62–63, 68–70, 81–83, 88, 96, 103–107, 116, 127–128, 131–132, 151, 156; as labile, 134–135; and light, 47, 96, 108, 124; as presence, 13–16, 94–95

willfulness, 3, 9–10, 18, 62–63, 91–92, 119, 131, 142, 149–151, 164; demonic, 3, 14, 46–47, 50, 79, 85, 125, 135, 139–140; Jezebel's, 55–56, 64–65; and sovereign will, 9–10, 30, 75, 105, 113, 144–145; and witchcraft, 65, 70–71

witchcraft, 6, 26, 37, 65–71, 78, 124, 162, 175; blackness and, 68–71; early modern, 26, 66–67, Jezebel and 56–58, 75, 135; and colonialism, 68

world, 6, 8–9, 18, 26, 28, 30–32, 35, 45–51, 63–64, 72, 76, 79–80, 92–93, 95, 110, 111–114, 131–133, 136–137, 140, 145–146; antiblack, 13–14, 95–96, 103–106; as demonic, 6, 26–28, 30–32, 47–48, 72; dependency on, 37; end of the, 83, 103–108, 153–157; worlding of, 45–48, 49–51, 76, 90, 91–92, 110, 111–114, 120–121, 125–127, 129, 131–133, 135, 140, 142–143, 152, 153–157

S. JONATHON O'DONNELL is a postdoctoral fellow in American Studies at University College Dublin.

www.ingramcontent.com/pod-product-compliance
Lightning Source LLC
Chambersburg PA
CBHW020108020526
44112CB00033B/1094